TOTAL MEDITATION

I ⟶ self

BOFFA

TOTAL

MEDITATION

Mind Control Techniques
for a Small Planet in Space

RAYMOND VAN OVER

Collier Books
A Division of Macmillan Publishing Co., Inc.
NEW YORK
Collier Macmillan Publishers
LONDON

Macmillan Publishing Co., Inc.
866 Third Avenue, New York, N.Y.   10022
Collier Macmillan Canada, Ltd.

Library of Congress Cataloging in Publication Data

Van Over, Raymond.
  Total meditation.

  Includes index.
  1. Meditation. I. Title.
[BL627.V36 1978b]   291.4'3   78–1685
ISBN 0–02–067900–9 pbk.

First Printing 1978

Printed in the United States of America

For Maya and Virginia—
two of Diogenes' lights in the dark night.
Without their support and understanding
this book could not have come into being.

Contemplation of my life
Decides the choice
Between advance and retreat.

      —*I Ching,*
        The Book of Changes

Contents

ACKNOWLEDGMENTS

*With any book many people beyond the
author become essential in its creation.
I am greatly indebted to C. C. Chambers for
her expert editorial assistance and to Cathy
Rennich for her patient work on the manuscript.
And, of course, S. D. G., without whom nothing
could have been accomplished.*

TOTAL MEDITATION

Meditation and Society

COLLECTIVELY AND INDIVIDUALLY, people have failed to deal with their internal lives while concentrating almost exclusively on altering external conditions. Many have suggested that the imbalance should be righted by learning to control our internal lives. In an inexorable and necessary way, then, inner space has become the next ground for exploration and development. Thus, the prime task of our age is not to conquer space or overwhelm nature, but rather to reintegrate our life-styles and value systems with our environment—an alchemical wedding between our internal and external worlds.

Meditation is perhaps the most profound and immediately available technique for achieving this union. It is a private process, dependent only on one's willpower and determination; yet, because it directly affects your inner life and behavior, it indirectly affects society.

Over half a century ago Swiss psychiatrist Carl Jung predicted that the reductive psychologies and materialism of Western science would create feelings of "loneliness in the cosmos." The centuries-old emphasis on competition, reductive analysis, unhesitating satisfaction of personal needs even at the expense of our environment isolates and destroys the individual's sense of integration with the world. Jung felt that for optimum health each person needed to integrate the internal with external, the conscious with the unconscious reality. The unconscious "inner nature" was a rare treasure that had, during its unnatural suppression, separated the individual from the true and full integration of the self. An individual's sense of isolation, loneliness, and despair could only be resolved by harmonious integration of these two symphonies of the self. Once united, both the outer and inner worlds are transformed; they then obtain what Jung called individuation—or recovery of "the original experience of wholeness." Jung's significance is greater than that of an exceptionally perceptive psychiatrist examining the hidden contours of our emotional life. He has become symbolic of the solitary quest that is ever more relevant to our age as the process of isolation continues, as a growing number of people seek answers to the eternal questions of identity, purpose, and meaning.

Many of the advocates of the new consciousness and the spiritualization of our culture are not simply far-out occultists, faddists, or practitioners of esoteric religions. Their number includes a great many exceptional scientists, writers, and philosophers—Arnold Toynbee, Pitirim Sorokin, Michael Polanyi, Pierre Teilhard de Chardin, Arthur Koestler, Abraham Maslow, and Sir Alister Hardy. The common thrust of their argument is that a humanized science must be in the forefront of change; it must respond to questions of basic human value and meaning and, finally, be more sympathetic to philosophies dealing with the inner human experience.

Some commentators see the phenomenon of new religions, exploding interest in occultism, ESP, and UFOs basically as a way of questioning traditional belief systems that no longer work. As sociologist Robert Galbreath has commented, "A serious concern with occult belief systems can very well reflect a fundamental questioning of accepted values and a largely healthy sense of urgency in seeking out viable alternatives." Galbreath suggests that the occult becomes "a symbol of unlimited possibilities, a means of stimulating a sense of wonder, awe, and mystery, a catalyst for scientific, aesthetic, or religious creativity, and not a set of beliefs to be accepted literally." Professor Galbreath could even have gone a step further and argued that if the occult becomes a generally accepted set of beliefs, its broadest application and its most creative function of stimulating new thought and questioning outmoded ideas would be diminished. To survive, therefore, the occult must remain mysterious, an outcast from traditional beliefs and practices.

Concern about contemporary belief systems is not limited only to the philosophically or psychologically inclined, but has become a major topic at many recent religious conferences and symposiums. At the Fifth Assembly of the World Council of Churches recently held in Nairobi, the world gathering of orthodox delegates heard Professor Charles Birch of the University of Sydney argue that "the world is a Titanic on a collision course and only a revolution in human relationships can save it."

The obsession with Western cultural values and the disruptions resulting from material growth in a technological society was one of the major topics of discussion. And the fact that the churches were not coping with the dismemberment of human values, which is its natural subject, was one of the meeting's primary anxieties.

The same concerns have been reflected time and again during the last few years at practically every church synod or humanistically oriented conference. That the establishment has done little more than talk about these problems is perhaps one of the reasons why the average person has sought relief in the nontraditional beliefs of occultism, Eastern religions, and meditation. The latter are all humanistically centered systems and have specific techniques with which a distraught or isolated individual can experiment. Whether or not the techniques objectively work is a question not initially important to the seeker; what these systems offer to the confused questioner is an "understandable," even simplistic, answer to basically complex human problems. That modern science rejects almost out of hand many of the provocative ideas that sustain Eastern religious and meditative systems has no doubt served to push many people more readily into the waiting arms of occult and metaphysical beliefs.

Can we blame such hungry, indiscriminate seekers? What are we to make of a culture that apparently replaces spiritual with consumer-oriented values, where the admired and desired goal is an insatiable acquisition of material goods? Values obviously become confused and we begin to place unwarranted trust in specific groups of specialists who seem to have clear answers to complicated problems. Our orientation consequently becomes ever more outer directed, and the ability to make strong independent judgments atrophies.

For example, even though it is an absurd premise, God has been proclaimed dead for some time now; yet, American ingenuity seems to have identified the problem and taken action. Business has become more value-oriented—not necessarily to improve its own standards, but as a means of selling products. Sales campaigns reassure the buyer that the product or company is trustworthy. The emphasis is not so much on the value of the product as on how the product can affect your life. The need for beneficent influence and direction in our lives is clear, and leaders of the consumer society have taken advantage of our spiritual anxiety and confusion in their sales campaigns. Buick advertises that they bring us "something to believe in." If you buy their car a difficult world can seem beautiful because a Buick is "dedicated to the Free Spirit in just about everyone." Union Carbide Company also touches our souls when they tell us time and again, "We've got the answers now. . . . Today, something we do will touch your life." "We'll take care of you," says British Airways. It seems that advertising writers are ever more frequently using these traditionally comforting words of trust, faith, and beauty. When politicians and ministers fall back on these terms, one has a sense of no foundation. They are just words and nothing more. With Buick at least we get a car. Do these corporations and advertising writers understand the public anguish, the general confusion, the fundamental loss in our lives better than our government, our religions, our basic institutions? At least these corporations appear concerned enough about us to try to assure us that their products can assuage our anxieties if we simply put our trust in them. And they are asking only for our dollars, not our souls.

It is ironic that many of the "new age" churches resort to advertising campaigns that are surprisingly like Union Carbide's and Buick's. Selling of spiritual wares is not new, of course, for proselytizing has always been the favored technique of the confirmed believer—whether of church, state, or commerce. But the movement of the product-oriented company into the spiritual marketplace *is* new. And so is the widespread corruption of the language by modern media. Lack of credibility thus has become a major problem for all the institutions of our culture, a problem which in turn may further explain the rapid increase in self-help books and personal experimentation with new ideas, experiences, drugs, and religions. These characteristics of our culture are important because they condition and create belief systems that often determine what individuals and hence societies will do in the future.

What, it has been asked, becomes of creativity as our culture's mechanization continues? What becomes of a human being's capacity for love, empathy, and self-sacrifice, the ability to give one's self in the service of others or even in the service of one's own well-being? What, in short, becomes of basic aspects of the human mind, such as intuition, insight, and judgment, as technologized man becomes more oriented to a mechanical view of himself and is conditioned to accept this as a true reflection of his being?

Society creates the average person in images already accepted; only the individual can create the fundamentally new. It is this premise that clarifies the evolutionary urge toward personal growth. The undistinguished self becomes a distinguishable only as it progresses toward fulfillment of what is fundamentally new within its own being. That this urge is not always realized in some lives is not proof of its nonexistence. There have been enough people throughout history who have been evidence of the more fully realized self.

Intoxicated with technological and material success, man no longer considers his own character or spirit a center of philosophical inquiry. Intellect has thereby become an instrument for manipulating the externals, for defending mankind from an enveloping alien world. The belief that reason, or intelligent examination, can lighten the shadows of our internal mysteries has been either demeaned or ignored. Extreme rationalism, which enjoys such renewed popularity today, creates an imbalance in our intellect because it avoids questions that deal with the inner being, the personality and character at the core of our existence. Meditation restores conviction in the idea that directing the conscious mind inward is a valid method for self-exploration and philosophic inquiry, for reestablishment of an inner balance between the individual and his environment.

Life is commitment, and to be committed it is necessary to become more aware of one's interior life. Without such awareness it is impossible to make mature decisions concerning the process of one's life. In a culture that does not give full support to the idea of inner growth and an evolutionary view of human life, what has been true since the dawn of religious and psychological awareness is particularly important today: Each individual has the duty to enhance those qualities within himself that create a more complete human being. Yet he has an equal responsibility to honor certain values beyond those affecting the individual self. Protestant theologian Paul Tillich has explored this moral paradox more profoundly than most other contemporary thinkers. He regards the contradiction as resolving itself when man comes to see himself as reflecting a larger, more universal harmony—as an integral particle in the cosmic process. This integrated, creative function is in direct contrast to our traditional Western culture and way of thinking. If Tillich is right, then we are a people badly out of joint and need a revolution in how we view ourselves. Such a personal reassessment has been one of the major benefits derived from the modern preoccupation with meditation. The fact that meditation aids self-integration is very important precisely because the tensions of our world are so intense and influence us constantly throughout our day.

An important question each person should ask himself is whether he experiences within himself the harmonious cooperation between his internal states and the external world. Most of us have experienced harmony between the warring factions within, for example, in moments of joy or high play, in moments of profound love when the smaller interests of the self are transcended. In such fleeting moments a limited form of self-consciousness is replaced by participation. Without these fleeting positive, melding, and unitive experiences, life would be unbearable: a dry battleground upon which the warring elements of the self thirst for a peace that each by itself cannot create. Meditation seems to be one of the most effective means of experiencing this unity and of extending its duration.

To summarize, it is cultural irritation that meditation helps heal. Since we cannot escape being a reflection of our environment, trouble develops when millions of people begin to relate their humanness to their urban culture—a process doomed to failure and disenchantment. The symbols, words, and thoughts of people reflect their surroundings. Often the very quality of human existence has been defined by its hard or soft, its harsh or pleasant qualities; by its flowing grasses and fields or its rugged peaks and awesome mountains. It is not surprising, therefore, that as we try to articulate our humanness within dehumanized surroundings we suffer ever-greater alienation—a separateness from what we *are* internally, from what we perceive ourselves to *be,* and from that which we have created around us. Our created physical extensions tend more toward a mechanical and technological expression, leaving the deeper natural symbols of our existence unarticulated, festering in a kind of psychic sinkhole. Under such conditions it is natural that alternative methods for expressing our inner human-ness would occur. In the Western world meditation has become one of the most recent, popular, and functional methods because it can benefit anyone in a relatively short time.

Since all human expressions, whether word, action, image, sym-bol, or thought, are constructed according to the shape of culture and reflect the multiple hues of human bias coloring our attitudes, growth becomes dependent upon freeing ourselves from our own particular logic. If we consistently view the world from a single preconditioned perspective, all our perceptions will be colored by that limited view. If we have breakpoints—moments of insight, flashes where the self-imprisoning logic of our created world is breached, and which allow a broad, new vision of our particular reality to impress itself upon our consciousness—then change and growth are not only possible but probable. In this sense meditation is a vital and important part of personal evolution, regardless of whether it carries one to the consummation of *nirvana* or *samadhi*. It is at these breakpoints along the path of personal growth that we perceive the world with unfettered vision. Meditation frees the individual from cultural restrictions and moves the human spirit into uncharted territory.

BELIEFS AND THE IMAGE OF SELF

To anyone who closely examines various life-styles it is clear that we are habit-ridden creatures who often follow self-defeating pat-terns. What meditation does initially is to replace the neurotic habit patterns with new, more liberating ones. In effect, the medi-tator sees the world in a fresh way. How many times, for example, have you seen—but not really seen—the apple you are about to eat. To view the world in a continually fresh way each moment is a radicalizing experience, precisely because we have come to depend so heavily upon expected perceptions. An apple is simply a round red object that we shove between our teeth. In this sense we truly are environmentally determined creatures of habit.

Each of us has constructed in his mind a personal view of the world, a miniature model in what William Blake called the "crystal cabinet of the mind." In this internal psychic crystal there is contained our preferences, our preconceived notions, our beliefs, and a predisposition regarding our reactions to the newest events that come into our lives. Responding automatically through such inclinations, we tend to fall into habits that are created and continually reaffirmed as we unthinkingly follow our unconsciously determined patterns.

As psychology has advanced, one thing that has become clear is the extent to which human beings are conditioned to perceive and believe certain things. *What* people believe is determined by their previous conditioning. A striking experiment conducted a few years ago by an American psychologist indicated just how much we create our own reality. The psychologist used a device that held two images, one before each eye. One image was a matador and the other a baseball player. He had a group of Mexican and American schoolteachers look into the device. The Mexican teachers saw only the matador, and the Americans only the baseball player. Our everyday perceptions are just as selective, and yet we go through life believing what we see, hear, and touch without question.

Psychologists tell us that we tend to stabilize around a set of secure concepts that we protect until overwhelming evidence forces us to modify them. These stabilizing concepts include friends, family, familiar groups in our neighborhood, favorite objects, abilities in which we feel confident, and ideas that support all of the former. The mind follows a similar set of associations that create a secure mental environment. The virtue in this structure is that we are able to function effectively when we feel secure; but the weakness is that we tend to become excessively conservative, limit our mental adventures to the familiar, and avoid the mysterious, unusual, or surprising.

What if certain experiences occurred that showed us our preconceptions about the world were mistaken? How would most of us tend to react? Some no doubt with panic, others with disbelief and rejection. And perhaps a small group would respond by accepting the new experience for what it is, and readjust their world view to incorporate it. For example, what would happen if a man lived in a world that had, say, only two colors—blue and gray—and suddenly as he was sitting under a tree he saw bright yellow in the sky? If he were an educated man, his first reaction would be that the new color was a hallucination. Upon reflection and if the experience were repeated, he would realize that perhaps his two-color world was not the complete truth he had assumed it to be, or the whole of reality. If he did not become terrified that his secure world of blues and grays were being shattered, and if he could integrate the new perception into his view of reality, his understanding of the world would be considerably greater than before. He might reason that if one other color existed beyond his world of blue and gray, perhaps there were also others of which he was not aware. This knowledge could lead him on a pursuit for a fuller, more complete, and hence truer picture of his existence.

The individual who sees his world in a new way also sees *himself* in a new light. Rather than a two-dimensional world of blues and grays, the universe has suddenly opened into an exciting, broad spectrum of possibilities. Such a vision of the world even changes the individual's relationship to the subtle shadings in his environment; they are all now tinted with yellow and golden hues that each bring an exciting new perception. Thus, each person expands his personal vision of the world and ultimately alters even his perception of himself only if he is capable of remaining open to the new and surprising.

Obviously, the meaning of a thing depends upon the extent to which one's personality responds to it, not simply on the thing itself. How one responds to life determines the grades of significance it carries. In other words, the human personality tends to limit itself, to construct a closed system within which it can comfortably function for the simple needs of the body and the ego. Yet people seem capable of responding to the world in terms greater than the limitations of their senses or their momentary ego needs. In those moments we express a greater awareness and adduce a greater significance in what we perceive than the object alone would normally reveal.

If these new experiences cause a revolution in our view of reality, they also create a new hope, even a thirst for change and evolution. The objective world of experiencing is melded into a personal evolution. In such a way science, or the objective examination of the world, is integrated into the innermost crystal cabinets of the mind and becomes the catalyst that helps us evolve into new and different beings.

But this process cannot be allowed to happen haphazardly. That is why structured education is usually better than haphazard learning. Not only does it save time and effort, but it creates a stronger foundation upon which the new and evolving can grow. Knowledge is thus related to action, to change, and to growth.

Not only do people fear the unusual and mysterious, but they also fear the uncontrollable. It is an ironic fact that we fear the uncontrollability of our own unconscious minds and thus are afraid of a major part of our being. This fear of the unknown psyche is unfortunately enhanced by those psychologists and psychiatrists who always emphasize the negative aspects of the unconscious. Some psychologists and psychiatrists give the impression that the unconscious is composed of a swirling mass of dangerous, uncontrollable urges and images from which only they know how to protect you. This negative evaluation of the unconscious is Freud's undesirable legacy. For the meditator, these attitudes imply that when delving into the unusual, or into the inner mind, you are taking your life in your hands.

In a sense this is, of course, true, for if the conscious mind is untrained and moves too rapidly into unfamiliar terrain, difficulties can erupt. But if the conscious mind is indeed the controller of one's destiny, the future is in our purposeful use of the mind's full potential. Those who automatically accept the contemporary negative and destructive vision of their inner psyche impede their own growth, for in effect they resist the flow of their own inner lives. To be terrified of inner emotions or internal imagery means burying even deeper certain thoughts and ideas from which one is already estranged. This psychic armoring can only reinforce negative belief systems and set up additional defenses between the conscious, striving, analytical self and the self-regulating, self-healing capacity of one's inner being. If you are consistently frightened of the inner content of your mind, there is little hope of ever communicating with it and hence little advantage in using certain forms of meditation that rely upon dealing dispassionately with your internal imagery. Such a person should probably use the simpler mantra or structured content imagery types of meditation.

We should ask ourselves why we usually accept so quickly every negative thought that pops into our heads; why we don't give equal weight and value to the more positive thoughts. Belief in the destructive powers of the mind implies belief in its curative,

constructive ability as well. That the body and mind acting together can heal itself is becoming more evident as scientific investigation continues. Each mental or physical symptom is beginning
to look more like a clue to the conflict in a body or mind that
contains its own healing potential. This does not mean that there
are no diseases afflicting human flesh, but rather that mind-and-
body conflicts help set up an environment in which a disease can
take hold and flourish. While the evidence for this analysis of
mind-body interaction is still developing, there are enough data to
say with assurance that each symptom suggests the presence of a
battle within a system that has disrupted its successful functioning
as a whole.

But if a man is committed to the idea that he has no control
over his internal bodily functions, his tendency is to reject the
thought—and even sometimes clear evidence—that some mental
control, say, over blood pressure, is possible. Too rigid adherence
to a concept can close off entirely fruitful new approaches to life.
Even one's life-style can be so limited that certain ideas in a culture
are automatically rejected as impossible or even dangerous.

We set up physical limits for ourselves in the same way. Even
our language serves these negative beliefs. "No one will ever break
the four-minute mile" was a common idea in the 1950s. Once it
was accomplished, the psychological block disappeared from our
language and our minds, and many athletes subsequently broke
the old "impossible" barrier. As one person broke the four-minute
mile, another pole-vaulted higher than seventeen feet, another
high-jumped over seven feet, and athletes continued to break other
old "impossible" records as well. The same limitations exist in
relation to our minds. If we think of consciousness as an elaborate
computer capable only of mechanical functions such as adding
columns of figures or analyzing an equation or logical syllogism,
then that is all the mind will be capable of doing. The same cultural biases that have crippled the full use of our bodies have
clouded and impeded the full use of our minds. But even with
these cultural barriers, the mind seems to have an inner dynamic
that occasionally brings forth exceptional insights.

This is not to suggest the abolition of all conditioning. Without autonomic function we obviously couldn't take a step, or
breath while we sleep, or control our bladder without first thinking about it. But to assume that all conditioning is good allows

people to rely too heavily on it, which eventually creates over-simplified beliefs and protective rationales.

Unexamined beliefs force us to rely exclusively on public wisdom, peer acceptance, and infantile conditioning. This is how beliefs can become oversimplified. Once we accept a set of behavior patterns as correct and never again bother to examine their origin or underlying logic—even when there is clear contrary evidence—we live a life lowered to mechanical responses and repeated situations. Santayana's perceptive insight regarding history—that if people ignore the past they are fated to relive its mistakes—applies here to our own psychology. If an individual ignores his conditioning or motivations, he is doomed to relive his neurotic or nonconstructive patterns over and over again. Once one's conditioning is brought into the open, we can see where our behavior needs to continue unhampered or where it needs to be changed. The complexity of human beings is so great that no amount of self-examination alone is enough to understand the whole mass of emotion, sensation, and thought that makes us unique individuals. But with techniques like meditation we can learn to influence whole areas of behavior without becoming excessively emotional, overly analytical, deluded, or intellectual about it. Often, analyzing something or relying too heavily on analytical technique does little more than substitute neurotic mental habits for emotional ones. The classical all-head-and-no-emotions individual suffers this kind of imbalance. What meditation and other self-modifying techniques attempt to do is to balance the various mental, emotional, and spiritual aspects of the individual into a more unified whole.

BREAKING THE BOUNDARIES OF SELF

It is a fact of life that we are bound creatures, but, paradoxically, our consciousness strives to break its fetters and soar on the energies of imagination. It is a part of human life that the bound person rebels, that a troubling inner awareness rejects its physical cage. It is this urge to break free of our limitations that both distinguishes us from other animals and causes us eternal dissatisfaction or despair—depending upon the depth of one's desire to be free. "Thou hast bound bones . . . fastened me flesh," writes poet Gerard Manley Hopkins.

Yet, oddly, there is comfort for some people in this prison of bounded bones and fastened flesh where no test is necessary, where the individual floats in a secured environment, living on the delusion that his life-plan has avoided the apprehension of surprise and the abrasiveness of change. But the price of this private prison is separation of the individual from his nature and his origins. Acceptance of this conditioned comfort is closer to the animal condition than the truly human. Alfred Korzybski, the creator of General Semantics, believed that animals accept the binding of their lives by time, space, and energy, while the human being attempts to mold these conditions to his desires, even uses them to break the boundaries of his imprisonment.

Some have argued, and with good cause, that "normalcy" is a concept for escapists, a comforting fixation, which allows one to avoid confronting vital and often disturbing issues of personal growth. Perhaps, others say, it is better to be *abnormal* if that is what it takes to understand the true nature of our inner character. Most people seem to crave normality in the belief that it will bring peace or contentment. But the art of living resonates in the ebb and flow, the light and dark, the life and death that punctuate our existence. Change is the grammar in the poetry of life. To circumscribe the limits of experience with static concepts is to reject the very essence of life, which must involve the acceptance of all parts of living—the good, bad, and indifferent. Metamorphosis is the real "dance of life." Acceptance of change, of life's variability, is the beginning of courage and the capacity to use life's energies as a positive force.

The boundaries that limit our sense of self, that capture our minds and hearts in small and often petty concerns are all false creations. English poet John Donne expressed the meditating mystic's perception of a human world that moved beyond the limited world of any single self. When Donne wrote that "no man is an island" he captured the psychological reality developed by mystics of both the Eastern and Western spiritual traditions. All the challenging psychological problems that accompanied studies of hypnosis, sleep and dreams, ecstasy, and other altered states of consciousness indicated that individual selfhood dissolved in an inner experience common to humanity. The symbols of interaction between different aspects of the self shone more brightly as psychology kept expanding the boundaries of the human experience. The perception of mankind as isolated—even that exhibited by saints themselves, such as Simeon Stylites standing alone above the rest of humanity on his exculpatory but exalted pillar—has disappeared in a view of humanity in mutual suffering and confused communality.

Greek philosopher Anaximander wrote that "every individual does penance for his separation from the boundless." Heraclitus, another fifth-century Greek and one of the fathers of Western philosophy, believed that the human personality has "no boundaries," implying that human life has aspects that reach beyond any momentary condition. The idea that there are dimensions within human nature that connect individual men with each other and mankind with the cosmos is a very ancient concept that is regaining its place in modern psychology and philosophy. For example, the distinguished American psychologist Gardner Murphy believes that the nature of man may be seen as a resonator of larger forces. To be properly understood the human being must be considered as a microcosm that, in Murphy's words, repeats "like the sympathetic vibration of wire, the vaster processes of the macrocosm."

A common goal of all forms of meditation, whether clearly stated in dogma or not, is to break down the limiting mental boundaries separating the individual from the surrounding world. In contrast to psychologists like Murphy, the predominate rationalist view of Western science states that there is nothing in the universe outside of man to which he can respond with a sense of oneness—or at least this was the popular view represented by Bertrand Russell in his essay "The Free Man's Worship." Humanity and the world are two, inevitably and eternally separate. But rather than being a description of true reality, this exaggerated alienation from the world is more likely an expression of mankind's insecurity, its historical discomfort when faced with an overpowering and seemingly undecipherable universe. Intellectual alienation like Russell's and other arch-rationalists' had blinded us to the deep affinities between the human and the cosmic.

Spanish philosopher Ortega y Gasset wrote that "life is a petty thing unless it is moved by the indomitable urge to extend its boundaries. Only in proportion as we are desirous of living more do we really live." The motivation behind wanting to meditate, to obtain greater control and effectiveness over our personal lives, is therefore considerably more dynamic than a simple exercise in self-improvement or a self-help course. The justification underlying the meditative discipline is more comprehensive and involves an evolutionary drive that expands its dimensions and thereby its role. There seems to be a fundamental force rather than a simple psychological motivation or egoist gratification.

Meditation is therefore an invaluable method for breaking the boundaries of the self and bringing the relationship between the conscious and unconscious drives to a fruitful merging. The process of meditation thus can transform the singular, self-oriented striving of the limited "I" into a broader concept of "self" that incorporates a far wider reality. As we expand our awareness, we come to realize and understand more, and as we consciously grasp the broader reality we *become* more than we were the moment before.

Meditation, prayer, intense concentration on creative tasks all contribute to inducing an altered state of consciousness. Thus unconscious dynamics are brought into creative interrelationship with our conscious life; unconscious forces are thereby integrated into behavior and motivation, extending the limited human personality into the depths of the psyche and the webbed corners of a potentially infinite nature. The unknowing insertion of unconscious influences into our daily lives has occurred from the beginning of phenomenal consciousness. The ancient shamans may well have originated the creative arts through such interaction. Music, for example, could conceivably have been born in the entranced rhythmic murmurings of the shaman. He may well have been the first dancer as he twirled himself out of his everyday world and into contact with another dimension; he may have created poetry as he fell into inspired trances and uttered epigrammatic truths that his tribe honored and immortalized in myth and legend; he may have guided humanity into the world of imagination, keeping the bridge between the conscious and unconscious world intact and open, thereby giving form and meaning to the boundless, the free and spontaneous relationship to life around him, to the intoxicated commitment to life.

It is in this shattering of boundaries, in the depth dimension of the psyche, that we find the stage upon which the human drama begins, flourishes, and still maintains itself. Understanding, writes Martin Buber, means "holding ourselves open to the unconditioned mystery which we encounter in every sphere of our life. It means that from the very roots of our being, we should always be prepared to live with this mystery as one being lives with another." That life is a mystery gives us hope we may one day understand it; that human beings have a capacity to change allows us a future.

Meditation and
States of Consciousness

THE "FELT" REALITY of our inner selves has always fascinated
human beings. We seem unique in our splendid self-awareness.
Other animals have forms of self-awareness, but none so subtle
and extensive as that of the human mind. This is not a sentimental
humanism, for self-consciousness in the human animal is not only
a blessing and a unique privilege, but also a confusing and sometimes oppressive burden. At times the human experience seems
caught in a web of complex realities, each mode of reality demanding exclusive attention. In this sense the world to which the
mind attends is a jealous and demanding tyrant: it demands attachment while the reflective mind constantly desires to step
away to get some perspective or larger view. So the labyrinthine
and perverse web we seem entangled in dictates that our bodies
and senses demand intimate attention—even attachment—to the
physical world; yet our minds and inner awareness urge us to de-
tach ourselves, to seek the larger view. Caught then as we are between the specific, particular demands of our senses and the larger,
ever-seeking universal perspective of consciousness, we exist in a
state of subtle torture. We cannot survive by turning off our
senses and ignoring the world, and we cannot indiscriminately extend the boundaries of our conscious awareness without threatening our sanity.
  But perhaps freedom from this web spun by our paradoxical

[17]

spider can be found in the centuries-old Chinese concept called
the "Golden Mean": the capacity to live in moderation in all things.
In the context of the classical dilemma between our body and
mind, the Golden Mean would suggest extending the boundaries
of conscious awareness slowly, cautiously, but inexorably to their
greatest dimension—whatever that might turn out to be. But in order to experiment with consciousness, the senses and the body
must be controlled and brought into a quiet state that does not
intrude upon the delicate experimenting with one's inner sensing.
This is where meditation offers a wide range of techniques, as well
as a long tradition of anecdote and personal experiences reported by
many who have gone before us. Such altered states of consciousness
are an important aspect of the modern meditation scene because
they introduce the idea of levels of consciousness and an evolving
intelligence into our world view. This point of view raises the
personal questions: "At what level of awareness do I exist?" and
"What level of consciousness may I obtain?" Such questions lead
to a new perspective of ourselves. And this is vitally important to
the modern age, for it reestablishes transcendent ideas; it once
again allows the individual to see himself as *in potentia*. This philosophy transcends the small, petty concerns that have choked us in
our mechanized age. Thus, the great ideas of past generations are
introduced again into our awareness—but this time through the
consciousness-expanding mental and physical disciplines of meditation.

Reflecting the paradoxical Janus-face of human life, two major
categories of altered states of consciousness have been distinguished: the everyday awareness by which objects and events are
separate from the mind perceiving them; and a state of consciousness in which everything is seen as part of the whole, as a cosmic
pattern with numerous interacting "fields." The first category of
consciousness is a functional one we use in order to survive in a
physical world. The second one is a strange state most familiar to
artists, mystics, saints, shamans, or madmen. This second state of
mind has been reported by creative people as a state of high excitement in which their minds suddenly resolve problems and
unify previously disparate facts. Between these two extremes are
numerous different states of awareness. The English language is
particularly deficient in words to describe altered states of consciousness. Other cultures are much more sensitive to the nuances

of these states. Sanskrit, for example, has over twenty words that relate to states of consciousness. One *sutra* in Buddhism lists almost a hundred distinct categories for the varieties of consciousness.

Many altered states of consciousness (ASC) are *not* all that strange; they are part of a continuum that permeates everyday life. When we watch a movie, become engrossed in a book and are oblivious to everything but what we are concentrating upon, we can be in a light trance. Our brain-wave patterns and brain chemistry are altering. While the *scope* of our attention has decreased, the *intensity* has increased. While concentrating we are unaware that the power or focus of our attention has altered, but the increase in attention automatically diminishes conscious awareness of our sensory and perceptual contact with the external world. Even if we are attending to something external to ourselves, such as a movie or book (in contrast to internal concentration such as daydreaming or meditation), all objects not directly connected to the focus of our attention will diminish.

The same phenomenon of "one-pointedness" is often mentioned in the traditional literature on meditation. Concentration increases the power of our focused awareness whether we exercise that concentration in the external or internal world. That is why practice in mind-control is so effective; it follows the mind's natural inclination. The more we practice concentration, the greater becomes our power to concentrate. There seems to be an accretion of strength as the instrument of the mind's focusing power is used. Hence daily practice brings a greater and more positive result than an occasional meditation, even though intermittent practice may also successfully increase to some extent the mind's capacity to focus.

Attention is one of those central mysteries that revolves around the human mind, that plays a vital part in learning meditation, that has been discussed by modern science *ad nauseam*. Yet very little is known about the mechanics of how the mind consciously directs attention. We do know that the human mind is capable of creating its own heaven or hell, depending on how it is applied. Its range covers a broad spectrum—from quantum theory to crossword puzzles, from the sadism of Hitler and horrors of Auschwitz to the sanctity and compassion of St. Francis, from the heavy-handed laborings of power politics to the subtleties of Bach's

The Art of the Fugue. Each mind seems to speak its own dialect of the human language. Some thoughts cannot be spoken in normal language but demand special symbols, as in music, mathematics, metaphysics, or the metaphor of intense human passion. What seems to occur is that people turn their attention from one type of reality to another. Our perceptions and understanding reflect in large measure how we view the world and where we concentrate our attention. Clearly, where there is a will, there is an intellectual way.

Our concentrated effort in the West has been traditionally directed toward conquering the external world of nature. The obvious advantages of this attention have been the advances of natural science. The disadvantage is the loss of contact with our internal life. In learning the flight dynamics of rockets we tend to forget the beauty of birds soaring. We have learned that our bodies react to stimuli by conditioned reflex, and have forgotten that before and after each response there still exists a complex whole being that flows on in its own unique process of living.

One of the most important revelations in modern thought has been the realization that *how* people perceive and reason about their world reflects the values that shape their culture. In other words, our reasoning processes tend to be self-fulfilling and help to create beliefs and values that we then analyze as deriving from the culture itself. Consequently, the very act of "how" we think or "where" we apply our attention determines largely what we will become.

Yet where the mysteries of the human mind—and more specifically, consciousness—are concerned, science is in a very difficult position, as in Bertrand Russell's description of electricity when he pointed out that science can *describe* what electricity does very accurately, but has no idea of what it really *is*. We all have intimate experience of our own consciousness. We understand it in descriptive terms but have no idea what it is. Great portions of the mind's landscape are clouded, and science can do little more than observe its effects; yet we get a hint of its contents during dreams, visions, creative highs.

Even though there is little scientific evidence to prove the existence of such exalted modes of consciousness, there is an enormous amount of personal testimony. So much so, in fact, that honest reflection on the problems of consciousness inevitably leads one to conclude that either there are forms of consciousness beyond anything science has imagined, or scientists have been extremely lax in not examining mental phenomena that have such widespread anecdotal evidence. If such modes of consciousness exist, then the modern "mind sciences" are somewhat in the position of eighteenth-century science—before the discovery of electricity, the atom, and subatomic particles—which claimed phlogiston to be one of the irreducible constituents of life. As physics has been forced progressively to advance the complexity of matter and energy from the phlogiston model, so it seems present attitudes are pressing contemporary science to reconsider consciousness as a "layered" or "aspected" mode that can become ever more complex and ever more all-encompassing. As Sir Charles Sherrington observed, the universe is looking less and less like a great machine and more like a "great thought."

If there is any truth in this analysis of the phenomena of consciousness, then three facts stand out as vital: (1) mind-control techniques like meditation will form the basis for further exploration; (2) the empirical testimony of mystics, seers, artists, and visionary scientists may offer the only adequate description we have of these unifying, highly creative modes of consciousness; and (3) both science and the average individual are in for a major, even traumatic change in how they view the world.

This eventual alteration of world views should preferably come gradually; not only because gradual change is part of the structural character of the scientific method, but because gradual change is psychologically healthier and safer for individuals and our culture at large. Radical alteration of belief systems and generally accepted theories of reality inevitably cause intense confusion and anxiety as well as potential backlash or rejection. That is why meditation and its theories of mind and consciousness should be approached with patience and cautious perseverance.

Although scientific attitudes regarding states of consciousness do seem to be changing, and there is even a thrust toward a theory of higher consciousness, attitudes are already polarizing. One group apparently believes that achieving forms of higher consciousness will, in effect, alter the history of the world, while the other tends to disregard the whole idea of higher states of consciousness as nonsense. The former group is composed of many occultists, some fringe groups in the humanistic psychology movement, as well as many serious scientists and philosophers. The latter types can be found even in orthodox scientific and medical institutions. The most obvious antagonism toward ASC seems concentrated in behavioral and clinical psychology where the favored experimental materials are those based upon the simple stimulus-response model. Concepts that cannot be easily measured such as mind and consciousness are considered nonproductive ways of examining the human mind.

An example of naive theorizing about ASCs is in the introduction to John White's book *Highest States of Consciousness,* in which he writes that "it is only through a change of consciousness that the world will be 'saved.'" This is such a clear, direct, and popular modern misstatement that it is worth examining. Many if not all the enthusiasts of otherworldliness make similar claims. The assumption is that an extreme ASC, a mystical or ecstatic experience, automatically and permanently alters character or personality. (Otherwise, how could the world be saved through a change of consciousness?) Alteration of personality does sometimes occur after such experiences, but this change is not always permanent nor is the end result of the experience always constructive. Even a cursory reading of the great mystics and sages clearly shows that many factors other than the mystical or ecstatic moment are involved in any alteration of personality. Many mystics, for example, continue to suffer from personal problems, psychotic episodes, demonic obsessions, and problems of character and will. All of these directly relate to their capacity to integrate the mystic experience into their personality, life-style, and inner being.

Second, the world cannot be "saved" by a change of consciousness in and of itself, for even after extreme ecstatic experiences there is the continuing need for application of willpower, disciplined behavior, and modification of destructive habit patterns that have built up over a lifetime. Most of all there remains the need for a clear, uncompromising honesty that will not succumb to the delusions of an ego likely to feel "special" or "chosen." Indeed, the dangers of ego involvement and "spiritual arrogance" are legion and well catalogued throughout religious history. It is naiveté, a kind of spiritual innocence (and not in the positive sense of Christ's "poor of spirit"), that involves many people in such sentimental, simplistic theories about ASC. This attitude is generally accompanied by a simplistic view of the human mind and by ignorance regarding the functions and tenacity of the ego to utilize new experiences for its own ends. Only a few modern "gurus" and religious philosophers warn consistently of this egoist danger: two examples are Krishnamurti as he preaches intense self-examination and self-reliance, and the young Tibetan monk Chogyam Trungpa, who continually warns of the strength and deceptions of the ego.

In short, different states of consciousness do clearly alter our relationship to, and perception of, the world, but it still remains for this new vision to be incorporated into our personality, belief system, and world view. Without such integration, ASCs can degenerate into a mere sensory circus, with consciousness as the center arena and self-deluding ideas as the trapeze act.

Disregarding the wilder claims of believers and nonbelievers, what evidence is there that ASCs are important and worthy of study? One way to find an answer is to look at the broad historical testimony of some of humanity's exceptional geniuses, leaders, and thinkers. Throughout the ages exceptional men and women who have changed the course of human history have reported experiencing higher states of consciousness—from Plato, Socrates, Christ, and Buddha to St. Thomas, St. Teresa, St. John, Henri Bergson, William James, and Albert Einstein.

There are moments when one feels that there is something great and breathing all around us, a vital ingredient to which our shuttered, fearful vision frequently blinds us. This sensation is usually a fleeting experience, and one that we can celebrate only passingly. To become sensitive to its presence is a difficult task for most of us. The outstanding characteristic of this sensation of a breathing, alive universe is its immersion in "significance." William James, for example, wrote to his wife of an altered-state-of-consciousness experience he had on Mt. Marcy, part of a wilderness area in New York's Adirondack Mountains: "I spent a good deal of it (the night) in the woods, where the streaming moonlight lit up things in magical checkered play, and it seemed as if the Gods of all the nature-mythologies were holding an indescribable meeting in my breast with the moral Gods of the inner life. . . . The intense significance of some sort, of the whole scene, if one could only *tell* the significance; the intense inhuman remoteness of its inner life, and yet the intense *appeal* of it; its everlasting freshness and its immemorial antiquity and decay. . . . In point of fact, I can't find a single word for all that significance, and don't know what it was significant of . . . so there it remains, a mere boulder of *impression*."

The mind in this experience, and in innumerable others recorded by inspired people over the years, reacts to the world with a spontaneous intensity, finessing the normal channels of logic and sequential thought, and searches out a peculiar kind of meaning. As James discovered, our daily consciousness is thus surrounded by modes of perception having little to do with the basic, everyday rational way of observing the world. The intense significance of James's experience, so representative of creative people, implies a structure and vitality not perceivable by normal cognition.

Yet there is also recent evidence that millions of people have experienced exceptional or higher states of consciousness similar to James's. The late American psychologist Abraham Maslow interviewed hundreds of people during the early stages of his research, characterizing what they reported as "peak experiences." After intense study and analysis Maslow concluded that these people's peak experiences were a natural and healthy condition rather than a peculiar anomaly. It was a fundamentally positive experience which enhanced their overall attitudes: "In the peak experience, such emotions as wonder, awe, reverence, humility, surrender, and even worship before the greatness of the experience are often reported."

Dr. Maslow described several dominant characteristics people reportedly experienced during these peak states of awareness. First, the peak experience is basically a cognitive one; it is perceived by the conscious mind. There is also a tremendous concentration of a kind that does not normally occur. As Maslow writes about it, "There is the truest and most total kind of visual perceiving or listening or feeling. Part of what this involves is a peculiar change which can best be described as non-evaluating, non-comparing, or non-judging cognition." An example is a mother lovingly examining every minute detail of her newborn child. Fascinated by each particle of the tiny body down to the toenails; every detail is as important and thrilling as every other. The mother's mind is concentrated so intensely on her baby that the rest of the world momentarily dissolves. Only the infant remains. The enthrallment at such moments can indeed be described as ecstatic, or perhaps even a religious awe or wonder. In the peak experience, this same kind of total noncomparing, noncritical acceptance of "everything" under attention occurs. It is as if everything within the focus of attention were equally important, and a person is then "most easily seen per se, in himself, by himself, uniquely and idiosyncratically as if he were the sole member of his class." Perception during the peak experience is also relatively ego-transcending, self-forgetful, egoless, unselfish. It comes closer to being unmotivated, impersonal, desireless, nonattached, not needing or wishing.

If frequent or long-lasting, this state of mind would naturally be repugnant to many in the activity-oriented West. It is, however, a more or less fleeting experience that does not impair effective outer-oriented activity. What occurs is that the perceptual experience is centered more on the object itself than upon more commonplace ego-needs. This means in turn that objects (including other people) are more readily perceived as having independent realities of their own and not merely extensions of our own psychological attitude.

Another major characteristic of the peak experience is its self-validating, self-justifying quality. It is felt to be not only a highly valuable experience, but one that is so great that sometimes even an attempt to justify its reality to someone else takes away from its dignity and worth. Maslow reports that some of the people he interviewed considered the experience so great that it validated life itself and made their lives more worth living. Because life is seen as so meaningful and worthy during the peak experience, it also transmutes the world into a place that is not inherently evil, where things are seen as valuable simply because they *are*. A thing's existence in itself is beautiful, good, and worthwhile. In effect, the world is accepted as it is without judgmental analysis. It is as if the peak experience reconciles people with the existence of destructiveness, ugliness, and evil in the world.

Practically everything that occurs in the peak experience can be categorized as a "religious happening" and indeed has been considered religious experiences in the past. The mystic's identification with God can be better understood in light of Maslow's analysis of the peak experience. Often the mystic perceives himself as not only united with God, but being transmuted into perceiving the world in godlike terms; that is, he sees the world and the universe as an integrated and unified whole with purpose, design, and meaning. It is indeed a godlike capacity to contemplate and encompass the whole of a being rather than just a part, and thereby understand it as inevitable, just, and good. Through such unclouded eyes evil might very well be perceived as the product of self-centered vision and limited understanding. As Maslow says, "If we could be godlike in this sense, then we, too, out of universal understanding would never blame or condemn or be disappointed or shocked. Our only possible emotions would be pity, charity, kindliness, perhaps sadness or amusement."

This is precisely the way *self-actualizing* people (a term Maslow uses for those who have had a peak experience) react to the world. For example, Maslow found that people were not only more "real" to the peak experiencer, but they took on a sacred quality —a feeling that mystics impart to all of life. To the peak experiencer, the world not only existed, but was also sacred. More than any other single factor, it is probably this vision of the world, perceived during these high states of consciousness, that connects the peak experience with religiosity.

In the past the peak experience has been called "revelation" or "mystical illumination," but with Maslow's work these experiences are being avidly studied by many contemporary psychologists. It seems likely that all the older reports phrased in terms of supernatural revelation are in fact natural human experiences that can be scientifically examined in whatever cultural, conceptual, or linguistic framework they occur. Maslow's research, however, is hampered by the fact that his sampling of those individuals reporting peak experiences was unsystematic and nonscientific. His analysis may have been brilliant, original, and provocative, but the small sampling itself makes one pause before accepting his conclusions.

Fortunately, this lack of empirical and properly ordered data has recently been corrected by Dr. Andrew Greeley and Dr. William McCready of the National Opinion Research Center (NORC) at the University of Chicago. Their research involved a nationwide, controlled sampling in which they discovered that some 35 percent of the American population over eighteen (approximately 46 million people) have experienced mystical moments or something akin to Maslow's peak experience. Eighteen percent had had the experience "once or twice," 12 percent reported it "several times," and 5 percent reported it "often." In addition, a second surprising fact was that the groups who reported having had these experiences were not overly young or counterculture oriented. In fact, those in their forties and fifties were somewhat more likely to report peak experiences than the rest of the population.

Some popular myths about mystics and their "oddball" personalities were destroyed by the Greeley-McCready study. A basic assumption about the mystic has been that he is an oppressed, unhappy, rigid person looking for the reassurance and relief provided by withdrawal from the world. In fact, the NORC study shows the most frequent mystical experiences are had by college-educated males over forty, making more than $10,000 a year. They are also substantially more likely to be black. In short, the data did not suggest unhappy, rigid, or guilt-ridden personalities. But one of the most striking findings of the study was the high correlation between the psychological well-being of the respondents and their frequency of mystical experiences.

The most frequent "triggers" of the experience (reported by 40 percent of respondents) were not drug related; instead they included "listening to music," "prayer," "the beauties of nature," and "listening to a sermon." All of these triggers had in common the concentrated intensity of Maslow's subjects; yet the *type* of activity seemed to be less significant than the individual's state of consciousness. Other descriptions that fit both Maslow's peak experiencers and traditional mystical experiences involved "a feeling of deep and profound peace," "a certainty that all things will work out for the good," "a sense of my own need to contribute to others," "a conviction that love is at the center of everything," and "a sense of joy and laughter."

Interestingly, Maslow's peak experiencers are similar to those described by Greeley and McCready and also to the practiced meditators. The ecstasy of mystics who also followed the meditative path is often identical to that of those who experienced a spontaneous mystical insight. Greeley and McCready reported that in one case a college professor had his "peak" experience as he was walking by some tennis courts. Another, who was a president of a university and a mathematician, had an ecstatic moment while shaving in the morning. A business executive had his experience while reading a book in a fishing boat. All three said the experiences were of "decisive importance" in their lives.

That the ecstatic or peak experience plays an important role in

Value, Purpose & meaning

one's life is not surprising considering its intensity and the fact that it resolves anxiety, gives meaning where there was none before, creates value and purpose where there might have been only despair or confusion a moment ago. If these experiences are only one tenth as potent as reported, then it is not so strange that meditators are enthusiastic and even proselytizing about their experiences.

A peculiar paradox exists in today's study of consciousness. Unlike Maslow, most scientists generally tend to study the objective correlates of consciousness rather than the experience itself. This is undoubtedly because there is no objective method by which science can investigate something like consciousness. Other "nonmaterial" things, such as certain particles of light in physics, suffer from the same paradox; yet techniques have been developed to study their objective "effects." With consciousness there is no particle to trace, no cloud chamber in which one can hope to catch a glimpse of what stimulates consciousness—there is only a ghostly sense within the chambers of our minds. Perhaps consciousness needs no "stimulation" but simply is, like the mysterious source of energy called life itself.

Consciousness is perhaps the greatest enigma facing the inquiring human mind. William James defined thought as "a moment of consciousness." And indeed "consciousness" is often considered a term for overall psychic functions or, as James illustrated, for separate aspects such as thought, awareness, visualization, etc. But recent research has indicated that consciousness has many broad definable phases against which individual manifestations occur. Hence, consciousness is more like a background, a night sky with attention and concentration a shooting star that is illuminating our minds.

As Teilhard de Chardin writes in his *The Divine Milieu,* "All the consciousness of my life are one consciousness." Just as you cannot separate various emotions from your overall life and call each emotion a "part" of your inner life, so the various stages of consciousness we have been talking about are separate yet one. In this sense all the various stages experienced in meditation are actually one; that is, all experience is singular in the sense that the experience is the single source of interpretation. In this sense we are our own creation or author, and the clear consciousness of our minds, the stage. Until we are fully conscious, the process of evolving awareness moves from a sybaritic infancy to an emotion-ridden, ego-dominated, blind adult struggling to understand the promise sensed within.

We cannot fully live our lives because we do not totally know ourselves. As long as we are driven, urged, cajoled, manipulated by the shadowed centers of energy within us, we cannot claim true freedom. This is the basic psychological and spiritual value of meditation, for it is an invaluable method for revealing the shadowed complexities of our inner natures.

Man clearly interacts with the world on many levels. The pinpoint of light we call consciousness flicks across the rooms of our lives isolating only small, specific areas materially important to our immediate or survival needs. Yet an enormous area of our brains is excluded from this thin beam of conscious attention. At best we sense these great alternative realities within. There are even moments when we become aware of specific images, ideas, powers that seem just beyond our reach. Sometimes there is the awareness that within us there is a "godlike chaos," a potential of enormous force that is both attractive and awesome. This sense of potential power is the opposite of the existential despair, the "nausea of awareness" that results from our sense of isolation. At such moments our isolated sense of self brings with it the panic of one locked into an alien world of physical objects beyond the direct touch of our radiant minds.

These are the two extremes of our relation with the world. They represent the passive and active modes in life. They delineate the choice available. Either we can respond in an evolutionary way and constantly seek to broaden the perspective by which our consciousness relates to the world, or we can simply allow the world to affect us as we passively experience it. Through conscious attending, by directing our will and energy, we turn the key that opens the door to alternative life-styles. I, for example, clearly have the choice as the sun sets to sit quietly in the growing darkness or take action to turn on the light. If I choose to sit in darkness in order to think or to dream, it is a freely chosen option. But if I become indecisive and unaware, more animal than truly human, and allow myself to be so benumbed, unhappy, and depressed that I *cannot* take the option, at that moment life acts upon me and I become a passive creature separated from all else but my misery.

On one end of the spectrum, then, we are alone and in an alien world; yet on the other we are the possessors of a potential force that seems godlike because it is creative and self-determining. As godlike beings we also experience moments of intense feeling when there is a more intimate connection between our normally separate awareness of self and the broader reality of nature; in effect, we become aware of our capability for a more meaningful relationship with nature. It is proper, of course, that we initially must live pendulumlike between these disturbing extremes, for as Aldous Huxley pointed out in his book *Doors of Perception,* a limitation of consciousness is biologically necessary if civilization is to continue. We cannot be exclusively enraptured with our inner life-processes and also till the fields that will bring our food for winter. There are meditative techniques that allow one to meditate and work simultaneously, but these are advanced techniques. Oriental religions in particular emphasize retaining the meditative state of mind while being physically active. For example, there are Ch'an Buddhist and Taoist walking meditations. (See the Appendix for examples of meditation exercises that involve more than using the inner mind exclusively.) In fact, most religions that use meditation encourage the carrying over of the meditative state of mind into one's everyday activities.

THE PSYCHOLOGICAL URGE TO MEDITATE

Western psychology often seems captured by its own theories. There is little room for broad or comprehensive personal growth. The ego is the central, primary aspect of Western psychology. A psychology centered on ego functions can only stumble when it tries to question whether the ego can get beyond itself. If the ego defines the boundary of human reality, nothing beyond those frontiers can ever be considered seriously. Eastern psychology, on the other hand, considers *consciousness* the basic phenomenon of mind, with instincts, ego function, perceptions to be aspects derived from ever more subtle forms of consciousness. Human development is not viewed as a process of learning methods for controlling instincts and ego functions, but rather as a growth process that uncovers ever broader and more pervasive aspects of consciousness, and that culminates with the realization that all consciousness is the expression of a single, unitive "awareness" that permeates the universe. Everything perceived by the individual is an extension of this "absolute awareness" that has given birth to and energizes all life.

In such a philosophy the human ego is necessarily diminished rather than simply controlled. It is not the guide for an instinctual animal self that must be manipulated, but rather an interpretive bridge over which the various aspects of the self must travel. Like the Chinvad Bridge of Zarathustrian myth that becomes narrower as the sinful try to pass over, the dynamic ego that human beings utilize to relate to the physical world must be slowly narrowed to the width of a thread that can no longer block our vision of other realities.

Myths and symbols have thus built up around the warring ambitions within the human heart and mind: conflicts between outer and inner goals, between ego, instinct, and conscious purpose have been a recognized human battleground since ancient times. The relationship between meditation and the control over subconscious powers were expressed in early symbols and myths. There is, for example, the uniting of the body and mind in the Greco-Roman religions that begin with the Pythagoreans and continue through Plato, Aristotle, the neo-Platonists, and on into Judaism and early Christianity. In this Western tradition (often called "Orphic"), the personality is thought of as a unit composed of many disparate parts, which are frequently in conflict with each other. This approach to the "unwhole," "incomplete," or "neurotic" individual is not dissimilar to theories of modern psychotherapy. The basic need of the Orphic psychological tradition was to find methods that would resolve inner tensions that were the by-products of the various elements in the warring personality. The Orphic tradition taught that the bodily aspect in mankind was composed of strong compulsions that had combined with the psyche, or mind. The psyche, however, was not the totality of a human personality, but had originally been a fragment of God, or a divine substance. Thus humanity seemed destined to suffer a divided self, eternally torn asunder by clashing impulses.

Early Grecian myths express this duality of mind and matter, of godly and fleshly reality, with stories of primordial monsters, or Titans, who represent the evil inherent in matter. Throughout these myths runs the subtheme of guilt, the need for expiation and salvation, for cleansing the human particles from those of divinity. But most central is the theme of man divided within himself.

Modern psychology has come to regard the relationship between mind and body as more intimate, and, with the development of psychosomatic medicine, there has been an ever greater tendency to see the misery of the mind as the source for bodily pain and disease. ∨

One of the most evocative myths expressing these central concerns of ancient psychology is Plato's description of the charioteer and horses in his dialogue *Phaedrus*. Plato conceived the bodily desires as distinctive inner "urges." The need for food and comfort are clearly physical desires, but "knowing" of our desire is a function of the mind. Since desire is at base a psychological experience, Plato was far ahead of his time. In his parable of the horses and charioteer, "desire" is the horse that gives the charioteer the greatest difficulty. This unruly horse is a symbol of the multiplicity of desires by which man's mind is constantly obsessed. The second horse in Plato's parable symbolizes the emotional aspect, with the charioteer himself representing reason or the intellect. Plato thus equated reason with divinity, for it was the enlightened guide by which the whole (chariot, man, and horses) could be moved. Unruly desire and fragmented emotions could only be saved by reason. Reason or the controlling mind, however, could not rule by force, but had to integrate the whole in a harmonious coordination.* Each mind had to find for itself the higher reality that would move it on to fulfill its evolutionary potential. But, most important, in Plato's vision of life the mind must be strong enough to contain the destructive, unruly horse. This is very close to the basic ideal sought in the Eastern mystical religions generally, but especially in those religions that emphasize meditation or mind-control as the foundation upon which the troubled individual can begin to find peace and "equilibrium."

Some psychological schools lend themselves more than others to this holistic tradition. For example, a basic premise in Gestalt

* An interesting social application of Plato's theory is suggested by the fact that he called such harmonic adjustment *dikaiosune*, which is a word from Greek social life meaning "justice." Many contemporary advocates of meditation also envision a beneficent impact upon society through widespread use of meditation. Maharishi Mahesh, in particular, believes that if only 1 percent of the population practiced his meditation, a better world would result. If 5 percent practiced it, the world would move into a golden age. This type of spiritual naiveté is common to many new age spiritual movements, as well as the quasiscientific groups involved in consciousness expansion, biofeedback, alpha creativity, etc.

therapy (as with other humanistically oriented schools of psychology) is that the mind *is* the body and the body *is* the mind. This view of the mind-body relationship neatly avoids the painful and traditional dilemma of Western philosophical mind-dualism. The human being is a *gestalt* (a German word meaning 'whole') or unified organism, and one's physical or mental characteristics are manifestations of the same thing—the individual's total existence. This intimate relationship between the mind and body is also common to practically every school of meditation or religion that relies on meditation heavily.

Further, Gestalt therapy has two main goals: self-awareness (being aware of what is happening within oneself, even at very deep levels) and self-responsibility (willingly making a choice regarding oneself and thereby guiding one's life with full clarity and understanding). These attitudes are reflected in the techniques used by various schools of humanistic psychology. Gestalt therapy states, as does Buddhism and most other psychologically oriented Eastern religions, that the only thing we can really be sure of is what we know through direct experience. Concentrating attention upon what you are sensing, feeling, on your body movements, internal imagery, visualization methods, dreams, and fantasies is, therefore, a preferred method that moves us toward greater self-understanding. The difficulty develops between theory and application (as always), when each school and teacher seems to believe it has an exclusive corner on truth.

What the humanistic psychologists emphasize is that paying attention to yourself involves paying attention to the continuum, or the ongoing processes of your mental and physical life. For this reason most humanistic psychologists are also phenomenologists. And even here the parallel with meditation tradition is striking, for the phenomenological psychologist or therapist will deal with what is going on at the moment, at the "now" point in a person's life.

In Gestalt there is a fundamental exercise called the "awareness continuum," in which the individual is asked to pay attention to him- or herself and report each detail of his awareness at that moment. This technique is even considered a "spoken meditation" in Gestalt because, as in the Ch'an Buddhist, Zen, and Taoist exercises, it focuses concentration on what the individual is feeling, sensing, or imagining. As the individual follows this "awareness continuum," there is an inevitable shifting from a wide-range focus to more singular events—a movement, a single image in the mind, a single feeling, memory, or whatever. As the technique becomes familiar, concentration on one's inner processes becomes ever more acute, sustained, and one begins to interact in meaningful ways with one's previous behavior or temperament. Practicing the "awareness continuum" is similar to other inward-directing meditation techniques, for the skill of inwardly focusing your concentration is always improved, and specific images or experiences begin to emerge as having more potency, energy, and meaning. These are pursued until their full meaning and impact on your life is revealed. It is very like the Ch'an (Zen) meditation method of pursuing images or ideas that disrupt your meditation until the final source, the "who" that is creating the idea or image, is uncovered.

While this may seem an excessive amount of self-concern and self-involvement, its final goal is a "forgetting of the self." To forget or diminish the self is fundamental to meditative religions, and it is generally believed to be an extension of a natural psychological state. For example, after daydreaming for several minutes we become aware that our "sense of self" has somehow disappeared. We wonder, "Where have I been?" during the last few minutes. Consciousness of the external time just passed is completely gone; only the remembrance of internal time and the fantasy we were involved in remains. There has been a major alteration in our ego-state. During the daydream the ego was attached exclusively to the dynamics of the daydream itself; it was caught by the power and fascination of our unconsciously motivated fantasy. Of course, this is also an ego function, but not the same as preening in front of a mirror as we prepare to go out for the evening. The ego has, in a sense, forgotten one of its functions of consciousness (external self-awareness) and become absorbed in another kind of fantasized, inner self-awareness. A similar forgetting of the conscious, alert, externally directed ego occurs during the early stages of concentration and mind-control training as one's attention is directed inward toward other goals. This is a forgetting of the self with a purpose, however, for we are now purposefully, alertly directing the forgetting of our "mirror-looking self."

During sports or other physically active moments when we concentrate intensely, we forget ourselves. We forget ourselves (sometimes) when we make love or are deeply moved by another person or an event. Intense emotion can automatically bring our attention to a sharp focus that excludes the mirror-primping self. D. T. Suzuki has described the "forgetting of self" that is deliberately induced in Zen sports. In Zen archery, for example, Suzuki writes that "the archer ceases to be conscious of himself as the one who is engaged in hitting the bull's eye which confronts him." The observing ego is diminished in the focusing of concentration. Perhaps this is what concentration is all about: the forgetting of the observing self, a reduction of the alert, demanding ego. The Hindu sage Patanjali described the yogic *samadhi*: "when alone the object of contemplation remains and one's own form is annihilated. This is samadhi."

Meditation and Religion

WITH THE RAPID GROWTH of meditation in the West, two areas of emphasis have developed. One involves the social and personal benefits of meditation: those practices that concentrate on and influence the meditator's psychological and physical well-being. The second deals with the philosophical-religious principles that underlie the traditional meditations of mystics, saints, and seers. ✓

The ultimate point of secular meditation is that the ever-expanding, ever-changing perception of the world brings new realities into the mind and heart. Art, music, philosophical and scientific ideas also have tremendous transmuting influences in our lives; but meditation seems to be a singularly practical and simple technique for melding all the ingredients of our daily lives into a unitive, meaningful whole. But the desire for meaning and union has, of course, its religious basis as well. Most experiences in life move from the external world to the internal, where they are integrated into the personality. Meditation is the inner world speaking to the inner world. It is a healing of disparate realities not yet integrated; it is the expansion of the gift of conscious insight. It is this melding of consciousness with the inner and outer worlds that serves the religious meditator.

Meditative religions hold a fundamental belief that man has

a purposeful destiny, that his uniqueness does not lack meaning. Many men in many cultures have accepted this belief but have not pursued its implications as the serious meditator does. The meditator who thinks beyond the comfort meditation brings to his body and mind generally comes to the same conclusion as Justice Oliver Wendell Holmes in 1913: "I think it not improbable that man, like the grub that prepares a chamber for a winged thing it never has seen but is to be—that man may have cosmic destinies that he does not understand."

There are two general religious tendencies in the West: to regard God as transcendent, outside the soul, and to be reached by stages; or to regard God as immanent, dwelling within the soul, and to be found by going deeply into one's own inner reality. The latter is the meditative way. In the "God is transcendent" tradition, the individual's dependence upon a higher power external to himself is fostered, whereas the meditative or mystical religious tradition tends continually to force the individual back into his own self, into what Rudolf Otto termed "introspective mysticism." When following this method, the inner self becomes the matrix, the center of intense activity by which the meditator hopes to first understand and then conquer his inner confusion. To accomplish this the mind becomes the medium of available power; it is the microscope through which new intimate worlds are revealed, through which new realities are introduced into our awareness. There is, of course, a close relationship between "things of the mind" and religion. This is no doubt why arch-rationalists are so forceful and overly defensive in trying to maintain the distinctions between the rational functions and the inclination to religious and spiritual symbolisms in the mind.

The connection between meditation and religion is intimate and ancient. Religion can be approached from several angles: from its psychological aspect, or as method, as devotion, as salvation, as a process of revelation leading to perfection, and so forth. But meditation *is* religion as a method; for while there are principles involved in each meditative technique regardless of the religion, the goals—and often the method—of contemplation are common to most religions.

Pope Pius XI commented on the importance and history of the contemplative life to the Catholic and, indeed, the Christian tradition:

From the earliest times this contemplative mode of life, most perfect and most useful and more fruitful for the whole of Christendom than anyone can conceive, took root in the Church and spread on all sides. . . . Since the whole object of this institution lay in this—that the monks, each in the privacy of his own cell, *unoccupied with any exterior ministry and having nothing to do with it,* should fix their thoughts exclusively on the things of heaven—wonderful was the benefit that accrued from it to Christian society. . . . In the course of time this pre-eminent institution that is called the contemplative life declined somewhat and lost vigor. The reason was that the monks . . . came by degrees to combine active life with their pondering on divine things and their contemplation.* (Merton's italics.) √

In the traditional Christian definition, contemplation means "simple intuition of the truth." This is its broadest definition, but, in its strictest Christian sense, contemplation is an intuition of God, induced in the soul by God, and allowing the soul a direct experience of God. The contemplative life, then, as practiced in traditional Christian belief exists when everything in one's life is directed toward the development of contemplation in its strict sense—union with God! The life of a contemplative monk is restricted in its external aspects in all religions—from Christianity to Buddhism—while maximum activity is directed toward internal exercises. The main distinction between this traditional Western definition of contemplation and the Eastern view of meditation is the Christian belief that the intuition of God is being produced by God Himself. In the East both the concept of God and the element of grace, which produce in the disciple the intuition of God, are practically nonexistent. Eastern techniques rely more on individual effort, more upon personal control of the mind and spirit, eventually inducing in oneself the experience of union. But in the East the goal is not union with God but rather a universal constant, or a principle without any experiential base to describe it, such as *nirvana* and *satori.*

PRAYER IN MEDITATION

Meditation in the West is also often considered "mental prayer," a process that aims to bring about union with God through reflection, proper thought, or concentration. In effect, the mind and will

---

* "Umbratilem" [Apostolic Constitution of July 8, 1924], quoted in Thomas Merton, *The Waters of Siloe* (New York: Harcourt, Brace and Co., 1949), p. xxxi.

cooperate with grace in actualizing God in the human soul. Meditation, or mental prayer, is prescribed as a matter of duty in Western and Eastern churches alike because in both the West and East meditation is considered essential to live a spiritual life. It is so important that it is advised for the isolated monk, cenobite, or layman.

Meditation was practiced possibly as early as 5000 or 6000 B.C. in India and China. In the West we know the monks in the deserts of Egypt and Syria from at least the third century A.D. practiced meditation. Later, in the Middle Ages, the Hesychast monks of Greece followed a system of meditation similar to Yoga, with emphasis on breath control and concentrating on points of the body—primarily the heart area (or heart *chakra* as they call it in Yoga). Christian saints such as St. Francis of Assisi and St. Teresa developed their own meditative disciplines. And the founder of the Jesuits, St. Ignatius of Loyola (1491–1556) evolved specific and stringent contemplative procedures in his *Spiritual Exercises*. In fact, the practice and even the ideals of contemplation held an important place throughout the history of Christianity. The *Philokalia*, a Christian book of the Eastern church first published in 1782, contains writings on meditation of the early desert monks. The writings themselves detail the methods and reasons behind Christian meditation, and advise the young monk on how to discipline and awaken his attention and broaden his control of consciousness. It provides mind training in the most effective methods for what the church "Fathers," or early priests, called the "art of arts and the science of sciences." The goal of these contemplative techniques is to lead an aspirant to the highest perfection open to him: union with the Lord. Jesus Ch

Appendix for examples

The meditation tech
sects of Christianity ha
meditation. The Roma
ample, attempts to dire
which result in the mec
meditator might, for ex
even Christ, might ha
his life. At its most e:
that his own "self" is c
object of meditation—wl

Other examples in Christian tradition involve silent prayer, which is somewhat similar to the Eastern "contentless" meditation, or the sense of "emptiness" striven for in the Buddhist *sunyata*. The Quakers in particular emphasize silence in order to listen and wait for God to speak. Their belief is, logically enough, that if you are constantly speaking or in prayer to God you can never hear a response. This is the Christian "prayer of the heart" found in the *Philokalia*, which seeks to keep one's heart expectantly open so that Christ can fill it. Put in simple analogical terms, if a bottle is full it cannot receive anything more. The classical form of the prayer of the heart is a meditative, repetitive invocation of Jesus' name in your heart, which is pictured as empty of all images and cares except the name of Christ. The prayer of the heart is therefore both an active placing of oneself in an open, receptive state and also one of intense expectancy and concentration. Because the Christian church emphasizes the relationship between man and God as one of the "created" to the Creator, the whole purpose of this meditation is to "deepen the consciousness of this basic relationship of the creature to the Creator, and of the sinner to his Redeemer." *

This belief is in strong contrast to many other Western meditative techniques that use very active forms of prayer, which sometimes even degenerate into a kind of speaking *at* God, or demanding, cajoling a response to petitionary invocations. The "I want" syndrome of prayer and meditation, however, is not limited to Christianity, for it is found throughout the world's religions.

In general, the Western meditation techniques developed combinations of invocation meditations, prayer, and meditation joined with song, chant (similar to Indian mantras), and even forms of arguing with God in almost legallike petitions. All of these forms of meditation-prayer rely upon words, upon communicating with divine forces external to oneself. And even while many monastic orders had rules forbidding or curtailing speech, there was still heavy reliance on internal dialogue and a dependence on words in communicating with God. Again, speaking generally, the Oriental more often rejected words or verbalization of any sort and preferred a complete absorption through experience. The Eastern meditator can be said to have rejected verbal or conceptual tech-

* Thomas Merton, *Contemplative Prayer* (New York: Doubleday & Co., Image Books, 1969), p. 83.

niques in favor of nonstructured or spontaneous spiritual experience.

There are, of course, many theological arguments about the differences—or lack of them—between meditation and prayer. But perhaps American psychic Edgar Cayce summarized the distinction between the two best:

Prayer is the concerted effort of the physical consciousness to become attuned to the consciousness of the Creator, either collectively or individually. *Meditation* is emptying self of all that hinders from the creative forces rising along the natural channels of the physical man. . . . As we (mankind) give out, so does the whole man become physically and mentally depleted. Yet, entering into the silence in meditation we may receive that strength and power that fits each individual, each soul, for a greater activity in this material world. In meditation you are seeking to know the will or activity of the Creative Forces; for you are raising in meditation actual creation taking place within the inner self.

In another place Cayce suggested that the difference between meditation and prayer is "Prayer is supplication to God and meditation is listening to His answer."

In analyzing Cayce's approach to meditation and prayer, Charles Wise has observed that meditation for Cayce seems to be a search for the Creator, a search that "begins in the mind and seeks knowledge (i.e., relationships), a search that culminates in revelation or cosmic consciousness, contact with the mind of God." Prayer is rather a search that begins with longing, that travels through the emotions and finds the answer to one's yearning in union with the Infinite, or "spiritual orgasm of ecstasy." In short, this approach leaves prayer dependent upon faith, upon a longing for union with a God believed to be waiting and receptive; meditation is available to anyone willing to undergo the discipline and practice, even if he is an agnostic or atheist. The meditator is in this sense pursuing a cognitive process, and hoping to find ultimate truth. It is an idea surprisingly like Mahatma Gandhi's when he described Hinduism: "A man may not believe in God and still call himself a Hindu. Hinduism is a relentless pursuit after truth. Truth is God."

"CREATURE" MEDITATIONS AND NATURE

However, there are many exceptions to the above generalizations. An example in the East is Pure Land Buddhism and its reliance on ritualistic chanting of special *sutras*, or sacred verses, in order to ensure salvation. One of the many exceptions in the West is the use of the creative experience—poetry, music, painting—in a religious meditation. A passage of The Epistle to the Ephesians (5:18–20) combines the creative and religious consciousness, justifying the use of meditation in the writing of religious poetry. "Be filled with the spirit; speaking to yourselves in psalms and hymns and spiritual songs, singing and making melody in your heart to the Lord; giving thanks always for all things unto God the Father in the name of our Lord Jesus Christ." Thus the meditative, creative, and religious experience all fuse into an *ars poetica*. √

In both the East and West the aesthetic impulse was utilized for sacred ends. The metaphysical poetry of late-sixteenth- and seventeenth-century English poets such as Southwell, Donne, Herbert, Vaughan, and even Milton is full of fundamentally meditative images. During these few centuries there developed a habit of meditating on "creatures" that was practiced intensely by many aesthetics like Henry Vaughan. This style of meditation stimulated poetic imagery and evoked what modern psychology would undoubtedly consider archetypal symbols from the poet's unconscious. There is little doubt, however, that "meditating on creatures" is a highly effective method of inducing an altered state of consciousness that bridges the protective boundaries between the conscious and unconscious mind. The technique itself is not complex. √

The basic assumption underlying the creature meditation is that the divine can be found in all objects of life if one "sees properly." When the meditator turns his attention to the external world he attempts to "see" the divine there. Seventeenth-century Puritan mystic Richard Baxter describes this meditation: √

Make an advantage of every object thou seest, and of every passage of Divine providence, and of everything that befalls in thy labour and calling, to mind thy soul of its approaching Rest. As all providences and creatures are means to our Rest, so do they point us to that as their end. Every creature hath the name of God and of our final Rest upon it, which a considerate believer may as truly discern, as he can read upon a post or hand in a cross way, the name of the Town or City which it points to. This spiritual use of creatures and providences, is God's great end in bestowing them on man. . . . O that Christians were skilled in this Art.

Baxter later adds in his book *The Saints Everlasting Rest, Heavenly Meditation* (1649) that the true Christian meditator not only opens his Bible and "reads there of God," but should also "learn to open the creatures, and to open the several passages of providence, to read of God and glory there. Certainly with such a skillful industrious improvement, we might have a fuller taste of Christ and heaven, in every bit of bread that we eat, and in every draught of beer that we drink, than most men have in the use of the Sacrament."

In simple terms, the meditator here attempts to translate his perception of divine things external to himself into his internal world. Another example is Henry Vaughan's poem "Vanity of Spirit" in which the speaker is exhausted from study and leaves his room to lie down beside a spring in order to find "refreshment in nature." He seeks to find God in external creation all around him but fails. Then he turns his attention inward to search within himself, where he finds traces of the creative power that moves all life. The narrator of the poem thus moves from admiration of the external world to seeking within himself a sense of unity between the inner and outer worlds. St. Bonaventure also describes the vestiges or traces of God "mirrored in the external world." In seeking God through "creature meditation" the meditator can "behold the reflection of God," and in that reflection find a resonance within himself. From this bridge-building between the external and internal worlds, a dialogue begins to take place within the mind, with the whole process concluding in the realization that "from this speaking to our selves we speak to God." The same sequence of enlightenment—and creature meditation technique— was also used by St. Ignatius and Fray Luis. As Francis de Sales adds, "all creatures do invite them to this. . . . all things provoke us and give us occasion of good and godly thoughts, from whence afterward do arise many notions and aspirations of our soul to God."

It is strange to read these seventeenth-century Puritans, who were often self-righteous and who cloaked themselves in rigid piety, as they sing the praises of nature and natural things, as they seek through intense concentration to find the divine through all forms of life—even the lowliest. How fearful they were to take the last step, yet how close they came to the Taoist and Buddhist reverence for life and nature. Their vision is almost as perceptive, but lacks the freedom and spontaneity so obvious in Taoist and Zen reverence for life. In Christian Puritan terms the Taoist would be considered a "creature meditator," yet no Puritan could ever free himself to speak of the divinity he saw in life in the same terms as the Taoist. In the fourth century B.C., for example, the Taoist sage Chuang Tzu recorded this dialogue on how he perceived God in nature.

Tung Kuo Tzu asked Chuang Tzu, saying, "Where is what you call the Tao to be found?"

Chuang Tzu replied, "Everywhere."

The other said, "Specify an instance of it. That will be more satisfactory."

"It is here in this ant," Chuang Tzu pointed.

"Give a lower instance," insisted the other.

"It is in this grass," replied Chuang Tzu.

"Give me still a lower instance."

"It is in this earthenware tile," answered Chuang Tzu.

"Surely, that is the lowest instance?" said Tung Kuo Tzu.

"No, it is also in that excrement," said Chuang Tzu.

But since Chuang Tzu knew that his questioner did not yet understand he said, "Your questions, my master, do not touch the fundamental point of the Tao. You should not specify any particular thing. There is not a single thing without the Tao. So it is with the perfect Tao. And if we call it the great Tao, it is just the same. There are the three terms—'Complete,' 'All-embracing,' and 'the Whole.' These names are different, but the reality sought in them is the same. They all refer to the One thing." √

China and Chuang Tzu were not unique in their complete commitment to a unitive vision of life. Intimacy between the divine in man and the divine in nature can be found in many ancient cultures. The Oglala Sioux Indians called the divine element in man *sican,* which is regarded as identical with the *ton,* or divine essence of the world. After death the *niya,* or vital soul, left the *nagi,* or personality, and disappeared into the material universe. The nagi, or soul, continues to exist in the ghost world while the sican, or divine aspect of the self, is reunited with the divine essence of the universe. The Maoris have a similar view of humanity. Every human being is a compound of four things: a divine element called *toiora;* an ego, which dissolves at death; a psyche, or ghost-part, that survives death; and the physical body.

All of these traditions can be considered crude formulations of a perennial philosophy, a spiritual doctrine that can be found in the belief systems of ancient peoples all over the world.

The perennial philosophy states that there is a "divine ground of all existence" which is "a spiritual Absolute." It is ineffable in terms of discursive thought, but can be directly experienced during exalted states of consciousness like *nirvana* and *satori,* and can be realized consciously and willfully by anyone. It is this Absolute that the spiritual meditator seeks. For this type of religious meditator (in contrast to those who simply seek freedom from stress, etc.), the ultimate reason for existence, the last goal of man is the unitive knowledge of this "divine ground." At the moment this is experienced the self dies and God fills the void. Talk of ego-death, of overcoming the attachments of the self, of expanding consciousness all come to rest in this ultimate resolution. All the metaphysical arguing, the floods of words drowning eyes and mind, the arid waste of emotion-laden seeking cease to torment the human awareness in this reentered (or never left) continuum. As described by saints, sages, mystics, poets throughout the ages, it is truly an experience that "surpasseth all understanding."

Only saints and mystics have the right to absolutes. All the rest of us who are still partially unmade must deal with a world of physical, ethical, and spiritual relativism. Our immaturity may lead us to believe moral absolutes are possible and necessary in an immoral world, but this is the theoretical piety of the inexperienced. The stages of moral and spiritual growth seem to move from the pietistic absolutes of youth, to the cynical relativism and compromise of middle age, and, finally, to a sad confusion and acceptance of mysteries beyond our capacity to capture in our life-style. As Robert Frost wrote, "We dance round in a ring and suppose,/But the Secret sits in the middle and knows." Once we cease in our mature confusion to dance and suppose, we allow the full mystery of life to begin seeping in between the rigid seams of arrogance and absolutes.

The mystic's perception of life is indeed strange when seen strictly from our businesslike everyday consciousness. In a small classic of Western mysticism, *The Candle of Vision* by A. E.,* the author considers meditation as both a prelude to and part of the end result of the religious awakening. This awakening starts

* Pseudonym of George William Russell.

with an "inexpressible yearning of the inner man to go out into the infinite." But that infinite we enter is living. It is our ultimate being. Religious meditation is a fiery brooding on that majestic self. "We imagine ourselves into its vastness. We conceive ourselves as mirroring its infinitudes, as moving in all things, as living in all beings. . . . We try to know as It knows, to live as It lives, to be compassionate as It is compassionate. We equal ourselves to It that we may understand It and become It." A. E. writes that the mind creates the reality that finally absorbs itself. "What a man thinks, that he is," says A. E. The mind is the builder, the creator of all reality, from how we perceive the world at our fingertips to how we conceptualize and envision the ultimate.

Most of the higher religions consider the relationship between the spiritual self and the personal self or ego an important description of the spiritual nature of humanity. In the Christian Bible, for example, there is the declarative statement, "I have said, ye are gods; and all of you are children of the most High." St. Augustine embellishes this idea when he says that "when the soul loves something it becomes like unto it; if it should love terrestrial things it becomes terrestrial, but if it should love God does it not become God?"

The Buddhist and Hindu religions especially emphasize the intimacy between the divine aspect of mankind and the larger, universal expression of the spirit. In fact, the core of the Advaita Vedanta philosophy in Hinduism is expressed in the single, simple, enigmatic *Tat tvam Asi* (Thou art That)—a phrase that we can be sure Chuang Tzu, St. Augustine, and even the Puritans would understand.

Though Judaism does not often emphasize meditation as a union between man and the universe, it has produced many mystics and specific meditative traditions. Some of Judaic meditations seem close to Yoga and Zen. Abraham Abulafia was a thirteenth-century mystic who used a system of meditation very like some yogic techniques. Abulafia developed techniques that used the Hebrew alphabet, with each letter possessing a numerical equivalent that imprinted their mystical meaning on the soul. But concentrating on these letters was also a device for dissolving the mind's numerous psychologically disturbing mental and sense images and for developing the ability to bring the mind to a single point of attention. The Hasidic Jews relied on "insight" techniques not unlike Zen *koans* in which the goal is to shock one into enlightenment or insight. A Hasidic parable that has a strong resemblance to Zen koans shows that the flash-of-insight technique used in Eastern meditation appears in Judaism as well:

A conductor once asked some Hasidim in a train for their tickets.

"Why don't you ask the engineers in the locomotive for their tickets?" asked the Hasidim.

"But they're driving the train," the surprised conductor replied.

"So are we," replied the Hasidim.

THE MEDITATOR'S "SACRED WAY"

Mysticism should not antagonize, frighten, or even disturb the nonmystic, for there is nothing inherently dangerous in it. To most people the most disturbing aspect of mysticism is its uncompromising admonition that the "self" must be altered, with the final result that the ego will be destroyed. But the mystic's way is not so clear-cut and rigid. There are many different personalities who accept the mystic's general vision, but differ in their personal philosophies and attitudes. In short, there are as many different people who are mystics as there are religious sects and philosophies. For example, not all mystics maintain that one must sacrifice one's ego to achieve enlightenment.

One of the greatest Islamic philosopher-poet-mystics argued fiercely that his everyday self, his ego, be retained in its entirety. "Even if one iota is to be diminished from my being, I shall not accept life immortal at this price," wrote Muhammed Iqbal. He adds, "The pangs of yearning constitute a priceless commodity,/I shall not exchange my humanity even for divinity." *

What Iqbal and others like him are saying is that the mystical transformation in which they have deep belief involves an altering of the individual, but it is an augmentation rather than a diminishing or destruction. In the transformation process, of course, some elements in one's temperament become less important—and therefore less active—even to the degree where they may disappear. In this sense, destructive elements in the personality are so diminished that they no longer play an active role in the everyday personality because they have been replaced by constructive

---

* Sir Muhammed Iqbal, *His Art and Thought* (Kashmiri Bazar, Lahore, Pakistan: Sh. Muhammad Ashraf, n.d.), pp. 47–48.

inclinations. This clarifies the fundamental wisdom of many ancient, esoteric books like the *I Ching,* which advises the reader:
"The best way to fight evil is to make energetic progress in the
good."

The meditator-mystic would appreciate Faust's reply to Me-
phisto: "In this your Nothing, I find my All." "Nothingness"
is the usual definition of nirvana, satori, and the ultimate goal of
the meditator's and the mystic's path. But "nothingness" is un-
satisfactory because it is misleading and confusing to the many
people who have never had such an experience. It is one of those
ineffable experiences of human intensity that seems impossible to
communicate to others. Consider how difficult it is to convey the
experience of intense love to someone who has never experienced
love, or to describe a color to someone blind from birth. How
much more difficult it is to describe the apex of human consciousness—which by definition means an exalted awareness—as a state
of nothingness. After all, to the average person the term "nothingness" conveys a wide range of impressions that has little to do with
what the mystic or meditator who has experienced satori or nirvana
is actually talking about. Nothingness can mean a state of "no relationships," a condition where no value systems and where no
frame of reference exist, or perhaps even total unconsciousness or
a state of death. It is important, therefore, to try to understand
just what the meditator-mystic means when he describes his experience as nothingness.

The concept of nothingness is a difficult idea to grasp. Perhaps,
as with other word-poor experiences such as love, analogies are
helpful. The rationale behind the Ch'an Buddhist's frequent reference to the cleansing of the mirror of the mind—the clearly desired Buddhist meditator's goal—is that even the slightest speck of
dust (i.e., mental or sensory attachment or discrimination) would
give the conscious mind an object, a frame of reference beyond the
single, clear state of its own surface to regard. Put simply, Buddhism teaches that when there are no conditions the mind returns
to its fundamental state. After all of the references to the world—
mind or body—have been dissolved, the meditator should have
only consciousness itself remaining. At that point, consciousness
is in effect paying "attention" only to itself: consciousness perceiving only consciousness.

To make this idea clearer, imagine your consciousness to be

a color and that that single pure color is then placed in an environment also totally of the same color. All objects in the room would blend together and no discrimination by your senses or your mind would be possible. This is the state the religious meditator seeks: pure white placed within an environment of pure white where no differentiation exists. The cleansed mirror reflects only itself. "If the doors of perception were cleansed," says William Blake, "every thing will appear to man as it is, infinite." The meditative illumination shows us, for the first time, that light can contain mystery—no shadows or dark covers are necessary. Light itself contains the illimitable.

Another perhaps even simpler analogy is to imagine your consciousness to be the *light* of a single candle, and that this candlelight is slowly moved into an environment of great brightness, equivalent, say, to the sun. The candlelight itself would, to all forms of normal perception, become extinguished; it would in effect be lost within the greater light. As the Sufi mystic Farid al-Din 'Attar writes:

> Come you lost Atoms to your Center draw,
>   And *be* the Eternal Mirror that you say:
> Rays that have wander'd into Darkness wide
>   Return, and back into your Sun subside.

The candlelight would still obviously exist as an independent light, but it would *also* become a part (or become "One" as the mystics say) with the larger, brighter light. If your consciousness were that single light of the candle, how would the world be perceived by you? All distinctions would be lost; objects or symbols by which we understand the world would have disappeared. While you would still have all the composite integrity of that single candle flame, of that "I" with its sense of personal history, of previous moments lived, the sense of singleness of the "I" would become totally lost. To retain it, you would have to divert your attention from the overwhelming, bright, awesome light all around you, back to your history, your childhood, your perceptions of the world a moment before immersion occurred in the greater reality of that sun-dominated moment. If your attention was completely concentrated on the light all around you, however, your own candle of consciousness would become totally absorbed by it—which is exactly what mystics throughout history have described in agoniz-

ing and exalted language. In effect, the experience would be of
"nothingness," for you would have nothing to relate to. There
would be nothing to see or perceive beyond the immediate same-
ness of you and the greater element so identical to yourself. As
Christ Himself said, "If, therefore, thine eye be single, thy whole
body shall be full of light."

When such an experience has been tested in the laboratory, the
sensory deprivation soon gives rise to mental hallucinations; the
mind begins to fill itself with random material floating up from
the unconscious. But the whole point of meditation and the disciplines of the meditator-mystics is to eliminate all perceptions—
including those from the unconscious. And if we accept this as
possible, it is far easier to grasp what the meditator or the mystic
means when he says that all differentiation has passed, that there is
no distinguishing aspect between himself and the rest of the world.
Under such conditions it is not too hard to understand that the
experience would indeed be perceived as nothingness.

The Mysteries of
Transcendental Meditation

DURING THE SECOND HALF of the 1970s, Transcendental Meditation practice had become so popular in the United States and elsewhere that even many of the meditators did not realize how quickly this method's impact had spread. *Time* magazine recently described the TM phenomenon as "the turn-on of the '70s—a drugless high." Prestigious universities are conducting experiments into its methods. TM courses have even been given at major American corporations (AT&T, General Foods, Blue Cross, and others) in the belief that meditation could improve corporate efficiency. The originator of the TM method, Maharishi Mahesh Yogi, has become widely known, and his face and manner have become familiar from frequent appearances on television programs. Still, both the man and the method raised questions that remained unanswered despite the many public appearances, lectures, and interviews concerning the TM program. Foremost among these questions were Who is Maharishi Mahesh Yogi? Where did he come from? Just how is his meditation method learned and practiced?

Answers to even these three key questions are not easily obtained because Maharishi avoids inquiries into his personal life and because the Transcendental Meditation teacher-initiators have developed a special terminology that, in some respects, beclouds rather than clarifies details of their system. They are, however, clear-cut and even vociferous on one major point: The Transcendental Meditation method can only be learned by the technique developed by the Maharishi; there is no other path, they emphasize, but that of attending TM group meetings and eventually receiving individual instructions by a teacher who has himself been taught by the special TM method.

Meditation as advanced by Maharishi Mahesh Yogi is a direct and, to a wide range of individuals, quite appealing merger of Eastern and Western thought. As Charles Lutes, who directs Maharishi's Spiritual Regeneration Movement, puts it, the TM technique provides a meeting ground, a "point of entry for the mutual understanding of two heritages and cultures," which in turn provides "a method for each to enter into, complement, and enrich the other, to the immediate and practical benefit of both." Writing in an introduction to Maharishi Mahesh Yogi's book *Transcendental Meditation* (formerly titled *The Science of Being and Art of Living*), Mr. Lutes has noted that Westerners have long regarded Eastern religious and mystical teaching as "essentially a museum piece to be viewed under glass and of little practical worth to Western man, who has to live in the world, deal with its problems, and meet the responsibilities which it thrusts upon him." Maharishi Mahesh Yogi himself believes that meditation is being rediscovered in the West "as a result of an unprecedented upsurge of interest in achieving states of mind in which the consciousness is expanded by various means." √

Measured against the combination of awe and occasionally fearful aversion that the image of the Eastern Holy Man has traditionally aroused in some Western observers, the message and method put forward by Maharishi Mahesh Yogi appeared too pat, too easy, and quite possibly too superficial to those who initially studied it. How could anyone, many thought, suggest that some fifteen or twenty minutes of meditation—once in the morning and then again at night—could change not only individuals but even aspire to advance worldwide peace and understanding? √

The global aims of the Transcendental Meditation movement remain, of course, unfulfilled at this point, but increasing numbers of men and women have taken TM instruction and found it to be individually beneficial in a variety of degrees. By early 1976, the number of TM meditators worldwide had exceeded one million. More than three quarters of these were in the United States, with lesser numbers in Western Europe, Asia, Africa, and Latin America. Communications media had discovered the movement; news magazines, women's service periodicals, and television personalities introduced millions to the basic concepts and personalities of the movement. Books on the subject became best sellers. At one point there were more than an estimated 30,000 people signing up for TM classes every month. There are now more than 370 TM centers and more than 6,000 TM teachers around the country. At the movement's peak its estimated revenue in America alone was over $12 million a year.

And while Maharishi Mahesh Yogi used such means of communication as television to put his message across, he continued to try to avoid or ignore some aspects of communication which, to Westerners generally and U.S. communicators in particular, were matters of course. Starting with the simple, everyday, personal statistics of Maharishi's own life, an irritating, trivial elusiveness began. When and where was Maharishi born? He didn't say, and by refusing to answer, he made the missing piece of information doubly intriguing—just as Greta Garbo had succeeded for years in continuing worldwide interest in her "mysterious" personality by seemingly avoiding all publicity. When asked about his past, Maharishi sometimes laughed. He told one reporter, "I am a monk and as a monk I am not expected to think of my past. It is not important where I come from, I am totally detached and peripatetic, like Socrates." He was, said Maharishi's spokesmen, born "during the early part of the twentieth century" (some estimate around 1918). They could hardly have been more pompously vague in stating the obvious. Information on his parentage and early upbringing tended to be unreliable, although interviewers were told that Maharishi had "studied physics" at the University of Allahabad in northern India and graduated in 1940.

The identity of the Maharishi's own teacher, or guru, is, however, not in doubt. In fact, a picture of "Guru Dev," or "Divine Teacher," is in evidence wherever TM practice is taught. This man was Swami Brahmanandi Saraswati, also of northern India. He is further identified as a Shankaracharya, or a person of highest spiritual authority. Maharishi has spoken of him as one "who expounded the Truth in its all-bracing nature" and said that he studied with him in the Himalayas for some thirteen years. When and where in the Himalayas, one wonders, thinking of this enormous mountain range and its adjacent territories.

Considering the Maharishi's other down-to-earth attitudes, it is difficult to explain why he remains quite so mysteriously elusive about what must, in fact, be fairly plain and even trivial bits of geographic and chronological data. That, however, is the way he prefers it; such mysteries add an otherworldly air to the TM program, no matter how secular or nonreligious it presents itself.

According to Maharishi Mahesh Yogi and his spokesmen, TM techniques are psycho-physiological rather than religious in content. This is partly borne out by the increasing number of scholarly studies that have measured such aspects as pulse rate, breathing pattern, blood pressure, and other physiological correlates of stress or tension. Less easy to measure are euphoric elements that seem to emerge from TM practice, either immediately—during the "honeymoon period of TM," as one practitioner termed it—or after longer and regularly repeated meditation. These feelings appear to encourage belief in the more expansive and visionary concepts advanced by Maharishi Mahesh Yogi and are designed to apply his method for worldwide benefits.

Certainly, if one assumes that something like a governing elite throughout the world could achieve peace of mind through TM practice, stresses and strains between nations would disappear. Maharishi's immediate aim is to have 1 percent of the population in each country enlist in his program, which is directed by a World Plan Executive Council. Several organizations, coordinated by the Council, exist to bring the method and its supplementary elements to different strata of the population. Whereas early on students were the mainstay of TM programs, emphasis has shifted to include other groups more and more prominently.

Maharishi Mahesh Yogi's aim of having 1 percent of a nation's population among meditators is certainly an attainable goal in the United States. The point at which more than two million people in the U.S. have gone through the TM process can be envisioned for the foreseeable future. However, the quality and lasting impact of meditation will certainly be a decisive factor in reaching Maharishi's aim for a World Plan, first outlined in 1972. What are the aims of this World Plan? Maharishi Mahesh Yogi has listed the following seven goals:

1. To develop the full potential of the individual.
2. To enhance governmental achievements.
3. To realize the highest ideals of education.
4. To solve the problems of crime, drug abuse, and all behavior that bring unhappiness to the family of man.
5. To maximize the intelligent use of the environment.
6. To bring fulfillment to the economic aspirations of individuals and society.
7. To achieve the spiritual goals of mankind in this generation.

Few would want to quarrel with such aims, even if they wonder how great an impact 1 percent of a society, the TM meditators, can possibly have on the remaining 99 percent—a vast majority that might well include millions of criminals, polluters, economic nonidealists, or educationally backward elements of society. Traditionally, however, it is necessary to aim high if one is to reach a goal; and no one can deny the loftiness of his aims. As the Maharishi says, "A good time for the world is coming. I see the dawn of the Age of Enlightenment. I am only giving expression to the phenomenon that is taking place."

On a less visionary level, scientific evidence for the psychophysiological usefulness of TM techniques is beginning to add to a respectable body of scholarly experiments and published papers. Among these are studies that show the use of TM techniques as an adjunct to psychotherapy and for rehabilitation of drug addicts and of certain criminal types. The usefulness of TM techniques in juxtaposition with other techniques, such as biofeedback and psychiatric treatment, is being explored. And while the gap between worldwide betterment and individual reduction in tension is a wide one, each case of lowered stress represents one pebble on the vast shores of mankind's oceanic desire for freedom from anxiety.

To understand the TM process fully, it is necessary to summarize the relatively brief history of the movement. It spans about two decades, beginning with Maharishi's realization in the mid-1950s that it would take the unrealistically long time of 200 years to bring the message of Guru Dev to the world. Maharishi found himself in Madras when he arrived at this conclusion: The year 1958 is a turning point. From then on, he began a series of travels and lectures. In his headquarters in Rishikesh, on the Gan-

ges River in the foothills of the Himalayas, he set up an Academy
of Meditation. Maharishi Mahesh Yogi then went on several
world tours that resulted in increasingly formidable waves of
support.

Success was not instantaneous, however. The Madras meeting
that marked the turnaround in Maharishi's efforts was called the
Congress of Spiritual Luminaries. Its external occasion was the
eighty-ninth anniversary of the birth of Guru Dev (who had died
in 1953). Maharishi said in Madras that results he had registered
up to that point enabled him to "envision the spiritual regeneration of all mankind." The Spiritual Regeneration Movement
(SRM) was the outgrowth of that congress. The following year
gave Maharishi the opportunity to go on a world tour, beginning
with South Asia and ending in Los Angeles, where the U.S. headquarters of SRM was established.

The 1960s were, of course, the decade of student activity, and
the rapidly increasing interest in meditation led to establishment
in 1965 of the Student International Meditation Society (SIMS).
It was followed by the International Meditation Society (IMS),
which expanded beyond the student range. Next, in an effort to
find a framework for the interest and activity of scholars and edu-
cators, the American Foundation for the Science of Creative Intelligence (SCI) was established. Since then, the words "Transcendental Meditation," the initials "TM," as well as the words
"Science of Creative Intelligence," the initials "SCI," and other
terms associated with the movement have become registered trade-
marks, so as to avoid confusion or imitation. Finally, to facilitate
education of TM instructors and others concerned with the scientific relevance of TM techniques, Maharishi International University (MIU) was established, with campuses at Fairfield, Iowa,
and at Livingston Manor, New York.

Important recognition of the life of Maharishi Mahesh Yogi
came in late 1968 and early 1969, when the rock group then known
as The Beatles became ardent supporters of the TM technique.
Because of their immense popularity, The Beatles were a widely
imitated model for ideas, styles of living, manner of dress, and an
open-minded as well as erratic approach to concepts of belief.
When The Beatles endorsed Maharishi Mahesh Yogi, the diminu-
tive Indian monk suddenly became a personality of international
standing. However, The Beatles, singly and as a unit, were as

restless in their spiritual affiliations as in their travels and human relations. Before long, they turned away from TM training and embraced other causes.

From this temporary setback, Transcendental Meditation methods made an undramatic but apparently lasting comeback. By word of mouth, personal experiences with TM study created an increasing number of followers, of teacher-initiators, and of meditators. A series of international congresses were held, and while the activity in the United States was clearly the most important in sheer number and organizational strength, the international distribution of the movement was also increasingly substantial. In the U.S. public curiosity was heightened by such events as a *Time* cover story on Maharishi Mahesh Yogi and his repeated appearance on the Merv Griffin television show (where Griffin and other show business personalities revealed their personal indebtedness to the TM method). All this resulted in thousands of inquiries at the meditation centers throughout the country.

What did an inquirer encounter? How did he proceed along the path to meditation in order to arrive at what Maharishi had successively called "bliss consciousness" and "pure consciousness"? Anyone visiting a center is usually received by politely enthusiastic women or men, most likely in their early or mid-twenties. Next, there are lectures providing an introduction into the teachings of Maharishi Mahesh Yogi, together with accounts of the history of the movement (involving a more detailed summary than on the preceding pages), plus preparatory conversations with a potential initiator.

The initiator-meditator relationship is very dear to Maharishi's heart, and in many ways it is crucial to the success of the TM technique. It is not, according to Maharishi Mahesh Yogi, a mere one-way street; it is not just a traditional teacher-student relationship. Rather, it is a delicate internal dialogue for which there is no substitute outside the actual experience. The ceremonial element of this initiator-meditator encounter is heightened by the instruction that the meditator bring the gift of a fresh white handkerchief, fruit, and flowers to the initiator; these are likely to be placed on a table in the initiation room, often under a portrait of Guru Dev, of Maharishi, or of both men.

The initiation ceremony is secret and individual. Much has been made of the TM movement's emphasis on the secrecy of the mantra that is selected for each person. It is this mantra, this single word—supposedly a Sanskrit word that has only neutral meaning for the meditator—that is used as a central part of the Transcendental Meditation process. (Mantras have been traditional meditation aids for thousands of years. A mantra can be either a complete thought or a single sound.) The actual method is given to the meditator at this point, together with the mantra, and instructions on how to employ it during the meditation process—some twenty minutes in the morning and another twenty minutes each evening. The initiator-meditator ceremony, while standardized in some respects, is sufficiently individualized to enable each person to fit the actual meditation period into the pattern of his or her daily life. By 1976, a fee of $125 was charged for each initiation. Each meditator could return whenever necessary for new instructions or clarification, for the kind of personal contact that in some way would seem essential for the strengthening and continued effectiveness of the Transcendental Meditation technique. √

HOW TO MEDITATE THE TM WAY

There is no question that the TM method is actually as simple as its advocates claim. First, the teacher-initiator himself meditates for a moment and then chants a Sanskrit mantra for the initiate. This single word/sound is to occupy the meditator's attention for the rest of his or her life. Even though mantras are traditionally assigned according to each personality, one report suggests that TM teachers are given a set of mantras by the Maharishi (seventeen according to one source), which are then passed on to the initiates. Presumably, many TM meditators, therefore, use the same mantra—which explains to some degree why the movement wishes to keep each person's mantra secret —it both adds to the uniqueness with which each initiate can view himself, and the aura of mystery around the TM method itself. (For finding a mantra to use while meditating, see the section on mantras.) √

Once assigned a mantra, the meditator-initiate attempts to experience it freely, without pressing mentally or concentrating directly on it. As other thoughts enter the mind, as they usually do, they may be examined without intensity and gently discarded.

Contrarily, some Buddhist techniques follow the image or idea to its source or, alternatively, examine it casually and then follow it within the mind until it dissolves under pressure from other thoughts or images pressing for attention. Such intruding images or ideas in TM meditation are not followed or allowed to lead one to any further associations. One is taught simply to push them gently from the forefront of consciousness, as if one were a teacher slowly and casually erasing a blackboard in order to write something else.

The mantra ideally comes into the mind automatically about thirty seconds after the eyes close. If it doesn't, the meditator gently inserts it into the forefront of consciousness and starts repeating the word to himself either silently or out loud. If it becomes difficult to hold the sound in the mind, it is considerably easier to chant it out loud, for this serves the dual purpose of concentrating the attention and conditioning the mind to repeat the specific sound of the mantra.

Unlike breath-counting or heart-rhythm types of meditation, the TM meditator need not repeat his mantra according to any special rhythm, although getting into a rhythmic pattern helps many people to concentrate better. At first the mantra can—and often does —slip away, but after at first nudging it gently back into awareness, it begins to automatically repeat itself. For this reason it is often thought of as an entirely mechanical process, which automatically attains its goals with faithful practice. Unlike many other forms of meditation it requires no faith, nor does it involve any control of mental imagery or exceptionally intense concentration. It is precisely because it does not require any of these traditional ingredients that it is such an easy method for the average Westerner unfamiliar with the mental disciplines of meditation.

Another valuable asset of TM-like techniques is that they can be practiced silently almost anywhere—in subways, cars, planes, hotel lobbies, or even when walking—although it is not advisable to walk streets in large cities such as New York concentrating on your mantra. Most city drivers are unsympathetic to meditators humming along the crosswalks.

As with all other meditation methods, the key to successful TM meditation is regularity. Once you establish a meditation, you must practice it regularly. This fact cannot be emphasized too much. Even the simple TM meditation cannot work if the twice-

daily fifteen to twenty minutes of practice is not faithfully followed. Yet, regardless of how often one warns of the need for
continual practice, many who try to learn even simple meditation
techniques like TM drop out after a while. One figure that TM
officials admit to is a 25 percent apostasy rate. Others place the
number of dropouts even higher. But for the majority, the TM
method seems to work so well that the federal government has so
far funded seventeen TM research projects covering a wide range
of experiments. ✓

While the claims of its advocates sometimes seem excessive,
according to well-documented research, TM meditators show
some impressive effects. Researchers from Harvard University and
the University of California found a significant drop in blood pressure with twenty-two hypertensive patients over sixty-three weeks.
Oxygen consumption was reduced by as much as 18 percent during meditation. Such a marked slowing of body metabolism has, of
course, many important medical benefits. ✓

Alpha-wave electrical activity in the brain became more pre-
dominant during TM meditation according to studies by a neurol-
ogist at Massachusetts General Hospital and two psychiatrists at
Hartford's Institute of Living. Still other studies indicate that
meditators can become less dependent on liquor, cigarettes, hallu-
cinogens, or drugs of any kind. Dr. Herbert Benson and Dr.
Robert Keith Wallace conducted a study of 1,862 habitual drug
users, and found that after twenty-one months of TM practice
almost 96 percent lost their drug dependence entirely. The TM
program has been so effective in drug rehabilitation that Stanford
University professor John Kaplan considers it a "nonchemical
tranquillizer with no unpleasant side effects."✓

The primary scientific criticism of TM techniques is not that
they lack positive effects, but that they are not the panacea that TM
promoters claim. For example, one of the pronouncements made
by TM advocates is that the meditator becomes more creative
after using their method. Creativity is, in fact, one of the most
complex, difficult-to-study traits in the human personality. Such
facile claims tend to make scientists justifiably skeptical. One
study that investigated the claims of greater creativity by meditators (including both TM and the "relaxation response" methods) was conducted by George Domino at the University of Ari-
zona. After experimenting with four groups of thirty-five adults,

each over a six-month period, he found that the TM group did not exhibit any greater creativity. The same negative results occurred with a group who participated in a relaxation program—similar to Herbert Benson's Harvard experiments—that involved repeating a single-syllable sound. What meditation apparently does do is allow the creative personality to express itself more fluidly; but it does not seem able to make the average or noncreative individual any more creative. Meditation may also enhance the relationship between the conscious and unconscious aspects of the mind, thereby opening up channels for the creative individual to use.

It is clear that many other meditative methods benefit both the body and the mind, and that TM promoters only weaken their valid claims regarding the benefits of their technique. One critic-psychiatrist, Stanley Dean, sums up the scientific community's suspicions with the direct and reasonable observation that "anyone who claims exclusivity is immediately suspect. The TM people's claims that theirs is the best of all possible worlds is nonsense. It is a sales gimmick. Meditation has been a way of achieving mental serenity through the ages, and they (TM) have no patent on it. TM is an important addition to our medical armamentarium, but it is not exclusive." Other equally critical psychiatrists argue that the TM organization does not screen their prospective initiates adequately and that unstable persons taking the TM course might be pushed over the edge by inexperienced young initiator-teachers. But there is little evidence that TM, or any other simple meditation method, causes mental breakdowns or even nervous disorders. In fact, all the evidence contradicts this fear.

A major criticism by religious groups is similar to the scientific one and again involves the movement's excessive claims. But a new twist is the complaint that the TM movement tries to walk both sides of the street at once and represents itself as something more than it actually is. On the one hand, TM advocates claim their movement is not religious, and on the other, they possess numerous spiritual accoutrements. Whether the TM movement is religious or not seems to depend upon whom you are talking to or on the point a TM promoter is trying to make. In Western public forums, TM spokesmen most often emphasize the practical benefits of their method, such as physical and mental health. But sometimes a religious fervor one has been led *not to expect* intrudes. In fact, as reported in a national magazine, one woman left the movement because of what she called the cosmic mumbo-jumbo she was subjected to as she got deeper into the TM program.

It does seem incongruous, or even hypocritical, for a movement to play down publicly its spiritual heritage while hanging Guru Dev's photograph at all their centers and practicing rituals that reflect Hindu beliefs. Maharishi himself frequently speaks about his method of meditating in graphic spiritual language and at other times claims it is simply a "natural technique for reducing stress." Part of the invocation ceremony for initiates, for example, is directly from the Hindu faith: "To Lord Narayana, to lotus-born Brahma, the Creator, to Vashishta, to Shakti, and to his son, Parashar, to Vayas, to Shukadava . . . I bow down . . . At whose door the whole galaxy of gods pray for perfection day and night, adorned with immeasurable glory, preceptor of the whole world, having bowed down to him, we gain fulfillment." Perhaps the TM hierarchy thought it would be harder to convince the suspicious, rationalistically trained Westerner to invest in a course if he knew beforehand that he had to invoke Brahma and Shakti. But by their timorous, even disingenuous, embrace of their religious heritage, they create more distrust than may be warranted.

Some TM believers have tried to bridge the gap between the muddied waters of science and religion by turning to Yoga, with its peculiar mixture of detailed, empirical/physical techniques and mystical goals. But Dr. Kumar Pal of the Yoga Institute of Psychology and Physical Therapy in New Delhi argues that TM "is merely a technique, a very limited technique, and it is not yogic because it lacks the prerequisites of yogic meditation. Transcendental Meditation does not reach the stage of giving you awareness of your real self." In response to the spiritual claims of some TM teachers, A. K. Krishna Nambiar, publisher and editor of *Spiritual India*, complains that perhaps "TM can make you a better executive, but it cannot give you the spiritual ecstasy that other more spiritual meditation techniques do. It can never lead the meditator to *turya*, the fourth and eventual stage of spiritual ecstasy which is the final aim of meditation and which makes the meditator one with and part of the universe." Further, the orthodox yogi would argue that since a moral and ethical life serves as the very foundation of all spiritual development, it is this *sine qua non* of yogic practice that TM ignores. The TM student, for example, need not sacrifice any of his physical pleasures and may continue as before with sex, liquor, or whatever. While this moral pragmatism may have added to the TM movement's greater popularity, a certain hypocrisy does creep in when TM is called yogic or Hindu. Yet, to be fair, many Western theologians have argued that sex, alcohol, and material concerns are not mutually exclusive with spiritual growth.

It would seem then that the better part of wisdom—both theological and scientific—would be for the TM movement to stay clear of any religious or spiritual ties. Stripped of the religious guise it occasionally wears, the TM meditation program seems a valuable, straightforward, and effective method for quieting harassed minds and bodies. But as a crypto-religious panacea, the movement takes on the unpleasant qualities of a promoter's media game. Yet whatever final judgment one makes about the TM craze, it is clear that it works in important ways, and that it has blended more successfully than any other modern, quasi-religious movement the technological, quick-success inclinations of the West with the more inner-directed and meditative ones of the East.

Meditating Alone
or in Groups

MOST SYSTEMS OF MEDITATION, such as Transcendental Meditation, sensory enhancement, sensory reduction, and so forth, involve some aspect of the group experience, even if it only consists of a teacher and one or two pupils. In some forms of Tantra Yoga, for example, a "group" meditation consists of a man and woman in sexual union. Therefore, questions involving the value of group meditation are really concerned with two different types of groups: those that are concerned with learning to meditate and those participated in by people who have already acquired some mastery and are using the group for other reasons. ✓

By nature some people seek insight or understanding in solitude, and others prefer traveling with companions. And even those who choose to start out alone or in a group may find it helpful to change along the way. The solitary path has traditionally been considered the more difficult, but most of us probably need guidance frequently throughout our lives. The question, however, is not so much whether we need a guide, but what kind of relationship we develop with others interested in the same things. (This will be dealt with in the section on gurus and disciples.) ⌣

When meditation works, it helps a person grow in desirable directions, and when a group practices meditation well enough, their experiences are genuinely shared and an added moral effect occurs. However, unless the group members are people one admires and respects, the benefits are not likely to accrue. It is wise to look elsewhere in such a case, regardless of how "expert" the group may seem to be in meditation. ✓

Some forms of meditation can *only* be practiced in a group or class and others only in private. Ultimately, each student must determine what is best for himself. It is better certainly to meditate alone than to have an unsuitable teacher. But a teacher and the members of a group can be of great help in sharing experiences; giving encouragement and an outward discipline for the beginning student; veering him away from many of the pitfalls, dead ends, and mistakes through which he would otherwise have to struggle by himself. At one time or another, most students will find meditation works both in private and in groups. It is probably unwise, however, to completely put aside private meditation. Valuable though it is to share with and learn from others, this learning relationship is sooner or later a limiting one. Ultimately, in meditation one learns from oneself; each has his own path and must travel it alone. ✓

In private meditations you set your own pace and select the subject or type of meditation. In groups a common purpose is set, and the individual rhythm is replaced by the group's. There are great difficulties for some personalities, for not all people find group meditation palatable, just as they would not find group activity of any sort acceptable. But for others the group consciousness and its common goals and needs support personal effort. For those who like to work with groups, meditation with others should be effective.

A fair question, however, arises: Since meditation is essentially a private experience, why would a person wish to meditate with others? One of the main reasons is that many people, especially beginners, have not yet acquired any degree of self-discipline. As noted earlier, one of the greatest initial difficulties is that of merely sitting quietly for twenty minutes or half an hour. This is especially difficult for the self-taught meditator. Patricia Drake Hemingway comments honestly on her problems with private meditation: "I know myself well enough to know that, regardless of how much of an individual I think I am, I really belong to the vast majority of *Homo sapiens* who usually require outside discipline, structure, and guidance to assist me in learning any intricate or complicated new subject. . . . One other way that I believe

makes me belong to the vast majority is that I usually approach
any new course of action with some apprehension, if not down-
right fear of failing in what I set out to do. And like most people,
I find that it is more supportive to begin these ventures in a group
rather than by myself. That probably has something to do with
the 'misery loves company' syndrome but whatever the reason,
it is nonetheless valid."

Ballet dancers also illustrate the power of mutual support in the
group, for no matter how long a dancer has been dancing, nor
how famous, each reports to class to practice. The discipline is so
difficult and so demanding that it is far easier done with others.
Only on vacations do ballet dancers stray from this self-imposed
life-style, for to do so jeopardizes the foundation of their careers
and the constant seeking of perfection through discipline and
practice.

This also applies for group and private meditation. Group work
demands regular attendance, so it is important to determine beforehand just what you hope to gain from joining. What are the
purposes and ultimate goals of the group? Are they the same as
yours? An affinity with the group's philosophical and psychological
aims is necessary to make the group experience work successfully. Again, it is necessary to consider whether your personality
needs and preferences are similar to the group's, whether you find
the people personally compatible.

In an effective group there is a binding together, where the
group consciousness supports each person's meditation and consequently creates a more satisfying experience for the individual
meditator. There is, then, a comforting aspect to meditating in
groups that is missing from private meditation. Unquestionably,
people can be mentally, emotionally, and spiritually transformed
in group meditations.

Another great virtue of group meditation is that if things get
confusing, if your meditations become sidetracked in some unexpected way—and they usually do—you can sit down with others and
discuss the problem. While group meditation (and, in fact, any
group activity) is often used by some as a crutch and can result
in others doing one's own thinking, it can also be mutually beneficial when some word or act clarifies a problem. When communication is good and the flow between people is constructive, the
end result can be truly enlightening. The same benefits as ex-

perienced in any personal relationship apply to group meditation. This was recognized and even emphasized in group meditations practiced in Eastern religions. Certain Tibetan Buddhist techniques, for example, consider the greatest problem for beginners is their laziness and need for considerable encouragement to follow through. In the Tibetan "Calm and Clear" technique, the antidote to laziness is continued exertion supported by confidence and aspiration. One assumes that aspiration is there in order to begin meditating; but in order to maintain and energize that desire, the problem becomes one of building the confidence needed. The Tibetans believe that the beginning meditator gains confidence and inspiration by seeing the benefits of meditation in others and through listening to an experienced master or friend. Group meditation is therefore an important part of this Tibetan technique and is considered highly efficient in providing the necessary desire and confidence needed to learn meditation.

Yet just as one can be inspired during group meditation by the example of others, one can also be stimulated to compete. To avoid this pitfall in group meditation, remember not to create high expectations for yourself, or to demand performances equal to what others are reporting. Above all, don't fall into the "theirs vs. yours" experience. It is a waste of time and goes with the "my guru is more spiritually advanced than your guru" game. Such game-playing, while all too human, has nothing to do with meditation and nourishes nothing but the infantile ego—which is exactly what you are trying to overcome through learning to meditate. (More will be said about this later.)

Be leery of groups which promise easy methods and immediate success in meditation. You will merely be disappointed if you expect to reach the highest levels of meditation at once. Serious change in your way of thinking can only come with growth. You will note an inner development if you practice the meditation which is right for you, but it will not come overnight. In your expectations, you must above all be honest with yourself. Psychotherapist Lawrence LeShan discusses this point in his book *How to Meditate*: "How much time *will* you spend on this discipline is the first question, not how much time you would *like* to spend on it. An important aspect of meditation is follow-through, keeping your promises to yourself. Short of an emergency, it is part of the program that you finish each meditation you start in the form you started it and that you finish each plan for a program of meditation in the form you planned it. . . . Take into account what kind of a person you are now (rather than the kind of person you wish you were) and how busy and complex your life is, and plan accordingly." *

It is important that you discover and follow your own pace, your own natural rhythms. As Dr. LeShan correctly points out, meditation is a creative growth process, not a rigid or formal therapy. Remember also that there are no set standards for either personal growth or effects from meditation, only general guidelines.

It may also be necessary to periodically change the form of the group meditation. As long as the basic goals and techniques are the same, slight variations can sometimes better involve the various temperaments in the group. The specific changes in form should be made by the group itself, for the moods and attitudes in a group are multiplied and in much greater flux than those of a lone individual. The greatest benefit in varying the group meditation is freedom from routine or rigid rules. It is also important to avoid role-playing, a danger in all group activities. If the forms are altered, role-playing is reduced, even if not entirely avoided. It is far more difficult, for example, to maintain a role when the rules are constantly being altered.

When one examines the components of group meditations, it becomes clear that there are basically two types of group activity: guided (structured) and unguided (unstructured). With a guided group there is generally formal material, such as ritual, dance, and song in which one person may lead the rest. Such groups also have a single leader who may talk to the group beforehand and explain the group's purpose or perhaps try to set the mood or inspire the members. Most church services are examples of structured group activity. Some sermons, for example, can be a type of guided meditation. The formality of ritual in structured meditations generally helps to evoke a common spirit. Without such controls or ritual, a group awareness often will not form at all or an individual or small group of people may take control of the meeting.

The unstructured group is less formal, and one will probably find less agreement among the members about common goals or beliefs. An unstructured session can be anything from a loose aggregate of individuals to a more cohesive group in which everyone

* Lawrence LeShan, *How to Meditate* (New York: Bantam Books, 1974), p. 103.

is familiar with the routine and practices. In the unstructured sessions each person can go his own separate way mentally, as long as each follows the general outlines of the group's goals. An example of this type of group would be experienced private meditators who meet together for unstructured sessions. The sessions may consist of little more than a place, such as a church, where persons who wish to meditate may gather without even knowing one another. Such sanctuaries may be set aside in unexpected places, such as a busy corporation headquarters. An interesting example occurs in the Pentagon. Charles Wise, Jr., a councillor in the office of the Secretary of Defense, has related that there is a meditation room in the Pentagon that is heavily used. Wise, who is a frequent meditator, has also observed that there are two rooms in the Pentagon's meditation chamber—and a sign that directs solitary meditators to the right and the group meditators to the left.

The problem with such unstructured group meditations is that a person whose personality is more compatible with a guided group activity may find it difficult to achieve a heightened personal awareness. Although I have known some who have succeeded, their success seems to have depended more in closing out the others in the group than in gathering emotional or spiritual sustenance from their presence. For example, it is hard to have a successful meditation in the unstructured group environment of, say, the waiting room of a city bus station, or the bleachers of a football stadium during a game. And even in the more sympathetic environment of a church, many find that their meditations are more successful if they are some distance away from other people. (This is especially true of beginning meditators.) On the other hand, if a group meets with a common interest that is acceptable and interesting to all members, it may be all the structuring the meeting requires.

There are, of course, some techniques to develop the necessary bonds. For example, at the onset of the meditation period, some will find that listening quietly to music creates a natural bond or union in the group. I personally find music one of the finest ways of preparing and even deepening a meditative session—whether alone or in groups. However, I know some meditators who find music distracting, even irritating. I, for example, respond to Gregorian chants, or *ars antiqua*, yet I have friends who find this music boring or even grating on their nerves. With a group meditation,

then, the additional problem of musical preference complicates
the music induction technique.

Once begun, however, and as the meditation proceeds from the
common basis, each person's awareness often seems raised to the
group level and probes more deeply into the meditative experience.
A communal spirit (whether of the group, or God, or whatever)
seems to rise on the communion of minds in harmony. There is
even some evidence that a biological communion may develop
during group meditation. For example, meditators at some biofeedback labs have found that group contact—sitting in a circle,
holding hands, and so forth—during meditation enhanced the presence of alpha brain waves. At the V.A. Hospital in Sepulveda,
California, Dr. Barbara Brown has conducted experiments using
EEG alpha feedback to train pairs of subjects to produce synchronized brain-wave patterns. The partners in the experiment are
given feedback only when they simultaneously produce alpha
brain waves. As the experiment progresses, apparently some kind
of rapport develops between the subjects. Dr. Brown is interested
in the question of "whether the partners who have learned to
synchronize their brain rhythms have correspondingly synchronized their feelings—and will they be able to guess which state
their partner is in?" There are initial indications that the answer
to both questions is affirmative. Dr. Brown suspects that the relationship between the biological rhythms occurs when this type of
"empathetic tracking" is learned. The implications for interper-
sonal relationships are enormous, and its applications in therapy,
in which a therapist and client sometimes take months to establish
a rapport, are equally intriguing.

In summary, then, a group's concentrated attention can often
draw each member into a deeper meditation than would be possible alone. Just as group meditations work for music, so they also
work for an abstract thought or a reading upon which all members
dwell in common. Often, too, a particular abstract picture or
sacred *objet d'art* may be substituted for either music or thoughts.
Although using a common thought may make the session re-
semble one of contemplation rather than of meditation, the tran-
sition to meditation is easily accomplished.

Another important point to keep in mind is that no matter what
one's personal preference, there is value in both private and group
meditations. If you have a strong preference for one type, it might

be helpful for you to purposefully seek the other in order to broaden your meditative experience. Since you can learn from both kinds of meditation, don't be too shy to experiment with alternative methods. In short, experiment wisely while seeking the proper balance between your personal preferences and needs. Since each person is unique and mysterious, group meditations offer an exceptional opportunity to explore the mystery of human nature—with others as well as oneself. It is in this sharing that the greatest common bond develops in group meditation; for to seek an answer to the mystery of human existence has been the common goal of every major religion and philosophy. During meditation you are exploring this mystery, and both the group and private meditations serve that important goal.

ON BEING ALONE: SILENCE AND SOLITUDE

There are several important keys that unlock the traditional secrets of meditation. One of the most difficult instructions to carry out is to "let your thinking cease," which is tantamount to living in silence. Silence has multiple importance in meditation: it is a method, a metaphor, a state of awareness. It is a metaphor because it exists only as an abstraction, for absolute silence is biologically impossible. A good description of this fact is an experience of the composer John Cage in his book *Silence.*

. . . try as we may to make a silence, we cannot. For certain engineering purposes, it is desirable to have as silent a situation as possible. Such a room is called an anechoic chamber, its six walls made of special material, a room without echoes. I entered one at Harvard University several years ago and heard two sounds, one high and one low. When I described them to the engineer in charge, he informed me that the high one was my nervous system in operation, the low one my blood in circulation. Until I die there will be sounds.*

By the body's very nature, silence seems to evade us. In addition, there are few silent moments in our lives, for even if one succeeds in setting aside quiet moments, the inner mental noise mimics the external cacophony of our modern life-style. Yet it is this inner silence that most methods of meditation consider vital to the process.

* John Cage, *Silence* (Cambridge, Mass.: M.I.T. Press, 1961), p. 8.

In the meditative discipline, however, silence is much more than the mere cessation of noise. For example, very early in meditation one reaches the point where the quiet of external surroundings is far less important than the quiet of the mind. And even though, as John Cage found, inner sounds bubble up from the internal workings of our body, the quiet mind of meditation succeeds in filtering out these inner sounds. One of the simplest methods is the mantra, in which a consistent sound overwhelms the more subtle inner noise. In fact, any consistent and patterned stimulus seems to organize itself into a nonsound by becoming part of the background that we all tend to ignore when concentrating on something else. There is a constant filtering of perceptions going on during our waking as well as our sleeping hours. We often sleep right through sounds from the street, wind, weather, sudden rain, one's own breathing, and so on.

As we see, an external quiet does not ensure internal silence, and an external noise can be ignored so thoroughly that it in fact becomes silence. The meditator, however, seeks control over both external and internal sounds. It is not until the meditator learns to disengage himself from external distractions (or, more simply, meditates in a quiet environment) that he can begin to learn to deal with a whole set of new sounds: mind noise. The unceasing activity of the mind does not seem to be a problem—indeed, many consider constant mental activity a virtue—until you attempt to control it. Once the meditator begins to "quiet" his mind noise, it rapidly becomes clear how little control he has over what goes on in his own head. This is why most of the early exercises in meditation stress gaining control over the innumerable images, ideas, words, and fantasies that intrude upon the meditator. This initial stage of mind-control begins to help the meditator understand the difference between the mind itself and its contents. We tend to view the mind as the sum of its contents. Yet, since we are never fully conscious of the mind's total nature, it is foolish to equate the chaotic noise of the mind with the mind itself.

What the meditator achieves through quieting the mind, through learning how to concentrate one's attention, is quite different from what we normally consider silence. The silence sought is not achieved simply by sitting in a quiet place; the meditative silence does not involve the normal discriminating process as much. To be accurate, the meditator's silence is more enveloping, and one *becomes* silent rather than observes it. To observe means that the meditator would retain the role of observer, of a separate ego dealing with his mind and its effects as if it were an object. Silence is something that occurs when the control of one's mind brings about the absence of mind noise or mental activity. At that point the meditator is no longer separated from silence by his mental noise, but becomes a part of the silence. Paradoxically, if the meditator is even *aware* that he is a part of the silence, the subject-object role is preserved and he has not yet silenced his mind noise. Silence, therefore, is not an awareness of silence; instead, there is no discrimination at all. Of the many metaphors used to describe this difficult-to-relate experience, the most common are no-mind, emptiness, the pure essence of mind. The tradition of this silence appears in cultures throughout the world. In the West, Meister Eckhart has written: "The central silence is there, where no creature may enter, nor any idea, and there the soul neither thinks nor acts, nor entertains any idea, either of itself or of anything else." * On the other side of the world, the Chinese Ch'an Buddhist describes it: "When no-mind is sought after by the mind, that is making it a particular object of thought. There is only the testimony of silence; it goes beyond thinking." †

One of the most widely practiced types of silent meditation is, of course, prayer. The effectiveness of prayer depends more on the spirit and involvement than on the form followed. As in other methods of meditation, if one loses sight of the prayer's purpose, following the form of the prayer becomes a hollow exercise. As E. V. Ingram wrote in his book *Meditation in the Silence:* "The silence is not in any sense the discovery of a new process of mind but is a practice known very well to every genius, every inventor, every philosopher, and in fact every individual who has in any degree outstripped his fellow men and brought back to the world some new idea or invention from beyond the range of habitual thought and experience. The silence is clearly taught in the scriptures, and is one of the most vital aspects of prayer. 'Be still, and

---

* Meister Eckhart, quoted in W. Stace, *The Teachings of the Mystics* (New York: New American Library, 1960), p. 144.

† Huang Po, quoted in Aldous Huxley, *The Perennial Philosophy* (New York & London: Harper & Bros., 1945), p. 73.

know' is a clear command to let the mind rest from its own activities and record knowledge that the Infinite waits to reveal." *

But these concepts of silence are difficult to grasp for the activity-oriented Westerner. Our culture has not educated us to the subtleties of inner experiences. In fact, silence and its counterpart, solitude, are often seen in negative terms. And the psychologically dark face of solitude—isolation—is even a less desirable reality. When a prisoner in the penitentiary is punished, he is put in "isolation." A child is punished by making him stand alone in the corner, or he is isolated by sending him to his room.

And yet, even as we struggle against the idea of isolation, solitude, and silence, as we suppress those unpleasant moments when we were punished by separation, an inevitable fact in modern Western society is that a peculiar type of isolation dominates our lives. As society continually expands, social solutions for new problems tend to involve mass techniques—which effectively isolate the individual. Mass social exercises are always based on the larger perspectives, leaving the individual the choice of responding to a solution not tailored to his needs. Even those who wish to conform to mass social actions begin to feel alien and heretical. The moral dissenter is thus born in isolation. Confusion is his only birthright. As the individual feels further outside his own history, an inner turning that seeks the stability so painfully lost takes place. The unbearable opacity of our lives begins to lighten even as the process begins, for a search for meaning presents in itself a small light that guides and comforts. Even though confusion or clarity is not the immediate result of this inner turning, at least we have a path to follow, a technique to explore that promises some clarification of our confusion.

Perhaps because the artist lives in a private world where communication is often limited to the artist and his medium, he exhibits a greater sensitivity to solitude and to the psychological isolation (i.e., alienation) in which our society enwraps us. French playwright Eugene Ionesco commented in his play *Rhinoceros* that the disease Rhinoceritis, which symbolizes the self-destruction of modern man in his conformity to mass needs, is the sickness that lies in wait for "those who have lost the sense and the taste for solitude." In fact, the individual who dares to confront

* E. V. Ingram, *Meditation in the Silence* (Missouri: Unity School of Christianity, n.d.).

aloneness and perceives the value of solitude is well on the path to his encounter with truth. Moments in the life of Christ, as well as many other spiritual leaders throughout history, can be interpreted as symbolic of every man's spiritual growth through solitude. When Christ went into the desert, his ordeals of temptation and loneliness became the pattern for every man. This perfecting of the Christ image symbolizes the goal of perfection for all men; yet in return for surviving the pain and dangers of solitude, Christ was rewarded with the gift of truth. His truth involved rejecting three kinds of illusions: power, reputation or fame, and great wealth or security. This truth can become everyone's truth if only we have the courage to survive solitude and the temptations within our own temperaments. But the freedom that comes from such a moment cannot be had without experimenting with the self. Self-reliance, self-exploration, self-examination, and self-modification do not come without effort. As Ionesco says in *Rhinoceros*, "It is the business of a free man to pull himself out of this void by his own power and not by the power of other people." *

SILENCE AND RECEPTIVE LISTENING

Indian philosopher-teacher Krishnamurti, who persistently refused to be encased in the role of guru or spiritual leader, often preferred to have open dialogues with his audiences. That way the individual could, hopefully, gain his own insights into what was being said, rather than rely on following someone else's teachings by rote. In one of these dialogues Krishnamurti stopped an intense young questioner by telling him to pause and listen both to his question and the answer. "Just a minute, sir, just a minute. You know, it is very odd that you come prepared with questions and therefore you are not listening to the talk. You are more interested in the question that you are going to put than in listening to what has been said. Sir, take time, have a little patience. . . . If you have looked deeply into yourselves you have not time to ask a question so immediately." †

It is this pause, the moment of silence when one can look more deeply into oneself, the question that puzzles, the motive behind

* Thomas Merton, *Raids on the Unspeakable* (New York: New Directions, 1964), p. 21.

† Krishnamurti, *Talks and Dialogues* (New York: Avon Books, 1970), pp. 44–45.

the asking, the emotions underlying one's communication with others, and the whole purpose of the present moment that serves to use silence in conversations as a tool for meditation. ✓

Silence is a forgotten virtue, an effortless resolution. Silence can establish new dimensions of reality for the meditator; an example is the religious monk existing in silence and isolation in the desert. Viewed simply as a psychological exercise, silence draws a clear distinction between our overly developed reliance on language and words and other culturally dominant symbols. For example, University of California psychologist Gerald Goodman argues that most people conveniently deal with closed-ended questions that call only for a yes or no answer, instead of open-ended questions that force more freedom in seeking a response. Silence—and its appreciation—forces one into an open-ended situation in which there is no fixed question that demands a fixed, prescribed answer. Such silence is a state of being that has no preset mental or physical demands. It can be a type of meditation when dealing with the world. Verbal information is not needed or requested. The only requirement is to translate the silence around the physical body into the inner self, into the fabric of the mind.

Professor Goodman, for instance, maintains that people rely so heavily on verbal reactions to the world that the habit of what he calls "verbal crowding" has to be unlearned. Such verbal crowding is not a meditative technique in the sense of absolute silence, but rather creates an opportunity to learn to appreciate the pauses that "need to occur during conversation." It is typical, for example, for many people to respond to someone else's sentence so quickly that there is no latency period. The responder launches so quickly into his own "verbal crowding" that there is no time available to see if he really understands the other person's viewpoint correctly. In effect, silence is sacrificed along with any attempt to see if there is correct understanding of the other's mind. This naturally inhibits communication. What normally happens is that the victim of verbal crowding becomes frustrated because his thoughts are misinterpreted and he begins to also speed up his verbal patterns in order to get in as many words as possible in the shortest amount of time. Soon the conversation has become a race between verbally dominated individuals, with neither properly communicating or understanding the other.

By learning to pause, to allow a few seconds to elapse between someone's statement and your response, (a reflectiveness) develops both around the other person's idea and your own beliefs. The small silence can at first throw off other speakers who give the typical pressured, rapid-fire speech pattern, but, interestingly, others begin to sense that you are dealing more seriously with their ideas. In response they seem to give more consideration to your answers because the small silence reflects your own attempt to take the idea under discussion seriously. It is, in short, like telling the other person that you have heard him and are letting what he says filter through your own mental and emotional system. As Goodman says, it is showing your empathy and attempting to grasp the idea in the other person's mind. ✓

Silence, then, can be utilized in a number of ways, ranging from a mental silence in meditation similar to the Zen no-mind, to psychological methods for bettering communication. But learning to use silence in communication is more than gaining control over one's own verbal habits or even simply improving communication. You also develop the ability to empathize beyond the self. The more you listen the more you hear, eventually perhaps even hearing others without constant reference to your own circumscribed world. ✓

In a meditation experiment conducted by Dr. Karlis Osis of the American Society for Psychical Research, one subject considered the high point of the week's meditation the realization that it is "an awesome thing . . . to feel oneself on the verge of the possibility of really knowing another person." Such a feeling is not possible while you are talking *at* someone, but only when you are in empathetic communion, when the silence shared with others has become long enough to be meaningful. Thus receptive listening is a meditative method that can be used during everyday activities. Former United Nations Secretary General U Thant described how he uses receptive listening (although he doesn't call it that) in both its practical and essential aspects. "When I enter my office in Manhattan," he wrote, "you will understand that I must forget that I am a Burmese and a Buddhist. Most of my visitors wish to leave with me a message, a deeply felt belief, or an idea. In order to receive and fully understand what my human brother has to say to me, I must open myself to him. I must empty myself of self."

In commenting on U Thant's practice, Norman Cousins, the

editor of *Saturday Review/World,* observed: "U Thant was right:
man can learn so much by simply opening himself to others, by
lowering the barriers of his self-sufficiency, a profoundly balanced
and integrated member of the human race. Humility and meditation lead in the end to integrity. It is perhaps the clue to serenity
in our bewildered, complex world." ∨

These comments by busy men deeply involved in world affairs
are witnesses to the idea that meditation in daily life is not only
workable, but necessary and valuable. Receptivity in every phase
of life, not just listening, enhances the effectiveness of one's daily
meditative periods and helps bring about changes in personality
and functioning that we all desire.

MOVEMENT MEDITATIONS

In recent years body movements have been considered an integral part, an expression, of one's total being. Paul Byers, an an-
thropologist, made a film recently that revealed some fascinating
rhythmic patterns relating to speech and motion. The film showed
a montage of different events: two Kung Bushmen in the Kalahari
Desert sitting and talking; Margaret Mead talking with her insur-
ance salesman as her students looked on; a group of Eskimos cut-
ting up a seal carcass. At first glance this jumble of impressions
seemed just that—a jumble. But when Professor Byers began beating out a rhythm and urged the viewers to observe the changes
in motion among all those in the film, a clear "pulse" interacted
among them: "The head of one Eskimo turning, the hand of
another going down, the shift of a third, the head turn of the
salesman, the arm movement of Dr. Mead, the leg cross of a student, the arm sweep of a Bushman and the nod of his partner." *
Each change of direction evoked a constant, pure rhythm of interaction among all the people in the film. The rhythms born out of
this human interaction seemed an evocation of a universal rite,
a cosmic ritual resonating to the underlying energies of life. Awareness of these rhythms is the common goal of all movement meditations, so that one can learn not to interrupt these natural functions but rather to flow naturally with them. (See Exercise 24 in
the Appendix for a specific "flow meditation.")

* Martha Davis, "Movement of Patterns of Process," in *Main Currents,* 31, no. 1,
p. 13.

Historically, before man expressed his experience of life through using materials, he did so with his own body. For example, early man used dance for almost every important occasion: to express joy, love, sadness, and every hope—that the sun would rise, that the birth would go well. Thus, movement in one form or another has always been an expression of mankind identifying itself with universal concepts and essential powers of nature. The dancer's movement provided him with a deeper sense of his life's experience. In his dancing, the world of sound, light, and emotion symbolized his feelings about the world and was a spontaneous communion with a powerful and mysterious universe. Only after long religious ritualization did the spontaneous dance of life become a fixed pattern of gestures, movements, and sound.

But what sacred dance and music have consistently attempted to encompass was the external world outside one's body, and at the same time put man in communion with his own inner being. In this way the external and internal world became one. In the sacred dance man brought together the disparate elements of his character and his world; and, thus, the movement meditations are all methods to transcend personal fragmentation and unify the conflicting elements in being. Indeed, harmony of the body and mind is the very foundation of all true meditation, both East and West.

In movement meditations the reliance on sound, posture, and rhythmic involvement are expressions of the symbolic essence of life. This tradition is found in numerous religions: in Christianity as the Hesychast "Prayer of Jesus"; the Islamic *zikr* practice in which the breath (and sound as its expression) is thought of as the vehicle of life; and in the Hindu and Buddhist mantra and *pranayama* systems. In these exercises the physical movement is repeated over and over as in sound meditations such as mantras. Consciousness is continuously focused on the act of making movements. These types of meditation take many forms, including Tantric Yoga, touching or sensory awareness, the practice of martial arts (aikido, kung fu, Zen swordsmanship, Zen archery, etc.), and dance styles like the Chinese t'ai chi chuan, Rudolf Steiner's Eurhythmics, or the Sufi Mevlevi (whirling dervishes).

Many of these dances and movement meditations are becoming increasingly popular in the United States—especially the Sufi and t'ai chi chuan. The Mevlevi meditation exercises include chanting and a dance based on spinning. Unlike the Zen or Yoga groups, the Sufi are reluctant to make their meditation exercises widely known, for they believe that publicity regarding the details of their practice would undoubtedly lead to misapplication of their methods.

The bodily movements of Mevlevi dancing are associated with a thought and timed to the rhythmic repetition of sounds. The thought focuses the consciousness; the repeated sound blends the mind and body into a new state of consciousness that is a oneness with the universe. Without conscious involvement, then, the body *is* movement. A similar purpose is served in the dancelike ritual that often precedes an exhibition of the martial arts such as aikido, jujitsu, or kung fu. The two "opponents" stand face to face, then in three turning steps pass each other, face to face, almost touching, and end up again facing each other. The movement may be repeated several hundred times, or until each feels himself a part of the other, as if they were a single body.

Like jujitsu and kung fu, aikido is a nonaggressive martial art. Hours are spent in meditation: centering the body's energies, sensing the approach of others, attempting to blend with cosmic energies. Some aikido exercises are practiced blindfolded, with the master moving a finger before his pupil's face and behind his head until he can learn to sense exactly where the finger is. In this way, the aikido student is taught that there is a different kind of seeing.

There is a Zen story that clarifies the relationship between a martial art and one's identification with the attacker. A student travels to a monastery in order to learn the martial arts. After hearing the young man's request to learn the sword, the master sends him to the kitchen to begin his labors. The young man cleans dishes, takes out garbage, works hard in the vegetable garden for six months. Becoming impatient, he approaches the master and humbly asks when his training with the sword will begin. The master tells him to be patient and sends him back to his kitchen. More months pass until, gaining his courage, the young man again asks the master when his training with the sword will begin. The master smiles and responds, "Soon." More days pass and the young man despairs that he will ever learn the secrets of the martial arts. But one day, when he is taking the garbage outside, he is suddenly hit with a great thump on his backside with a large stick. As he picks himself up from the ground, he sees the master slowly walking away.

In the following weeks the young man is surprised by the master many times. The old man silently and swiftly springs from behind a bush, a rock, or a door, and strikes the young man with resounding whacks. The student soon becomes a nervous wreck. He begins second-guessing. He pauses before passing any corner, before going out a doorway, before going to the privy. But as careful as he is, the old master never says a word but succeeds in giving him so many thumps that he occasionally breaks out in sweats and trembling. The old man continues to stalk him until one day the youth is walking down a path, and without knowing why, he suddenly ducks; as he does so the master's staff cuts the air over his head. He looks up. The master smiles and says, "Now you may begin to learn the sword."

As with most of the martial arts founded upon meditation, aikido erases those distinctions we customarily make between mind and body; action and meditation; body and body; mind and mind. Aikido assumes an immaterial reality with which one can merge through "body consciousness" as well as through more traditional meditation methods. Whereas TM and such approaches teach that "higher reality" can be assimilated into the body through mental discipline, aikido stresses that our minds can be brought to know this reality through the experience of our bodies.

Despite its seemingly martial nature, aikido teaches the true meaning of Christ's words: "Turn the other cheek"—an admonition to nonresistance to evil that has puzzled many. The aikido master *helps* his attacker. He has been taught to be so sensitive to his opponent's intentions that he knows exactly what his opponent wants to do, blends with him, and when the aggressive gesture is completed, it is the attacker who has fallen. Through his acceptance of aggression, the aikido master remains in harmony. Despite the apparent conflict between meditation and the martial arts, between contemplation and action, we see that in aikido opposites are brought into balance. We then can understand the words of Heraclitus: "That which opposes, fits. Different elements make the finest harmony."

As with meditations involving sensory awareness techniques, the movement meditations are difficult to learn without a teacher. But because there are so many self-proclaimed experts in these new disciplines, approach each new contact with caution. If you decide to try movement like the Dervish dance or the t'ai chi chuan, choose an established teacher or group first. Most of the new age journals and books list such groups. The qualifications of the leaders are generally clearly stated; and often people who are teaching movement techniques have had long-established reputations, such as Charlotte Selver in sensory awareness methods, or Sophia Delza or Dr. Da Liu in t'ai chi chuan.

Even though the movement meditations are probably best learned with a teacher, I have included descriptions of several such meditations in order to help the reader develop an impression of them. A general familiarity with these meditations will guide you in choosing the proper meditation for your particular needs.

T'ai chi chuan is an ancient Chinese system of slow, flowing, and subtly arranged motions. It had a fleeting moment of attention when former President Nixon made his trip to China and the television public witnessed both small and large groups of young and old exercising in a slow-motion movement of their arms, legs, and bodies. Not only has t'ai chi been considered an important, valuable physical exercise for the general public, but it has been used as physiotherapy in hospitals, sanitariums, and nursing homes. A leading exponent of t'ai chi, Dr. Da Liu, describes how former students of his have organized t'ai chi chuan exercise and meditation programs in hospitals as an adjunct to Western therapy.

The origins of t'ai chi are obscure. Traditionally, its creator was Taoist master Chang San Feng, who was reputed to have lived many years and who could walk hundreds of miles in one day. Magical and fantastic claims aside, the benefits of t'ai chi have been well documented in recent years. It was probably created for the same reason as other exercise systems—in order to improve one's general health and to use in self-defense. T'ai chi is usually translated as "grand ultimate," and chuan means "fist" or "boxing." It is reputed to prevent illness in the healthy and cure ailments ranging from heart trouble to hives. It is also supposed to extend life well beyond the norm. Used as self-defense, t'ai chi chuan is similar to aikido in principle; yet the specific defensive moves are quite different. They both, however, are defensive, pacific, and use the aggressor's own energy and force against him.

But because it is Chinese and Taoist in origin, the inclusion of meditative techniques was inevitable.

The basic principle of Taoism is that a fundamental harmony pervades the universe. The Tao, or "Way," as it is usually translated, is the harmonious path of universal law in action. The wise man pursues meditation and techniques like t'ai chi in order to learn to live in harmony with these flowing energies of nature. Thus t'ai chi students attempt to transform the world and open their minds to their own intimate and natural connection with the universe around them. Taoists believe that all static concepts are the last refuge of impotent thinkers. These exercises and meditations are therefore designed to unite the mind, body, and spirit. Thus better mental and physical instruments are achieved in order to pursue the ultimate wisdom of the Tao.

This philosophy is an integral part of all Taoist exercises, including the Oriental arts of archery, boxing, fencing, and self-defense techniques like kung fu. Specific movements of t'ai chi chuan are designed to regulate the functions of various parts of the body, to relax tension or stiff muscles, to aid digestion, to increase blood circulation and oxygen supply to the lungs, heart, and blood. The breathing techniques have the same basic goal of yogic breath control: to bring in new air and release old air with maximum efficiency. (See Exercise 23 in the Appendix for a t'ai chi chuan exercise.)

Taoists respect the physical body in the same way Christians believe that the body is the temple of the spirit. They use the analogy of a fertilized egg, with the shell likened to the body and the yolk to the inner life-force. When the chick is hatched the shell is, of course, broken and then abandoned; but if it breaks before incubation the chick will die. Therefore, says the Taoist, the student "should preserve his physical body with the same care as he would a precious gem." But there is a paradoxical aspect to the Taoist attitude toward the physical world. In Taoist meditation there is a practical recognition that the body is necessary. "Without the body the Tao cannot be attained," says one sage, "but with the body Truth never can be realized." This apparent conflict exists because in the early stages of meditation the practitioner of Tao must use his body in order to train his mind and spirit. Therefore, he must respect and preserve his body as much as is humanly possible. But when his training reaches its goal, concern and attachment for the body will be abandoned, for the Taoist believes that, while the body is a vital tool, if dependency on it is not given up at the right moment, "Truth" cannot be attained.

USING T'AI CHI IN MEDITATION

T'ai chi is one of the most effective moving-meditations. Those who are used to *zazen*, the Japanese method of meditating while facing a blank wall, and to the Tibetan practice of lying on one's back and meditating on the empty sky will recognize the extreme difference in effect when practicing t'ai chi meditation. All of these methods, including t'ai chi, seek to let the mind dissolve its dependency on form and to identify with a cosmic unity. For many, however, the slow, flowing, unfolding movements of t'ai chi are a preferable form of meditation.

As with other forms of meditation, the student must give complete attention when performing its movements. All inhibiting, interruptive thoughts that intrude, which inevitably happens in the beginning, should be gently ignored. The mind must remain focused on the correct execution of each separate t'ai chi form—of which there are dozens. Each form flows out into the other until the meditator moves so fluidly between the different forms that it is like movie frames, each a complete still photograph, but when run together present a fluid, smooth picture of action. As the student progresses he will find it easier to keep his mind focused on practicing the form. With experience, he can begin to concentrate on the lower belly. In t'ai chi—as in Taoism generally—the lower belly is considered the body's center of gravity as well as a focal point for vital energy. It is thus one of the most important points in the body, both when relating to the body's movements and when concentrating the mind during meditation.

Unlike many other physical exercises, t'ai chi does not press the body to perform beyond its limits. Because the exercises are so simple and easy, any physical limits a person has are gradually extended. Breathing, for example, is not forced; the exerciser-meditator takes in as much air as his body needs. The amount of air is regulated by whether the body is relaxed, tense, or is pushing too hard; so it is important to learn to move without tension. In the beginning, be aware of minute changes in your breathing as you move through the exercises. As you begin to flow into the movements, your breathing will become deeper and slower.

A simple but basic fact involved in all movement meditations —but especially in t'ai chi—is learning to distinguish between "trying" and "letting" the body move. When one psychologically pushes, the inevitable result is tension and unnecessary nerve responses. When one "lets" the body respond in a natural way, the initial relaxation continues throughout the exercise. It is a clinical fact that when an effort is made in a tense way, the muscles shorten. When one relaxes and allows the body to move easily and without tension, the muscles lengthen. It is important, therefore, to learn relaxed movement. This is harder than it might sound. If you observe yourself even in the simple movements of everyday life you will notice that the slightest action begins with tensing your body, particularly your shoulders, neck, legs, and stomach. Watch yourself as you get up from a chair or bed and register the amount of tension you feel build up. If you imagine your body rising effortlessly from the chair before you even move, and if you breathe slowly and evenly and then follow through with your body with the thought of "relax" in your mind, you will see a quick and surprising difference. In t'ai chi the same basic technique applies in the beginning until one gets the knack of relaxed motion. In t'ai chi one must "let" the muscles flow and never "direct" them. This does, of course, take some practice.

Because Taoism is based upon principles of universal energy, of which the human body and mind are integral parts, the t'ai chi meditative exercises are meant to teach a mental and emotional energy conservation technique that allows us to focus our life's forces more productively. In a sense, all exercise is meant to accomplish this same goal, but t'ai chi overtly seeks to integrate the physical reality with its philosophy and spiritual values. Most important, t'ai chi helps the Westerner to develop a closer bond between his mind and his body's actions: they learn to function in harmony, which is carried beyond the meditation period into our everyday lives.

T'ai chi is one of those exercise-meditations that cannot be taught adequately in a book or without a teacher. However, I have included the first form (or position) in the Appendix (Exercise 23). It is a simple meditative exercise that you can perform by yourself and will give you an idea of what t'ai chi movements are like.

Gurus and Disciples:
Is This Marriage Necessary?

DIFFERENT PEOPLE OBVIOUSLY SOLVE their problems in different ways. William Sheldon has shown that some people prefer action —even if just taking a walk—while others need personal contact and emotional comforting. Still others need intellectual understanding. But because human beings are so uniquely isolated within the prison of their physical and psychic beings, there is no universal prescription for overcoming stress or problems.

Obviously, we all need personal guidance at one time or another. Help may come from a teacher, psychotherapist, priest, or friend. But the more original or difficult the problem, the harder it is to find a competent guide. This is especially true when dealing with the human mind and spirit. The mind is as unexplored as outer space and is probably even harder to examine, not only because there are so few guides familiar with this strange terrain, but because there is no easily acquired technology to rely on as with physical, mechanical problems. In a technological sense, only biofeedback has begun to give us a glimpse.

One of the most charismatic gurus of the modern age, G. I. Gurdjieff, argued that everyone has an emotional blind spot. To uncover this shadowy area of the psyche, Gurdjieff said, something or someone outside of oneself is needed. To find such a guide is the problem. Since each individual seeks his own missing center, his relationship to society and other people is one of constant searching, a continual questioning glance into the eyes of strangers to discover what profitable secret might be hidden there. The teacher-guide-guru has supposedly already found his missing center, and can theoretically communicate its nature to others. Perhaps this belief is the reason why gurus have become so popular in recent years. But do gurus really have the secret? Can they communicate what they know? And just what is a guru?

The image created by the numerous gurus now flying around the Western world in their private jets is a confusing and misleading one. Without careful and extensive investigation, there is no way of determining which of these atomic-age swamis is genuine. Since this is impossible for most of us, we are forced to use alternatives, such as measuring them against the traditional or historical Eastern guru or swami. Contrary to the life-styles of our Western gurus, the traditional swami lives a life of extreme hardship. It is not a life merely of chanting mantras twice a day for fifteen minutes or exercising with a few Yoga postures in the morning, but rigorous study of the holy scriptures; wearing simple garments; and eating simple, unadorned foods. Most swamis renounce all worldly pleasures. Of course, this is not to say that total renunciation is the only way to spiritual growth.

The Eastern swami who follows a life-style of acute sacrifice has as his goal the complete "mastery of self." His next task is to sustain his mastery. In order to achieve this state of constant "self-hood," the swami must exercise constant discipline over all aspects of his life—both inner and outer. He exemplifies a saying in the *Dhammapada,* a *sutra* (sacred scripture) revered by Hindus and Buddhists alike: "Irrigators guide the water; fletchers straighten arrows; carpenters bend wood; wise men shape themselves." The end result of this life of rigor and self-shaping is not only the spiritual grace or bliss discussed so often, but powers over mind and body that seem awesome compared to our own confused, undirected "normal" mental abilities.

For example, at the Menninger Foundation in Kansas, experiments on an Indian guru, Swami Rama, conclusively showed that he could manipulate his heartbeats up to 300 a minute—which can be fatal over extended periods—while meditating. In a further attempt to separate the myth from fact about gurus, B. K. Anand and Gulzar Chhina, at the All-India Institute of Medical Sciences, documented some remarkable abilities induced by Yoga training.

One yogi, for example, could place his hand in near-freezing water and keep it there for twenty-five minutes, whereas a normal person could do this for five minutes at most. The yogi had prepared for this feat with a long period of meditation, half-naked, in the Himalaya Mountain snows. A second yogi could break out into a sweat on any part of his body by meditating on it. Others showed they could stop their heart sounds and pulse beats for a few seconds—not actually stopping the heartbeats entirely, but reducing the movements to a "rapid flutter" that was extremely difficult to detect with normal instruments.

Interestingly, these swamis, who persistently and passionately pursue their daily discipline, often express reservations about and even distaste for the gurus who travel to foreign lands and embrace the glamor, gimmickry, and commercial life-style. In sum, they feel that the task of a swami or holy man is diametrically opposed to that of being a successful businessman.

In other ages, gurus have been considered saints, men so exalted in spirit that simply to be in their presence altered one's inner self. True or not, these powers are claimed by many contemporary gurus. There is little doubt that some individuals have a charismatic power that truly does move the spirit of those around them. What is all too often forgotten, however, is that charisma can result from megalomania as well as a uniquely developed personality. And although some are adored for their peaceful aura and a mellow personality projection, which is refreshing in our aggressive society, after listening to them speak one begins to sense that something is missing. One suspects that at least some are placid because half of their personality is unplugged and they are actually operating on only one or two cylinders.

The test of these individuals' spiritual credentials is not—and should never be—absolute trust in them. The only true "master" can be one's own inner awareness, even though trust in one's inner impressions is also notoriously difficult, misleading, and even dangerous. For without honest self-criticism delusion is often the result. A form of discriminating awareness when dealing with one's inner feelings can be developed, however. A good teacher helps you to learn this process of inner discrimination; a good teacher guides the meditator toward a general method suited to the meditator's temperament, helps him avoid possible pitfalls and dangers, and eventually lets each person find his or her way through personal experience. As Jesus said (Matt. 23:8–10): "Call no man your Father, but God only; and be not called 'teacher' or 'master,' for you are all brothers."

Buddha emphasized the same thing. Each person's salvation is his or her own. People can be helped, but ultimately it was each person's own hand that fashions his own end. As Buddha lay dying in the arms of his favorite disciple, Ananda, he is reputed to have whispered, "Life is full of sorrow, Ananda; work out your own salvation diligently."

In the positive sense, a guru can help many by virtue of his own understanding and personal development. At his best he represents an ancient tradition. He directs our gaze into our ignored inner history. We look back to ancient cultures and religious traditions and are guided by their pointing fingers. Our path becomes merged with the heritage of all seekers, with the innumerable others who have phrased our longings even before we encountered them in our own questing. Thus the guru's role is ideally one of guidance, or a creative translation of the abstruse into the understandable and functional. Since each individual is in fact a unique universal theme, the guru-teacher must be adaptable enough to play the various instruments that come to him for tuning. The authentic guru-guide seeks to demonstrate the spiritual element within his followers in order to help them perceive their own inner wisdom, to awaken the inner light that the meditative religious heritage claims is the core of every human being. To exalt the positive inner self of the human animal—who is a complicated, irrational, neurotic, immature, starving, striving creature—is a task only a saint or a fool would undertake. Make sure, therefore, that you don't follow the fool or fraud.

Since gurus are notoriously self-perpetuating you will find many who claim that you will fail without them. These types play the role of a demanding, authoritarian figure who allows no self-expression. If you meet teachers like this, and no doubt you will, be suspicious, for these gurus have probably succumbed to their own advertisements. In some very specific disciplines, such as Zen, the master actively tries to destroy a disciple's rigidly held assumptions about the world. But there is a valid reason behind his seemingly arbitrary actions, for he seeks to introduce an alternative view of reality. The master in Zen is still an authoritarian guide and the opportunity for abuse exists, since the human temperament remains a volatile mixture of power and vulnerability. But the Zen master is usually a highly disciplined individual with many years of hard work and training behind him. Dependency of the unquestioning sort desired by egocentric gurus is not only frowned upon by traditions like Zen or Sufism, but is actively discouraged. There is an ancient Zen parable that touches on this point.

"The master would never speak a word when asked to explain the Tao (Way), but would simply stick his thumb out. The master's young disciple seeing this, began to imitate his master, hoping thereby to gain understanding and enlightenment. One day when the boy mimicked him, the master suddenly hacked off the boy's thumb. The shocked boy ran off crying but the master called to him. The crying boy stopped and turned, whereupon the master again stuck out his thumb."

Not only is dependency rejected in this parable, but so is the shortcut to insight we are all so prone to take. The Zen master speaks or acts metaphorically in order to turn the disciple in upon himself. He directs the seeker to find his own answer—even if it takes years, which it often does. But the student often starts out his Zen studies confused. What the Zen master knows is that there is no master and no student. Yet the student doesn't recognize this. Another metaphor has the disciple questioning the master: "How can I ever get emancipated?" The master responds: "Who has ever put you in bondage?" For the Zen master the teaching task is to free the disciple of any dependence on him. In fact, this is a wise principle to keep in mind when dealing with all gurus.

One of the greatest values in having a guru derives from the fact that meditation has just as many dangers as other systems of self-exploration such as psychotherapy. The trial-and-error approach to meditation can lead to the same self-defeating behavior patterns and excessive self-absorption that you have taken up meditation to correct. And it should be remembered that self-obsession is just as dangerous as object-obsession. Each sets up patterns that exclude a balanced life. In fact, the guru can act as a guide in the same sense as a psychotherapist and supply the confused seeker with a *temporary* structure around which he revolves until he is strong enough and secure enough to stand alone. With the security of an outer force—that is, a personality stronger than one's own and more capable of handling what is at the moment unknown—the disciple often feels freer to plumb the mysterious depths of his unexplored psyche. The same supportive function is given by the therapist while patients seek answers for their troubled lives.

In Eastern religions, however, the guru is considered someone closer to God than the student and therefore wiser, stronger, and more divinelike. Sikhism is an Eastern religion that particularly emphasizes the authority of the guru. Traditionally, the Sikh believes that since the guru has already achieved spiritual enlightenment, the disciple can only benefit from being in the guru's presence and from emulating him. Consider the difference between the Sikh attitude toward the guru and the Zen master chopping off the disciple's finger because of his imitation. The purpose of these meditation disciplines is not to learn mimickry, but to pursue self-discovery. Relationship with a guru in these religions becomes a strengthening and healing force for the disciple. An illuminating description of the guru-disciple relationship is in Lama Anagarika Govinda's autobiography: "The moment we try to analyze, to conceptualize, or to rationalize the details and experiences of initiation, we are dealing only with dead fragments, but not the living flow of force, the inner relationship between guru and chela [disciple] and the spontaneous movement, emotion, and realization on which this relationship is based."

Contemporary Sufi philosopher Idries Shah believes that the guru is spiritually unnecessary. He may be a valuable social tool similar to the therapist, but there is too great a temptation for the guru to play the god-role. Another longtime observer of the contemporary occult scene, Dr. Gina Cerminara, states that she has seen many who are patently interested in self-inflation. "Hardly anything," Dr. Cerminara observes, "can match the heady feeling of being regarded as omniscient!"

Idries Shah is one of the more realistic and enlightened modern experts in esoteric religions, and while he is primarily concerned with the Sufi tradition, he has had broad experience with many types of gurus. His final judgment is harsh: He considers that most gurus are "frankly phonies." If the guru "had a sufficient outlet for his desire to be a big shot or his feeling of holiness or his wish to have others dependent on him, he wouldn't be a guru." In the Sufi tradition, Shah points out, those who don't want to teach are the ones who can and should. But the most trenchant and disturbing point in Shah's criticism is that gurus have come to him as if he were a guru of Sufism—a role he rejects—and question him openly about how Westerners can be manipulated or exploited. "It's time somebody took the lid off the guru racket," Shah says. "With many of these gurus it comes down to an 'us and them' sort of thing between the East and West. Gurus from India used to stop by on their way to California and their attitude was generally, let's take the Westerners to the cleaners; they colonized us now we will get money out of them. I heard this sort of thing even from people who had impeccable spiritual reputations back home in India."

But Shah is not completely negative regarding gurus. In fact, he points out, the followers and the guru need each other. But it is a form of therapy, a social function and not a spiritual one. According to Shah, the guru cannot communicate the Sufi experience; it "has to be provoked in a person. Once provoked it becomes his own property, rather as a person masters an art."

Other Sufis echo Shah's feelings. The thirteenth-century Sufi mystic Jalal ad-Din Rumi was keenly aware of false gurus who are on ego trips: "The real guru," Rumi wrote, "is one who has killed the idol you have made of him." Pir Vilayat Khan, who is one of the most respected of modern Sufi leaders, also warns about the guru who is domineering or tends to be overly directive. This type of guru "weakens your ability to come to your own decisions and that is what this work is all about." As one astute commentator on meditation, Haridas Chaudhuri, professor of philosophy at the California Institute of Asian Studies, says, "a guru is no doubt a great help, but beyond a certain point he may become a hindrance. So the mature guru withdraws at the right time with a loving act of sacrifice, just as the mature mother does when her child grows up."

Another point to consider when judging a guru is to try to assess the accuracy and honesty of his teaching. Gurus who have found America fertile territory have tended to water down their disciplines to the point where their teachings actually misrepresent their tradition. The result, in the eyes of one Indian yogi, Baba Muktananda, is that the guru then has nothing left to give. Of course, this watering down of difficult disciplines is what has contributed so greatly to their success in a society addicted to instant gratification. Have these disciplines been so simplified that they offer the disciple misleading Eastern techniques, or are they Americanized versions of Eastern philosophies?

Another difficulty is that there appear to be almost as many different methods as there are gurus. One teacher prescribes a mantra (chanting), while another gives a detailed argument for following the tantra discipline. Still another argues for concentration on images or symbols, while another asserts that images are no good. In short, the gurus seem to be getting richer while their disciples end up with a long-winded discourse and a depleted bank account. Baba Muktananda believes this is because Americans are rather "simple and credulous and naive . . . so any guru can be a smash hit here." Muktananda tells the story of a guru that he recently met who is quite respected and has a large following. "He had a pot belly and he said that he has been teaching yoga. I asked him where he himself was practising any yoga and he said, 'Oh, I gave that up long ago. Now I only teach it.' "

This is not an exceptional story, for one often finds people teaching Yoga who do not practice it, or teaching meditation who do not meditate. Muktananda, it seems to me, offers some sound advice about approaching a guru or new teacher. Assuming that you keep your wits about you and you are not one of Barnum's minute-born suckers, Muktananda advises that you try and determine if the guru is self-centered or absorbed in his own personality. Be suspicious and see if he is putting on an act. Muktananda asserts that a true guru does not make things so easy or cheap and does not initiate people quickly into his teachings. "He would first test them thoroughly," Muktananda says, "before initiating them. Likewise students should also test a guru thoroughly before accepting him. Anyone who claims to be a guru must be totally disciplined. He must exercise self-control in food and drink and in talking and in every other thing." In other words, a guru should have certain visible characteristics of spiritual insight, mental and bodily discipline, specific personality traits, and living habits.

Finally, because it is so difficult to find a true guru, Muktananda wisely recommends being patient. "One should not be in a hurry to accept a guru," he advises, "because taking a guru is the most significant, the most important event in your life." Anyone who has had a superior teacher alter his life or raise the dimensions of his consciousness realizes the impact and influence such people have. Caution, intelligence, and prudence are obviously necessary when committing oneself.

Before seeking a guru, you must clarify your goals: Why are you interested in learning to meditate? What benefits do you hope to obtain? This implies, of course, a certain amount of personal psychological insight even before starting to meditate. But all of us are much more capable of understanding our needs and motivations than we give ourselves credit for. Balances have to be struck between a realistic assessment of your particular needs and a critical, discerning awareness of the character and nature of the group or teacher to whom you are attaching yourself. This is where judgment comes in, for an intelligent decision cannot be made without it.

A little common sense is also immensely helpful when dealing with gurus. There is no reason to give up one's critical sense or abandon one's powers of discrimination when learning how to meditate, joining a group, or choosing a teacher. The blockage one gets from too much analysis or critical thinking comes during meditation itself, not when one is dealing with the physical and mundane world. It is one thing to learn to set aside the critical, analytical thought-process when meditating—for there are definite benefits at that time—but it is an entirely different matter when a guru or teacher expects one to become dependent upon him and give up one's critical insight or common sense. (Of course, few gurus are so obvious or direct in their demands.) Setting aside the critical mind is necessary in later stages of meditation, *not* while one is shopping for guidance.

The key to finding the right teacher or group is understanding human relationships. If you sensitize yourself to what actually occurs between two people, not to mention the multiple, complicated relationships interwoven in groups, you can see that for the most part relationships are based on expectation; the frequent result is frustration, resentment, and anger because your own fantasies make it difficult for another to match your desires. The more specific your expectations, the more unlikely that they will be fulfilled. So, it is wise to become aware of your expectations and try to reduce them to realistic levels.

Reducing expectations, however, is not to be confused with the specific aforementioned criteria for approaching a teacher or group. For example, you may be seeking a teacher or group to help you with a specific problem—say, you want to create a more stable emotional life. It would be unrealistic to approach others as if they had all the answers and all the discipline. Such an attitude sets you up for dependency, for it shifts the burden of correcting personal problems to others. Reduce your expectations to the level where you recognize yourself in others, and at that point the interaction between you and the group improves. Mutual respect (and sometimes support) grows as everyone recognizes that we are all walking wounded, for we see others in the context of our own lives. If you interact as the only person with problems—or as the person with the most important, the largest, the most pressing problems —you delude yourself and the relationship suffers from the imbalance. At once you aggrandize yourself by claiming an exaggerated importance, and ultimately a greater dependency develops; for you are also in the position of constantly absorbing advice and direction from others. You become as a dependent child who looks to the group or teacher for your answers rather than finding them for yourself.

The worst attitude you can develop is to expect the guru or group to carry you through personal trials and experiences necessary for growth. No one can pull another through the self-indulgences and muddied waters of his life. You can only succeed in getting along with others after you have success in struggling alone. Once this is understood—unpleasant as it is to face—liberation follows. All substantive change must come from within— even if one feels a part of the most stellar, godlike guru—and this leads to real action and the ultimate truer definition of self.

There is also a deep fascination for the "psychic" world, which often becomes an obsession or cosmic infatuation that leads the devotee to spend too much energy and time in a shadowy realm in which blatant and unchecked superstition nourishes more primitive emotions. Those caught up in this cosmic fascination fall prey to an uncritical acceptance for anyone with apparent credentials, such as Reverend, Swami, Sri, or Ph.D. There is a misplaced faith that being the author of books or articles is equivalent to superior intelligence or "illumination"; an erroneous conviction that to be psychic is to be spiritual; an absolute homage to whatever is vaguely paraded as "scientific findings"; a thorough confusion between simplistic slogans and profundity; and a thoughtless acceptance that someone can have "The Truth" once and for all, and consequently has the right to dispense this singular "Truth" to his disciples for payment in dollars, devotion, energy, or time.

An example of blind fascination is the convert who enthusiastically relates how "perfect" his new teacher (master) is, and how profound the new truths he has discovered through "Him." Eventually such conversations become filled with subtle—and sometimes obvious—hints that you must come to their next meeting and meet their guru or, they warn, you may never get out of the blind rut you are in. Such proselytizing can be motivated by deep conviction, delusion, or calculation. But the subtle threats and innuendoes often seem to have a desperate tinge, as if the new convert was deepening his own conversion through convincing you. Such blind, unthinking commitment is extremely dangerous; a disciple thus becomes a storm trooper for a kind of spiritual fascism, with the guru in the role of the fuehrer.

The dangerous delusion inherent in this unthinking acceptance is seen in the attitude toward apostates. All too often the ex-disciple or ex-follower of a group is emotionally rejected and derided as "sick," "dangerous," "spiritually undeveloped," or worse. One devotee of a popular religious group is quoted as saying that a spiritual group is not a "swinging door. Once a disciple goes, he's dead. There would be nothing to speak to him about." And what is so terrible about this ex-disciple? Has he become a beast? Why is there nothing to say? Unfortunately, many groups, while proclaiming ego-reduction on the one hand, are wallowing in their uniqueness on the other. To be special in terms of "being better than" is to set oneself apart from one's brothers. Our particular culture is viciously competitive and it is no surprise that psychological alienation results. As Krishna in the *Gita* says: "All roads lead to me." Such immature defensiveness and aggressive intolerance is perhaps the clearest evidence that a group or individual will not provide spiritual insight or help. The judgmental attitude of "them" and "us," plus the dependence on spiritual jargon, is to be avoided sooner rather than later.

A typical example of such jargon is the popular, blanket dictum that "you must destroy your ego." On the face of it, it is unwise and impractical, even foolish, to advise ego-ridden personalities to destroy their egos. There are many approaches for dealing with the disruptive elements of the ego; some are positive and constructive, while others offer only an equally limiting preoccupation with the self instead of release. The prescription "get rid of your ego" accomplishes nothing but confusion: How can I destroy my ego when I don't even know what it is or where it is? What are the helpful, positive aspects of my ego? How can I destroy my ego and be left with nothing to replace it? Usually the pat answer of contemporary gurus is to replace it with their teachings.

Another danger signal is an excessive reliance on ritual and gaudy costume. Such groups tend to prefer style over substance and often succumb to word games and spiritual cant. This is often justified by arguing that true spiritual insight depends on grasping the esoteric meaning in their garbled syntax. What is really meant is that they will accept you into their group only if you will completely accept *their* interpretation. Such word games are, of course, a corruption of the genuine tradition of spiritual paradox so often described by true leaders and mystics. Another rationale for this type of posturing generally includes the assurance that costumes and esoteric ritual are a sign of respect as well as a technique for continually reminding the disciple of his new vows. It is also supposed to indicate the disciple's continuing commitment to his new beliefs. These rationales do have some truth in them, but this only misleads the unsophisticated newcomer into accepting language and posturing that as yet have no real spiritual significance for him.

Undoubtedly, ritual can evoke strong spiritual involvement, but its value diminishes when it is used as an arbitrary rule. In its important traditional role, ritual involves the believer in the essence of religion. However, there is an invisible line after which reliance on dress and ritual degenerates into empty form and redirects attention away from the essence of a religion rather than toward it. Religious practice thus becomes a constant dress rehearsal, but there is no spiritual wedding. This invisible line is difficult to find, but with the enormous number of frauds who set themselves up as gurus after learning a few pieces of authentic ritual from an ancient religion, it is necessary to try. Any group that seems to rely on ritual and costume or that emphasizes the external trappings more than the hard discipline and inner labors should be suspect.

Furthermore, too much attention on externals creates competition. Example: If X meditates for one hour and Y only meditates for fifteen minutes, X is considered more spiritually developed than Y. Not wanting to seem to lack humility, X will never mention this obvious fact out loud, but will manage to let everyone in the group know that in his meditations he sees wonderful lights and illuminated figures. In a further effort to prove that he is humble and deserving of such special effects during his meditation, X tries to help Y meditate more effectively. Such an absurdly obvious egotism is unfortunately not limited to members of a group, but is often seen in its leaders.

With the exception of a few highly specialized meditation methods, it is better not to join a group in which the communication between you and the leader is poor. If a teacher or guide cannot answer a question to your satisfaction or puts you off with "wait until you're ready to receive this secret knowledge," it is better to head for the door. Communication with your guide and among members of any group is vitally important. There is little purpose (beyond an intellectual one) in spending money to be treated like a child. If the teacher cannot stand up to your valid questioning, then he is probably hiding his ignorance. A good teacher accepts you as you are at the moment. There is no projection of how far you will travel spiritually or whether you are a chosen person. All of that is nonsense. A good teacher also has the added responsibility of preventing you from falling into various traps along the way. And it is precisely because many such traps exist that you must be careful in choosing the right teacher.

About ten years ago a friend enthusiastically urged me to meet his new guru. When we arrived the guru was dressed in bright-colored check pants, a plaid shirt, and white loafers. There were pictures of Hindu holy men on the walls. He charged a couple of hundred dollars to teach a mantra system of meditation. The guru's main technique was to lock the disciple in the closet for a few hours chanting his new mantra. While I was sitting in his office, the phone rang and he started a cursing harangue at the hapless disciple on the other end of the line. "Then sell your fucking factory," he yelled into the phone, "and move to the forest." After he hung up he explained his toughness to us by observing that his "children" needed a firm hand. It taught them discipline. Closer to the truth, it served his own inflated ego and made his followers ever more dependent. He obviously relished playing the stern-father role and had, as far as I was concerned, no conception of what a spiritual guide was.

It is not really surprising that the guru is so successful in domineering his disciples; our culture traditionally has not only accepted but created a parent-child relationship in spiritual matters. A 1906 Roman Catholic guide for proper conduct is written from a paternalistic perspective: "You must endeavor always to please your parents and superiors by prompt obedience, a cheerful demeanor, and industry at your work; in regard to going to dances, or plays of doubtful nature, you must always ask and follow the advice of your spiritual director."

This paternalistic attitude is found throughout many religions and prepares the inexperienced or immature seeker for the guru syndrome. In a newspaper interview, one follower of a popular guru readily accepted the parent-child relationship between guru and disciple: "The guru is like a father, leading a child. His highly developed consciousness enters our unillumined mind and actually lights our consciousness. He guides us through the inner circuits of our psyche to the God that is within. All we have to do is surrender our minds to him." In other words, simply surrender your discriminating intelligence and all the discipline and hard work of spiritual growth is done for you. A perfect religion for a baby.

Surrendering your mind to a guru, or even to a belief system, immediately places you in mental and spiritual bondage. Clearly, no single value system can encompass absolute truth, and anyone claiming to express absolute truth has to be talking nonsense, for the simple reason that no number of words can communicate the infinite nature of an absolute. Indiscriminate identification with one system over another may provide one with a sense of intellectual, emotional, or spiritual security, but one should not be fooled into thinking that absolute truth has been communicated. Infinity in words is like encompassing the sun in a light bulb: A relationship may exist but the difference is so great that all comparisons are woefully inept. At best any system can only help to diminish one's understanding of the vastness of our universe and emphasize the limits of our conceptual prison house. To believe in its reality is to delude oneself into accepting less for more, the cover for the book, the clothes for the person. In fact, along with their ability to clarify, all theories and systems have built-in dangers because they imprison us; they mentally limit future vistas.

Advocates are always captured by their own theories. This is true of doctors, therapists, scientists, politicians, and even artists who succumb to the temptation to describe their art in verbal aesthetic terms. The numerous schools of meditation, and the religious tradition that they flow out of, also often succumb to self-created traps. That is why Buddha emphasized self-criticism and a constant questioning of all one's attachments—which, of course, include one's fantasies and unrealistic expectations. Buddha emphasized the need for earnestly striving after truth and for avoiding deception by the numerous games of both one's ego and the pressures of one's peers or society. In his famous "believe nothing" statement, he creates a wonderful rule of thumb for independent self-inquiry:

> Believe nothing because a wise man said it,
> Believe nothing because it is generally held,
> Believe nothing because it is written,
> Believe nothing because it is said to be divine,
> Believe nothing because someone else believes it,
> But believe only what you yourself judge to be true.

Meditation and Your Body

IN THE EARLY SIXTIES an interest in altered states of consciousness, including meditation, swept across the country. For the first time serious and widespread scientific study of the meditative states became possible. At the Menninger Institute in Topeka, Kansas, a woman learned to raise her skin temperature ten degrees in three minutes just by thinking about it. While in meditation, students at Harvard were able to lower their blood pressure. Experiments with the entranced Swami Rama revealed he could increase his heart rate to an average of 300 beats per minute by thought control. A yogi in a lab actually stopped his heart from pumping blood for seventeen seconds. Another yogi was wired to instruments and buried by a group of scientists for nine hours; he survived on a level of oxygen low enough to endanger the average man's life. All of this is not only part of the consciousness revolution, but more specifically, it is part of the surge of interest in biofeedback training and meditation.

Until the advent of biofeedback techniques, the feats of mind control mentioned above remained only delightful, titillating anecdotes not to be taken seriously. Then science began to notice the incredible claims of mind-control. Subjects could be taught to manipulate inner bodily functions previously thought to be entirely involuntary. Meditators could be wired and their bodily functions monitored.

One of the most intriguing initial findings was a correlation between a commonplace brain wave called alpha, which manifested
when one was in a relaxed, reverielike condition, and the internal
states involved with the fantastic exploits of the yogis. One of the
earliest and most persistent ideas was: Since alpha was so easy to
induce by using biofeedback equipment, why not use it as an
adjunct to or even in place of meditation? People who produced a
well-defined alpha wave also seemed to have a superior aptitude
in learning certain kinds of meditation. It followed, therefore, that
alpha-wave training would be an aid in learning to meditate.

But whether biofeedback is a shortcut to meditation is still
heatedly argued by researchers, for it was soon discovered that
alpha correlated only with an early stage of the meditator as he
plummeted into his psyche's depths. Another brain wave, the
theta, seemed to correlate with the deeper stages of meditation.
In fact, the mind began to seem like a bottomless well as researchers soon found that their instruments lacked the delicacy
to record the numerous subtle variations of the meditating mind
and body. Yet certain general characteristics about the relaxed-
alert state of alpha seemed clear. Dr. Eleanor Criswell, director of
the Humanistic Psychology Institute, noted that all techniques of
meditation have one condition in common: Attention is restricted
to one unchanging stimulus like an image, a word, a chant, or
the rhythm of breathing. As she explains: "There is a close similarity between alpha and meditation and what happens in perception when a stimulus is closely restricted. By putting a little
mirror over the eye or inserting a special contact lens, you can
create a situation where a person sees the same thing no matter
where he looks. You can see the similarity with meditation where
you restrict awareness to one object or thought. In both, you get
a phenomenon, subjectively, of loss of contact with the world."

Many other authorities, however, agree with Marvin Karlins and
Lewis Andrews, authors of *Biofeedback*, that if voluntary control
of brain waves can simulate the effects and advantages of meditation, whether or not it is the real thing is irrelevant. Still others
have suggested that feedback techniques in meditation might
teach the "blank mind" state of Zen or Yoga "within months or
even weeks."

Much of the relationship between biofeedback training and
meditation seems to be one of convenience: Americans are not a

patient people, nor are they attracted to the disciplines necessary for successful meditation. Biofeedback is therefore considered to be an easy way to develop meditation skills without investing all the time and labor. The reasoning is that meditation, as do other states of consciousness, has specific correlates in the nervous system and that these can be found and used in learning meditation. One of the originators of modern biofeedback research, Dr. Joseph Kamiya, believes that "once we have the complete physiological pattern that characterizes meditation, there is no reason why we can't train people, with feedback, to mimic it in a relatively short period of time." Meditation purists, however, continue to assert that brain-wave training, or simulation of the physical effects of meditation, cannot duplicate true meditation. They argue that Zen, Sufism, various yogic techniques, Transcendental Meditation methods, and so on, are states of being which cannot be defined by mere physical description. Be that as it may, others retort, "It's not enough to know you can contemplate your navel. There is the inevitable question of 'what happens then?' "

Even if the relationship between brain waves, biofeedback training techniques, and meditation cannot now be fully clarified, we can discuss those few meditative states that have been scientifically investigated and see how they relate to what we know about the mind and its control over the body. The categories of meditation researched during the last decade include yogic and Zen meditation, Transcendental Meditation, and what, for want of a better description, we may call "free" meditation. Free meditation refers to those innumerable students who have volunteered to "meditate" for experimenters. The main problem with the free meditators is that the subjects had no prior training and could only furnish the vaguest verbal descriptions of their mental processes ("I was thinking about a deep blue ocean"; "I was thinking about an argument I had with my son-in-law"). Nevertheless, such "free" meditations are the basis for most of the scientific studies that have so far been conducted.

Even within accepted disciplines, such as Yoga, wide differences exist among meditative states, at least in their physiological characteristics. Professors Robert Keith Wallace and Herbert Benson have stated the problem well: "Some [meditators] seek the goal through strenuous physical exercise; others concentrate on controlling a particular overt function, such as the respiratory rate;

others focus on purely mental processes, based on some device for concentration or contemplation. The difference in technique may produce a dichotomy of physiological effects; for instance, whereas those who use contemplation show a decrease in oxygen consumption, those who use physical exercise show an oxygen-consumption increase. Moreover, since most of the techniques require rigorous discipline and long training, the range in abilities is wide, and it is difficult to know who is an 'expert' or how expert he may be." *

Since Transcendental Meditation technique is a widely used and standardized practice, "expert" students were selected so that the Wallace-Benson experiments could be carried out on a large scale and under reasonably uniform conditions. The physiological effects of meditation that they observed appear to be confirmed by both earlier and later experiments, so that it is possible to draw some tentative conclusions.

ORIGINS AND DEVELOPMENT OF BIOFEEDBACK

Scientifically, the linkage between meditative states and brain-wave research goes back to the discovery of the alpha and beta waves by German psychiatrist Hans Berger in 1929. Berger established a relationship between brain-wave patterns and mental states. The alpha waves seemed associated with passivity, or nonconcentrative states of mind. The beta wave showed up when the brain was occupied with concentrated thought, as when doing an arithmetic problem in one's head. Berger thought the brain waves he discovered might be the cause of telepathic experiences. Realizing the waves were not strong enough alone to account for telepathy at a distance, Berger theorized an energy conversion in the brain which would result in a psychical energy that could be directed over distances without interference or absorption. While science accepted Berger's discovery of brain waves, it did not pursue either his investigations into altered states of consciousness or his telepathy theory.

Isolated fragments of the power of the mind over the body have been reported for generations. They have not, however, been formulated into any systematic study (except by parapsycholo-

* Robert Keith Wallace and Herbert Benson, "The Physiology of Meditation," *Scientific American* (February 1972), p. 86.

gists) until very recently. Perhaps such studies have been frowned upon because they imply something akin to religious beliefs, to such "unscientific" practices as Yoga and Christian Science. Investigation in psychology has been especially slow in researching the autonomic functions of the body. Psychologist G. H. Estabrooks wrote that during the 1940s and 1950s a tenuous start in this direction was born. N. Antoni, for instance, reported achieving an increase in urine as a result of hypnotic suggestion; Schultz, an increase in bodily temperature; W. S. Kroger in Chicago and M. Abrahamson in Minneapolis used hypnotism in all phases of obstetrics.

In one early experiment, a Russian psychologist, K. I. Platanov, gave his hypnotized subjects large quantities of alcohol with the suggestion that they would not get drunk. And they did not—either while under hypnosis or after coming out of the trance! Yet, surprisingly, even today the idea that the mind can affect physical changes in the body, including involuntary visceral modification, is anathema in many orthodox medical circles. Indeed, Neal Miller of Rockefeller University Hospital has discussed the difficulties he has faced when simply trying to get students to assist him in his biofeedback experiments in the early 1960s. The bias against anything smacking of Yoga in the laboratory was too strong.

Whatever the reasons for the slow progress, it was not until 1935 that serious scientific inquiry was resumed into the implications of Berger's discovery and the psychosomatic effects of meditation. In that year, French cardiologist Thérèse Brosse went to India equipped with a portable electrocardiograph. From the monitoring of the heart, Brosse concluded that one of her subjects could actually stop his heartbeat. What most probably occurred was the now well-known Valsalva maneuver. By holding the breath and straining downward, the yogi is able to increase the pressure within the chest and simulate heart stoppage.

A more extensive investigation with more sophisticated equipment than that used by Brosse was conducted in 1957 by two American physiologists, M. A. Wenger of the University of California at Los Angeles and B. K. Bagchi of the University of Michigan Medical School, in collaboration with B. K. Anand of the All-India Institute of Medical Sciences in New Delhi. They concluded that the heart stoppage shown in Brosse's test was probably an artifact, since the heart impulse is sometimes obscured by electrical signals from contracting muscles of the thorax (the Valsalva maneuver). However, they did discover that some yogis could *slow* both heartbeat and respiration rate. At approximately the same time, Dr. W. Grey Walter, experimenting with the late Irish medium Eileen Garrett, established a definite connection between alpha waves and the mediumistic trance state (even though there were no psychic phenomena during his experiments).

Then suddenly, like a chain of firecrackers, experiments began to be conducted that suggested that man may, after all, have a mind resource to control the most minute aspects of his physical being. In 1958, Dr. Joseph Kamiya, a psychologist engaged in sleep research at the University of Chicago, decided to see if his subjects could distinguish alpha and beta waves, produce and sustain alpha, verbally describe their alpha-meditative state, and then designate when they thought their alpha rhythm was strongly present. In the 1960s, Dr. Neal Miller experimented to determine if involuntary functions could be influenced by learning. He and his assistants conditioned rabbits to control blood pressure and to dilate the blood pressure in one ear more than the other, so that one ear blushed a bright red and the other turned to an almost transparent whiteness. Still another historical source of present experimentation grew out of Akira Kasamatsu's work (which is described later). Kasamatsu attempted to determine what happened to brain waves in yogis and Zen monks during meditation. ⱴ

From these small and dissimilar beginnings have grown the increasing scientific curiosity about the physiology of meditation: notably the work of Robert Keith Wallace and Herbert Benson, Elmer and Alyce Green, John Basmajian and Barbara Brown.

During a typical meditation experiment, the subject is isolated and asked to sit quietly for an interval and then invited to meditate for a 30-minute period. At the end of this period the subject is asked to stop meditating but to continue to sit quietly for an interval while the recording of his physical responses continues. Throughout the experiment the subject is connected to an instrument array that continuously records such physiological variables as heart rate and blood pressure. A catheter in the subject's left arm draws samples of arterial blood at ten-minute intervals; these samples are analyzed for oxygen and carbon dioxide content and for blood acidity and blood-lactate level. The subject's arm is screened from his view to minimize the psychological effects of blood withdrawal. The experimenter will also usually employ the GSR (Galvanic Skin Resistance), which measures the sweat-gland activity at the surface of the skin, correlated with arousal level; the EMG (electromyograph), which measures muscular activity; and the EEG (electroencephalograph), which measures brain-wave activity.

The EEG, essentially, is an amplifying system that receives and records the shifts in electrical potential that occur within the brain. These shifts are from positive to negative charges and create brain-wave patterns detected by electrodes attached to the surface of the head. With each bioelectrical shift within the brain cells, a pen is moved by the signal, swinging up when the charge is negative and down when it is positive. A sheet of graph paper slides under the oscillating pens and records the tracings of the brain waves.

For convenience, the usual brain-wave patterns during sleeping and waking are classified according to the amount of voltage in the electrical charges (amplitude) and the speed of change (frequency). The four known brain waves include the beta wave (13 to 26 cycles per second), which is associated with mental concentration, visual tracking, and problem-solving; alpha (8 to 13 cycles per second), signifying states of relaxed alertness and defocused attention—floating, peaceful meditation, pleasant blankness of mind; theta (4 to 8 cycles per second), which is linked to reverie and creativity—half-conscious awareness of subconscious imagery; and delta (.05 to 4 cycles per second), occurring during deep, usually dreamless, sleep.

The Brainwaves

Beta   13–26 cps   Focused attention: the fastest brain wave, linked to concentration, mental processing, problem-solving, and anxiety. The intense, jangling state of our brains while coping with the everyday world.

Alpha   8–13 cps   Unfocused attention: a relaxed, yet alert mental state. Floating, pleasant blankness, or shifting consciousness, peaceful meditation.

Theta   4–8 cps   Reverie: related to dream part of the sleep cycle, drowsiness, and creativity.

Delta   0–4 cps   Deep dreamless sleep. The slowest brain wave.

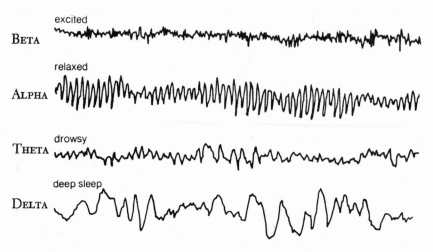

Norbert Wiener, one of the founders of cybernetics, concisely defined feedback as "a method of controlling a system by reinserting into it the results of its past performance." Biofeedback is simply a particular type of feedback—feedback from different parts of the body(the brain, the heart, the muscular structure) in which electronic instruments are used to amplify and monitor changes in the body's rhythms. These changes are translated into light or sound signals or the fluctuations of a needle on a paper drum. In a standard biofeedback session, a subject is "fed-back" his body signals through various instruments to which he is connected. The signals from the instruments—a flashing light, a steady tone, the squiggle of a needle—allow the subject to "see" his heartbeat or "hear" his brain waves. Once he has this information, he can begin trying to control them. For example, if an alpha brain wave feeds back a steady tone into his earphones, the subject begins experimenting with his inner mind until he succeeds in holding the tone steady, which is evidence that he is also holding his alpha wave steady. Through repetition a subject learns to identify these external cues with internal changes—the first step toward learning to *will* them. In its simplest, most natural form, a dart player, for example, *feeds back* trial-and-error information regarding the accuracy of his throw in the same way another person learns to manipulate his fingers to play a Chopin prelude or his legs to kick a field goal.

The similarity between the way the body and mind learn by natural conditioning and by instrumental conditioning is crucial to an understanding of how biofeedback training relates to meditation. Natural conditioning, or learning, always requires a stimulus that brings forth an innate response. Just as the dart player, by *visual* feedback, learns to adjust his throw, so the once-thought involuntary functions of the body may be brought under the mind's control by instrumental learning. However, the process of instrumental learning is much broader in scope, since it requires no specific stimulus to evoke a response or readjustment.

MEDITATION AND BIOFEEDBACK

One of the earliest demonstrated effects of meditation was the reduction in the rate of metabolism. Two Japanese researchers, Y. Sugi and K. Akutsu, found that Zen monks in meditation could decrease their oxygen intake by 20 percent and consequently reduce their carbon dioxide output. Further, scientists at the Komazawa University in Tokyo have recently made some surprising discoveries using modern biofeedback tools to explore the meditations of Zen practitioners.

Forty-eight Zen priests and nuns, together with 100 ordinary people used for control purposes, were tested by a research team led by psychologist Dr. Yoshiharu Akishige and psychiatrist Dr. Akira Kasamatsu. When the subjects assumed the stiff-backed, cross-legged sitting position of *zazen* (Japanese for "sitting in meditation"), the respiratory rate dropped rapidly to four or five breaths a minute (seventeen or eighteen would be normal), and their pulses fell ten to fifteen beats a minute below their average rate. In some cases, body temperature dropped several degrees. Dr. Akishige explained that this effect is partly due to the sitting position itself. "The strain that is placed on the diaphragm by zazen affects the autonomic nervous system and the over-all result is a calming influence, a slowing down of the bodily functions."

The biggest surprise to date is that the Zen practitioner, traditionally thought to be in a meditative trance that blots out the world, is actually very much aware of what is happening around him. He simply *chooses* not to let anything that occurs disturb him. The importance of this finding for the psychological aspects of meditation is profound, for there has been a perpetual argument over the role that "intention" and "will" have for the optimum function of the human personality.

Kasamatsu reports that "when one of the lay people sitting in the Zen position heard an electric bell, the normal pattern of his brain waves was interrupted for 15 or 16 seconds. But as the sound was repeated, he became used to it and eventually stopped reacting to it." The Zen priests and nuns also reacted to the bell, although their brain-wave activity altered for only two or three seconds. However, they continued to respond in the same way each time the bell was rung, regardless of how deep their concentration appeared to be. On the other hand, in experiments with yogis it was found that they did not react to outside stimuli at all. One can bang on a pot or sink their hands in ice water and their alpha wave continues uninterrupted.

Stimuli thought to have inherent emotional importance (such as the name of Marilyn Monroe, greatly admired by Japanese males) made no difference: The same low-level responses were recorded, supporting the contention of Zen Buddhists that they perceive all stimuli equally and allow none of it to disturb them.

The Japanese researchers feel that Zen could be an effective aid in helping an emotionally disturbed individual to "dispel his anxieties and achieve a feeling of detachment." But it appears that even the Zen Buddhists themselves are not entirely free of anxieties, for when there was some opposition to the testing, one nun admitted, "Many were afraid that the experiments would reveal insufficient depth in their Zen training and faith—or that the brain-waves of other priests would be better than theirs." Spiritual pride, it seems, is not limited to Westerners.

In New Delhi, B. K. Anand, working with G. Chhina and Balden Singh, later confirmed the findings with Zen monks in an examination of a Yoga practitioner, as did Elmer and Alyce Green of the Menninger Institute.

Commenting upon these tests, R. K. Wallace and Herbert Benson wrote that they "strongly indicated that meditation produced the effects through control of an 'involuntary' mechanism in the body, presumably the autonomic nervous system. The reduction of carbon dioxide elimination might have been accounted for by a recognizable voluntary action of the subject—slowing the breathing—but such an action should not markedly affect the uptake of

oxygen by the body tissues. Consequently, it was a reasonable sup-
position that the drop in oxygen consumption, reflecting a decrease
in the need for inhaled oxygen, must be due to modification of a
process not subject to manipulation in the usual sense." * At Harvard University, Wallace and Benson undertook their own experiments with twenty and fifteen student subjects respectively. After
their Harvard subjects were invited to meditate, both the rate of
oxygen consumption and carbon dioxide elimination decreased
markedly. (Consumption and elimination returned to their previous level soon after the subjects stopped meditating.) During
meditation, oxygen consumption fell from 251 cubic centimeters
per minute to 211 cubic centimeters. Similarly, carbon dioxide
elimination decreased from 219 cubic centimeters per minute to
187 cubic centimeters. The conclusion drawn from the Wallace-
Benson experiment was that "The ratio of carbon dioxide elimination to oxygen consumption (in volume) remained essentially
unchanged throughout . . . which indicates that the controlling
factor for both was the rate of metabolism." †

The measurement of arterial blood pressure in meditating subjects has been found by Dr. Neal Miller and others to fall to a low
level simply by "thinking it down." On the other hand, the rate of
blood flow into the forearm by subjects engaged in Transcendental Meditation has been shown to increase by 300 percent in
studies conducted by H. Riekert at the University of Tubingen.
The degree of control exhibited in these and other experiments
with blood pressure have indicated two things: that the rate of
blood flow is controlled basically by dilation or constriction of
the blood vessels, and that persons suffering from hypertension or
migraine headaches can "learn" relief through meditation.

Measurements of the lactate level in the blood (a known measurement of the body's "alarm system") have shown that these
levels decline rapidly during meditation. Patients with anxiety
neurosis show a large rise in blood lactate when they are placed
under stress; conversely, an infusion of lactate has been shown to
bring on anxiety attacks in normal subjects. But during meditation,
the lactate level fell nearly four times faster than the rate of decrease in people normally in a resting position or in the subjects
themselves during their premeditation period of relaxation.

* Wallace and Benson, p. 87.
† Ibid.

Perhaps the most remarkable experiment dealing with the mind's control over the body has been that of neuroanatomist Dr. John Basmajian. As described by physiologist Barbara Brown, "ordinary people are shown oscilloscope tracings of the spontaneous electrical activity of various small groups of their own muscle cells, activity detected by sensors on the skin over a muscle. With almost psychic power, these ordinary people begin to control, selectively, the minute electrical activity of different groups of muscle cells—involuntarily—just as they can voluntarily control the whole muscle when they want to move it. However, now they are activating as few as three muscle *cells* simply by deciding to do so." *

When the electrical impulse in the cell is fired, it is amplified by instruments to provide an audio feedback to the subject. In this way, Dr. Basmajian has trained subjects who became so skillful that they can actually fire off cells in rhythmic sequences so it sounds as if they are playing the drums. The subjects of other investigators have duplicated his experiments, with many of the subjects learning to activate these single cells in less than fifteen minutes. In Barbara Brown's evaluation: "The precision of control is extraordinary: to activate *one cell* independently means that other related cells, normally involved in muscle movement, must simultaneously be suppressed." †

Another physiological response tested by early investigators was the resistance of the skin to an electrical current. This measure is thought by some to reflect the level of anxiety: a decrease in skin resistance representing a greater anxiety; a rise in resistance, less anxiety. It appears to be established that meditation increases the skin resistance in yogis and somewhat stabilizes the skin resistance in Zen meditators. During the meditation of student subjects in the Wallace-Benson experiments, skin resistance to an electrical current increased notably, in some cases more than fourfold.

In experiments with yogis, Dr. Anand and other Indian experimenters (N. N. Das and H. Gastaut) observed that as meditation progressed, the alpha brain waves gave way initially to fast-wave activity (40 to 45 cycles per second) and these waves in turn subsided to slow alpha and theta waves. Tomio Hirai and Akira Kasamatsu of Tokyo University noted similar results in their experi-

---

* Barbara Brown, "Biofeedback: An Exercise in 'Self-Control,' " *Saturday Review* (February 22, 1975), p. 23.
    † Ibid., pp. 22–23.

ments with Zen monks. They found a high correlation between EEG patterns and the numbers of years of actual Zen meditation practice; there were progressive changes in the EEG of Zen masters during meditation. There was a high alpha activity with the monk's eyes half-open, such as is normally found in a person thoroughly relaxed with his eyes closed, but an increase in amplitude and regularity, particularly in the frontal and central regions of the brain. In monks with two decades or more of meditation practice, there was the appearance of theta activity.

Kasamatsu's experiments with the Zen state were duplicated in the West by Elmer and Alyce Green, research psychologists at the Menninger Institute. In 1970, the Greens conducted biofeedback experiments with an Indian yogi, Swami Rama. Since there was no way of describing with words the mental states they wanted him to explore, they allowed him to proceed at will, signaling to him when he produced the brain waves they wished to examine. The theta wave, which Kasamatsu had observed in the more practiced Zen masters, was particularly unusual. Theta is usually found only in states of near sleep and in EEG's of young children and pathological adults. Further experiments revealed delta waves beginning to emerge, characterizing the deepest, most oblivious sleep. Describing this state as his "yogi sleep," Swami Rama proved that he was able to enter it at will, producing an EEG record with 40 percent delta waves.

While in this entranced state, Alyce Green softly recited a number of prepared sentences, such as, "It is raining today, but tomorrow the sun will shine." While most people remember nothing that is said or done around them when they are sleeping, Swami Rama, despite the random and inconsequential nature of the meanings, could repeat from memory 85 percent of the sentences verbatim and paraphrase the remainder.

To sum up, persons in meditation experiments manifested the physiological signs of what has been described as a "wakeful, hypometabolic" state: that is, reductions in oxygen consumption, carbon dioxide elimination, and the rate and volume of respiration; a slight increase in the acidity of the arterial blood; a marked decrease in the blood-lactate level; a slowing of the heartbeat; a considerable increase in skin resistance; and an electroencephalogram pattern of intensification of slow alpha waves with occasional theta-wave activity. Similar physiological changes were observed in people who had been practicing Transcendental Meditation and what we earlier called "free" meditation, in highly trained experts in Yoga, and in Zen monks who had fifteen to twenty years of experience in meditation.

Regarding the physiological effects of meditation, the conclusion appears to be that traditional learning is limited to producing specific responses and depends on a stimulus and feedback, while meditation is independent of such conditions and produces not a single response, but a complex of responses that mark a highly relaxed state beneficial to the body overall. Further, the pattern of physiological changes suggests that meditation generates an *integrated* response, or reflex, that is mediated by the central nervous system.

In putting forth a description of the physiology of meditation, and the conclusions that may be drawn from it, the problems of experimentation should be noted. While researchers in the field are increasing, there are actually fewer than 300 persons doing active work, many of whom devote only part of their time to the subject. There is a bewildering variation in much of the literature as well as vagueness in reporting the results, which makes replication of an experiment difficult. There is also a failure on the part of many experimenters to follow through on their experiments and check the continuing effects of meditation on their subjects years later. There are also numerous methodological errors in many of the experiments themselves.* As Dr. Barbara Brown has argued, "Concluding anything about alpha is perilous. The EEG machines and electrodes used to capture only the external manifestations of the operation of the brain (which is what alpha does) are like the Mariner probe peeking at Mars from its thousands of miles' distance. Brain energy runs the whole mind and body; it cannot be expected that we can learn its secrets solely by examining its electrical topography. The 20 billion cellular inhabitants of the brain have nearly as many diverse ways of behavior as does the entire human body and there is as much variation in their behavioral profiles as there is in the universe of human beings." †

Even with such reservations in mind, the importance of medi-

* David A. Paskewitz and Martin T. Orna, "Visual Effects on Alpha Feedback Training," *Science* (July 27, 1973), p. 360.

† Barbara Brown, *New Mind, New Body* (New York: Harper and Row, 1974), p. 329.

tation and biofeedback techniques in alleviating or curing psycho-somatic illnesses can no longer be denied. It has proven effective (sometimes only temporarily) in the treatment of hypertension and high blood pressure, migraine headaches, epilepsy, facial tics, bruxism, asthma, Reynaud's disease, as well as introducing a more holistic relationship between doctor and patient. In the past, ac-cording to Roy Menninger, psychiatrist and head of the Men-ninger Foundation, the physician's position has put the patients in a dependent, even infantile, role. They are kept that way, as Dr. Menninger points out, but "there should be parity in the relation-ship—a therapeutic alliance, not a therapeutic autocracy." * Be-cause of the psychosomatic discoveries that have resulted from the study of meditative states, patients have acquired more responsi-bility and control over their own health, no longer finding them-selves treated as defective organisms, but as people with life-styles and habits that affect their bodies daily.

INFLUENCING MIND-BODY THROUGH IMAGINATION

Despite the known effectiveness of meditation and biofeedback upon illnesses related to tension, there is little, if any, concrete knowledge about how the "will" turns into action or how the mind is able to actually cure the body. Whatever subjects think and feel that enables them to control their bodies during medi-tation remains a mystery. When Dr. Bernard Engel, a psychologist in Baltimore City Hospital, followed in the footsteps of Dr. Jo-seph Kamiya and asked his subjects about their mind-body con-trol, one woman replied that she imagined a swing, while another thought about running down a dark street. Such imagery, while typical, is conflicting and confusing, but the facts remain: People in meditation (and in other unique mental states) are able to exercise a kind of psychic control over their bodies.

In A. R. Luria's remarkable book *The Mind of a Mnemonist,* the celebrated Russian psychologist presents a striking clinical por-trait, created over a thirty-year period, of a subject who not only possessed an extraordinary power of total recall but suffered from acute synthesthesia: that is, he saw, felt, and tasted each sound instead of simply hearing it. This created a bizarre situation; his

* Roy Menninger, quoted in "Quo Vadis, Medicine?" *Brain-Mind Bulletin,* 1, no. 1, p. 1.

mind would become clogged with vivid imagery and impressions
—so much so that the brain's normal power to coordinate and
organize impressions was lost. He became the victim of his own
extraordinary perceptions. "What a crumbly yellow voice you
have," the mnemonist would report, distracted totally from the
sense or meaning in the words said to him. So powerful was this
man's mental imagery that he could, according to Luria, "easily
drive his pulse up by [simply] *imagining* running." As the mnemonist imagined he was running, the *involuntary* organs of his
body responded to his imaginings. While this feat seems awesome
at first, it is probably not dissimilar from other forms of unconscious manipulation—whether it is hypnotic suggestion in a trance,
autosuggestion of the medium, or even the flushing of the left or
right ear by Neal Miller's small rabbit. ✓

Luria pointed out that his subject's vivid imagination broke
down the boundary between the real and the illusory. His mnemonist had so many moments of "magical" thinking—when his
imagination succeeded in absorbing his attention so completely—
that its reality was equal to that of the external world. He was
a rational man, so his reason would push away the "irrational"
connections. He sometimes thought he could cure himself if he
"imagined" clearly enough. Further, his experiences seem very
similar to those of modern mediums such as Edgar Cayce and
Eileen Garrett. I quote from Dr. Luria's report:

One time when I was planning to go to Samara, Misha [his son] developed stomach pains. We called in a doctor, but he could not figure
out what was wrong with him. . . . Yet it was so simple. I had given
him something cooked with lard. I could *see* the pieces of lard in his
stomach. . . . I thought to myself I'd help him. I wanted him to digest
them. . . . I pictured it in my mind and saw the lard dissolving in his
stomach. And Misha got better. Of course. I know this isn't the way it
happened . . . yet I did see it all.*

Anyone who has attended a healing seance or read a medium's
account of healing will be familiar with this type of report—except for the disclaimer at the end. For most mediums accept
such clairvoyance as well as their ability to heal in this fashion.

Recall the Hopi's, the shaman's, the entranced subject's experiences, the child's approach to reality, and it will be seen that

* Luria, *The Mind of a Mnemonist* (New York: Basic Books, 1968), pp. 174–78.

the mnemonist's condition parallels that of other states of consciousness we have been discussing. But in his case (as with the child and the shaman), the borderland between the conscious and unconscious was considerably expanded. He seems to have been living on that bridge between "essence" as perceived by the unconscious and organized "forms" as ordered by consciousness.

"Would you like to see me raise the temperature of my right hand and lower that of my left? Let's begin. . . ."

Luria used a skin thermometer to check his subject's hands and found they were the same temperature. He attached the thermometer to the skin of the subject's right hand after a minute and found that the temperature had risen two degrees. The mnemonist paused for another minute, then announced that he was ready; the temperature of his left hand had dropped one and a half degrees. Previous to work that has been performed by Miller and Shapiro, this experiment would have been deeply suspect. How did he do it? He imagined it. He thought it. He wished it.

"There's nothing to be amazed at. I saw myself put my right hand on a hot stove. . . . Oh, was it hot! So, naturally, the temperature of my hand increased. But I was holding a piece of ice in my left hand. I could see it there and began to squeeze it. And, of course, my hand got colder. . . ."

The medium, the yogi, the hypnotized subject most often need trance to perform this type of feat. The shaman possesses a profound conviction of his union with the world. The hypnotized subject is open to unconsciously perceived suggestion. They all have in common the fact that the conscious, critical faculties are set aside; belief, conviction so great that there is no question of something *not* happening, dominates the real world. The real world responds in kind. Faith like a mustard seed can move mountains.

The mnemonist lived a life of intense inner imagery, but he lacked the dynamic to break the boundaries of his present condition. So enraptured was he by the vividness of his inner world that he was dispossessed of the basic organic drive: the *conatus*, or "hormic" quality of life that is characteristic of evolving man. He did not suffer complete withdrawal from activity into an inner world as with the cataleptic or mentally deranged, but he incapacitated himself by becoming apathetic toward the rest of the world. Many of us seem as apathetic with less justification; we lack his

rich inner tapestry and consequently suffer both from apathy regarding the external world and from an inner dullness, an existential ennui, as well. It would be a mistake, however, to think that
this man could be a great poet because of his vivid imagination.
Luria reported that the mnemonist had great difficulty understanding some poems of Pasternak that were used for testing. He
would often be too taken over by the "color" or "quality" of a
word to finish the poem. He could not get behind the surface
images that dominated his attention. In reading a simple passage,
a phrase would turn into a palpable series of images. As he described it:

. . . I was read this phrase: "N. was leaning up against a tree. . . ." I
saw a slim young man dressed in a dark blue suit (N., you know, is so
elegant). He was standing near a big linden tree with grass and woods
all around. . . . But then the sentence went on: "and was peering into
a shop window." Now how do you like that! It means the scene isn't
set in the woods, or in a garden, but he's standing on the street. And I
have to start the whole sentence over from the beginning. . . .

Imagine how difficult it would be to have one's attention constantly, obsessively interrupted by realistic images impinged on the
senses before an idea is even fully expressed?

That a balance between the internal world of wishes, imagination, and speculation and the external world of "tangible" reality
is vital for our well-being is poignantly seen in this case. Luria observed that "his unstable grasp of reality, and the realistic overtones of his fantasies, had a . . . profound effect on his personality
development. For he lived in wait of something that he assumed
was to come his way, and gave himself up to dreaming and 'seeing' far more than to functioning in life."

This capacity of dreams to vitiate the thrust of life is what we
in the practical, hyperactive West see in Eastern religions and fear
so deeply—and with some justification, as can be seen from this
example. But two thoughts come to mind. That this is, in fact, an
inaccurate characterization of Eastern philosophy, and that our
society has overcompensated and turned too far away from the
phenomenal inner world that was both the mnemonist's blessing
and curse. Human life undoubtedly demands a balancing of these
two worlds; but it is precisely this need for balance that mandates
recovering our relation with the subconscious aspects of our selves.

Another case that illustrates the peculiar connection between the mind, imagination, and meditation is that of Jack Schwartz and his startling capacity to endure pain. In fact, one of the most enigmatic aspects of meditation, and least often noticed, is an insensitivity to pain. A forty-eight-year-old Dutchman who immigrated to the United States in 1957, Jack Schwartz is perhaps the most investigated subject in this area of research. In addition to sticking unsterilized needles through his arm without infection, Schwartz has placed burning cigarettes against his skin for periods of ten seconds. During these experiments with Dr. Elmer Green, instrumentation included a galvanic skin-reflex monitor, which showed Schwartz experienced no noticeable increase in stress. The rate of Schwartz's heartbeat increased by only a few beats during the needle experiments. Thermistors attached to his fingers revealed that his hand temperatures were high, a usual physiological sign of deep relaxation. During these experiments, Schwartz's brain-wave patterns showed as much as 80 percent alpha rhythms, further indicating his relaxed state.

During the first experiments Dr. Green recalls being worried not only by Schwartz's apparent lack of pain but also by his lack of bleeding. "So when I asked him if the wound was going to bleed, and it did, I was more relieved than disappointed. This enabled me to see that there was nothing peculiar about his skin or blood, after all. By asking him whether there would be any bleeding, I introduced a possibility that he had obviously shut out of his mind. This upset him a little; he went back into beta, and the bleeding began. Still, he demonstrated his control by stopping the bleeding instantly." *

Schwartz's own explanation is remarkably ingenuous. Pain, he says, is "man's servant . . . an alarm clock that wakes you when something goes wrong in the body that you should know about. But if you're doing something to the body of your own free will, something that you know is not really going to hurt you, then there is no reason for the alarm to go off, is there?"

So the mystery remains. In our present state of knowledge there appears to be no physiological equivalent of meditation that will distinguish it from other states of mind involving relaxation. Perhaps the main contribution physiology has made to the study of

* David M. Rorvik, "Jack Schwartz Feels No Pain," *Esquire* (December 1972), p. 209.

meditative states has been, apart from little-understood therapeutic effects, to remind us again how much we have to learn about the reality-shaping possibilities of the mind. Recall that the informational possibilities that may be stored in a single, average-sized gene can be arranged in some 10^{600} different ways. A gene is made of DNA, the basic blueprint for all life as we know it. A virus, the simplest form of life, consists of a gene or genes with a protein cover. Thus, it may be said that the world of viruses—submicroscopic entities so small that they will pass through most filters—has informational possibilities that would stagger the largest computer. Expand your imagination then from viruses to a single human being with 100,000 or more genes, as well as trillions of individual cells that can be arranged in any number of complex patterns. Add to this complex picture the human brain with its approximately 10 billion cells contained within the ten cubic inches of skull, with each cell capable of around 10,000 separate information functions. The actual number of possible interactions within the brain alone—without even calculating the cells of the skin, viscera, bones, and the organic world around us—is beyond the skill of the most brilliant mathematician to compute meaningfully. In short, in order to express in layman's language the total creative capacity of the human central nervous system (and the mind's coordination of data from it) one must call it "infinite."

How to Meditate ✓

○　○
　○

WHY MEDITATE AT ALL? Many who have tried it complain that all
they experience is a confused, muddled rehash of their problems
during meditation. Such people consider meditation futile, a waste
of time in a busy world that demands intense attention and a
competitive edge to everything they do. Periods of introspection
are little more than frustrating, restless, and wasted moments. In
the past there was no answer to people who had these negative experiences beyond commenting that they had not approached their
meditation period correctly. *tease, torment*

People are simultaneously frightened and tantalized by the unknown. Meditation, or any form of deep self-experiencing, has a
dual impact: one of excitement and one of apprehension. The less
disciplined and more ardent this free fall into the shadows of the
self, the greater its evocative power to engender awe and fascination. If it is a productive experience, the individual becomes a
passionate advocate; if negative, a disillusioned critic. But the fact
is that meditation itself does not require any forcing, any exercise
of the will. Willpower and perseverance, while fundamental principles of learning to meditate, are used *before* the actual deep
meditation. Concentration involves the exercise of willpower,
where the mind must be kept on specific tasks. Meditation is a
dwelling quietly within the "process." Meditation is a transforma-
tive art, a discipline whose purpose is a transcending modification

of the personality and inner self. Meditation is an intimate part of life; its involvement is a moving one that flows into life as life is lived. It fuses, melds, and becomes a part of the dynamics of living.

DEVELOPING WILL IN MEDITATION

A great mystery to me is why we, the peculiar human animal, forget to cherish what we already have. We seek incessantly and ignore what is already at hand. We concentrate on and complain about the past and fantasize about the future. How rare, and yet simple, it is to cease all that emotional activity and live in the present, cherishing what already is. The reason it is mysterious to me is that I know these things intellectually, yet have often failed to create the reality in my own life. One of the few things I have tried that works is meditation. But even here one must persevere and use one's will. Nothing is possible without will to carry it out. It is ironic, therefore, that in most books on meditation the crucial role of will, or intention, is ignored. The word *meditation* in fact has two basic dictionary definitions. One is an incomplete description involving musing, reflecting, or thinking contemplatively. The second definition is to intend or will, to do or achieve.

A French writer once said that the will means "to choose in order to act." This is only partially true, however, for the will does not choose; elements within the individual choose. In this sense the will, or rather one's power of choice, involves some justification or reason; and, most important, the motive must be sufficient so the will may be strong enough to act. Without sufficient justification or motivation, one can desire something and it may always remain beyond reach. Once a person has sufficient reason to act and the conscious-unconscious mind approves the motive, the will can be brought into action. This may sound involved, and even unnecessary, but it is very important in trying to understand the role conscious willing has in determining successful meditation.

Several steps must be taken in order to initiate something: an urge must exist within the mind that something be done; the presentation of reasons or motive must be made to one's own conscious satisfaction; and, finally, the will must be put forth in order to act. Will is, in short, the mind's *power* of self-direction. If we wish to meditate successfully, the desire must first exist; then the motive or conscious reason for wanting to meditate must be clear, and the conscious attention applied toward that goal. In the first instance, the meditator must determine why he wishes to meditate, and in the second instance he begins the action that will determine whether or not he is successful. Anyone will be successful in obtaining the benefits of meditation if he can apply his will consciously and faithfully. There is no escaping the fact that meditation takes effort and purpose. It is, however, no different than anything else in life that demands faithful attention in order to influence one's life-style and effect meaningful change.

The idea of personal evolution is not, of course, original. Many religions and philosophies include this concept. Often it comes under the guise of a religious manifestation: grace altering the inner heart. In Christianity, metanoia, or change of heart, is an important principle leading one eventually to salvation. The same principles occur in most developed religions, including even those god-reduced religions such as Buddhism and Taoism. In Zen Buddhism the change is recorded in enigmatic phrases indicating someone is "coming home."

More recently, P. D. Ouspensky, a controversial Russian philosopher-mystic, raised this question: If all men have the capacity to change themselves, why have they not done so and thereby eliminated all the injustice, cruelty, and stupidity in the world? Ouspensky answered briefly, "Simple, because they do not want it." The chief idea, Ouspensky argues, is that in order to become a different being, one must want it very much and work at it for a very long time. A passing or vague desire to change because one is dissatisfied with some conditions of one's life does not create sufficient impulse to either sustain the interest to change or do the necessary labor involved. The evolution of human nature depends on fully understanding what is received and what must be given up for it. If you do not want something strongly enough, no amount of cajoling or playing games with yourself to finesse your lack of willpower is adequate.

This whole approach to change applies to meditation. It is popular to say that there are easy ways to achieve one's goal in meditation, that there are special techniques, simple methods that can achieve wonders with minimum effort. This is only partially true. The basic techniques of meditation are not difficult to learn, and there are many methods that are indeed quite simple and that will bring quick and beneficial results. But even these simple methods require a minimum, daily effort. Expending *time* and *energy,* in a word, "will," is necessary no matter how simple the technique. That is why a short amount of time spent every day is better than an hour or two once in a while. Oddly, it is harder to maintain the smaller daily discipline of twenty or thirty minutes than to sit dramatically in a trancelike state for an hour once a week when you feel like it.

Commitment is one of the major elements when beginning the practice of meditation. Without the proper motivation and full effort, there can only be limited or no success. Zen masters have repeatedly responded to questions such as "How do I do *zazen,* or sit in meditation?" with the simple response "Just sit." The student then asks, "What do you mean, 'just sit'?" "Just that, sit," replies the master. The student more often than not walks away shaking his head in confusion: "How does he 'sit'?" "What does he *do* while sitting?"

An explanation of this succinct direction is in a beautifully simple saying of the Zen master Yunmen: "In walking, just walk, in sitting, just sit. Above all, don't wobble." Above all, don't wobble! In wavering we lose direction; we forget our purpose; we succumb to confusion and the ragged "mind noise" that meditation is meant to quell. An inner balance is needed, but to achieve that quiet inner state, discipline is required.

In the New Testament the importance of controlling one's attention and unwavering concentration is also recognized. "But let your response be 'yea' or 'nay,'" says the Bible, "for whatsoever is more cometh of evil." In commitment to doing something, there is an enhanced quality of attention that, once started, helps concentration and mind-control to flow on, ever more easily, ever more undisturbed. Accept or reject, but do not wobble! If you make a wrong choice it will become apparent soon enough and you can change course. But because you will have experienced the power of commitment, you can be confident of possessing the power to succeed in each new attempt.

As the mad but shockingly perceptive Nietzsche wrote, "How must one ascend the slope? Climb and don't think about it." Just do, says the Zen master, with total commitment. The will should not be used as a tool in meditation and should be clearly distin-

guished from desire. The will is trained in meditation only to eliminate the interruptions, not to seek anything. For this reason initial
concentration exercises should use objects that have no intrinsic
interest. When students complain that it would be easier to concentrate on something of interest than on a match or a pencil, it
often becomes clear that concentrating on what is interesting is not
truly training the mind but leading emotions. The will is not used
for creating new drives toward something of interest, but rather is
retrained to obey the conscious choice of the mind.

In a brilliant essay on the human will, "On a Certain Blindness
in Human Beings," William James describes the energies of man as
part of a psychology of vital forces. James restated the long-ignored
idea that human beings do have individual will and the capacity to
direct their personal lives. But he also argued that neurosis causes
one to give up the powers of "willing." This abrogation of will is
caused by what James calls "habit neurosis." Once the will is
weakened by indulging neurotic needs, the individual tends to fall
into habits or patterns of behavior that are further determined solely
by neurotic motives. But there is a solution to break the self-
destroying cycle of rote response and the dull, lifeless habits we
fall into. James says the solution is to bully ourselves to push beyond the "habit neurosis," which results in a new range of
power within the individual. Because of the bullying treatment we
force upon ourselves, we achieve a renewed level of energy and are
better able to freely exercise our will. The will is no longer quietly
acquiescent, but seems filled with a new zest for life, a new vigor
when facing challenges and taking action.

Italian psychologist Roberto Assagioli makes the same point in
his book *Psychosynthesis*, in which he outlines steps by which the
will can be strengthened and conscious command of one's life
once again asserted. The keystones of his method are (1) clarify-
ing your goals, (2) being deliberate in your planning, (3) and
using constant affirmation to follow through on your decision. An
affirmation carries an intense "psychological voltage" that determines how effective your action will be. It is necessary to repeat, or
rather renew, the affirmation continually. All of this mobilizes the
energies of the body and mind to reach goals. (See Exercise 1
in the Appendix for a specific method on developing the will.)

The great psychologist Otto Rank equates the will with the individual's definition of his existence; hence, will or intention be-

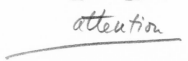
attention

comes a pivotal part of one's being. "The being experiences his in-
dividuality in terms of his will, and this means that his personal
existence is identical with his capacity to express his will in the
world." In summary, the important point here is that the individual who is not consciously, alertly aware of the "self" is
necessarily unaware of and unable to exercise the vital function of
the self—conscious will! The function of the will is to uncover and
utilize the *energies* of the unconscious. It is these energies with
which the meditator fills himself. In order for the will to be re-
sponsive, it must be trained—which means, in short, to use it consciously toward a specific goal or purpose, as in meditation. Will is
important in meditation, therefore, because it supplies immediate energy, a deeper commitment that can carry you through the
low points, and the ability to persevere.

CONCENTRATION

One of the major problems for beginners is learning to concentrate; because proper concentration is so difficult as well as a
fundamental part of learning to meditate, it is perhaps the single
most important lesson one has to learn. For the purpose of meditation, it is valuable to characterize concentration in two ways: one
kind is a spontaneous, emotional, or mental motivation that drives
your attention along on the unstable wings of impulse. Another
type of concentration is one in which your awareness is deliberately
and consciously controlled. With the first kind, concentration seems
to act under its own volition and responds primarily to the feeling
or emotional aspects of the psyche. With the second kind, you
direct your attention with purpose and with clear intent.
   In his *The Travel Diary of a Philosopher*, Hermann Keyserling
wrote that the power of concentration is the real propelling power
of the whole psychic mechanism. Nothing heightens our capacity
to perform as much as its increase, as its intensive focus beams in
upon its task. But because our minds have basically been left to
function according to nonunderstood energies, the mind rebels
at hard discipline being imposed on it. For the meditator, however, it is essential that the mind be pulled back to the tasks at
hand. There are, in fact, very few people (if any) that have had no
difficulty in controlling the mind. It is a universal problem. Those
who find they cannot concentrate on their meditation and are too

distracted by the demands of the world should not be too critical of themselves. The successful meditator is he who overcomes his distractions and follows through no matter how often he fails. ✓

Concentration has been defined as the consciously willed narrowing of the field of attention. There is a famous anecdote on the virtue and characteristics of concentration told by Sri Paramananda in his book *Concentration and Meditation.* During an archery tournament in ancient India, a wooden fish was set up on a high pole. The eye of the fish was the target. One by one many valiant princes came and tried their skill in vain. Before each one shot his arrow, the teacher asked him what he saw, and invariably all replied that they saw a fish on a pole at a great height with head, eyes, tail, etc. But when Arjuna took his aim and was asked what he saw, he replied, "I see the eye of the fish," and let loose his arrow. He was the only archer to hit the target exactly. ✓

In the *Bhagavad Gita,* Arjuna cries out to his Lord Krishna. "The mind wavers, Krishna. Turbulent, impetuous, forceful, I think it is as hard to hold as the wind." The Lord Krishna replied, "Without doubt, the wavering mind is hard to hold; but through assiduous practice it may be held firm. For him whose mind has been brought under his sway, who is controlled, it may be won." ✓

Meditation thus involves a fundamental fact of our everyday experience: focused attention. Since none of us can absorb everything that is striking our eyes, ears, and other senses, there must be filtering of some kind in our brains that protects the central nervous system from being overloaded and short-circuited. This filtering process is somehow tied to the mechanics of consciousness and its primary tools, concentration and attention. Attention in its most simple form is that machinery in the brain that decides every split second what is going to be noticed and what is ignored. While science does not understand the subtle strategies of the mind in its selection process, certain things do seem clear. For example, we can think clearly only about one idea or piece of information at a time. When we concentrate on something we tend to automatically focus on a particular feature which gives us an identifying point upon which to build. We concentrate on specific objects or specific people rather than on groupings or aggregates. And we tend to look for information relevant to a predetermined idea: a piece of information that we can identify with and integrate into what we can recognize. ✓

Attention is a most peculiar and mysterious characteristic of the mind. It is intimately tied up with emotions, memory associations, conscious willing. A sleeping person may not wake up for an errant sound, but a mother who may normally sleep through the sounds of a convention of loading garbage trucks will wake suddenly if her baby gives a faint cry. For meditators the important fact about attention is that its focusing mechanism is an inherent part not only of seeing and listening, but of the mind's capacity to direct itself. It can be programed to obey our conscious will. This is the key to the fantastic and peculiar nature of human consciousness and self-awareness. Just as the mind focuses on singular and simplified aspects of the outer world, so does the meditator learning concentration focus his attention on single points, on simple images, ideas, sounds. In this sense the student learning concentration takes advantage of the mind's natural talent to focus itself. It is the single greatest fact of learning to meditate; its successful exploitation is what makes it possible to learn how to concentrate— and it is only through proper concentration that meditation can happen.

Until the mind has been trained in concentration it is useless to try to meditate. Practically all early stages of mind-control training are for developing the power of concentration (and even many of the "meditation" exercises in the back of this book are in fact concentration exercises). Following the normal, regular relaxed breathing pattern, for example, is one of the simplest and most basic concentration exercises. Anyone who thinks he can learn meditation without first learning to concentrate deludes himself.

In her book *The Light of the Soul*, Alice Bailey itemizes seven stages of concentration the meditator must learn: (1) the choice of some object upon which to concentrate; (2) withdrawing the mind from the periphery to the center so that the avenues that the outer perception and the senses contact are stilled, and the consciousness is no longer outgoing; (3) the centering of consciousness in the head; (4) application of the mind to the object chosen; (5) visualization of the object; (6) extension of the specific mental concepts that have formed to more universal concepts; and (7) attempting to perceive and identify with that which lies behind the form.

Since the mind wanders at random, a good method for bringing it back to the task at hand is to begin to circle the object with your mind. For example, if you are concentrating on an ashtray and your mind wanders, as soon as you decide to bring it back to attention, begin to move your focus around the object in a circle that grows ever smaller until finally you are circling just around the edges of the ashtray. Then bring the mind to a stop on the object and begin to one-point your attention again.

A simple Yoga exercise for learning to focus one's attention is called *trataka*, or steady gazing. Write the word OM (or a big black dot, a black circle, etc.) on a piece of paper and pin it to the wall. Sit in front of your drawing and concentrate on it with open eyes until tears cloud your vision. Then close your eyes and visualize the picture in detail. Open the eyes again and go through the same process. Some students learn to gaze at pictures like this for an hour or more. This exercise is extremely good for steadying the concentration and stops the mind from wandering. (For other exercises see Exercise 25 in the Appendix, "Ten Yoga Concentration Exercises.")

A good test of "how" you are concentrating is to do the following exercise. Choose a special piece of music and listen to it over and over again. Try to follow every nuance of the music; each rise and fall in the volume, pitch, quality should carry you along. Listen to the music as often as you can within the time available. You shouldn't become "sick" of it if you are listening to it properly. If you literally try to identify with the sound so thoroughly that when it moves you "feel" it happening, the music should seem to become a part of you and you a part of it. You should not become tired of that piece of music any more than you would become tired of a single mantra sound, of a single candle flame, or a symbol held before your inner mind—if you are concentrating properly.

The importance of proper concentration is illustrated in a story told by Alexandra David-Neel. She describes how the Tibetan Lama or Master tests the degree and quality of the student's concentration. The Lama places a small, burning lamp on his head. The lamps are all filled with butter and last a considerable length of time, but are positioned in such a way that they will fall off with the slightest movement. One Lama who was trying to train his disciple to concentrate properly set a lamp on the young man's head. All through the night the novice kept the lamp in place and took it off his head only when the butter was burnt out at dawn. That morning the Lama returned and asked the novice why the lamp was on the ground. The student explained that it had burnt out during the night. The Lama retorted: "How could you know that the lamp went out, or even that you had a lamp on your head, if you had reached true concentration of mind?"

In contrast, William James relates a charming story in one of his essays that shows the impact of true concentration. There is a fable about a monk who stops in a wood to listen to the singing of a bird. Its song is so beautiful that the monk soars on its sound, immersing himself in what Wordsworth calls the "authentic tidings of invisible things." Sometime later the bird ends his song and the monk returns to his monastery only to discover that he has been away for fifty years.

There is another story about a surgeon who was so engrossed in an operation that he was totally unaware that a large part of the ceiling in the operating room had fallen right next to him during his surgery. This acute state of total attention is what the yogis call "true concentration." And if it is transferred from the operating room, the schoolroom, the reading of a book, or one's enchantment with a bird's song, the true essence of meditation can be felt. *Awareness* is a word that builds a strange and subtle bridge from fact to knowledge, from understanding to wisdom. It is over this bridge of intense awareness that we all must tread alone, as we move toward individual identification with the inner and outer worlds surrounding us.

VISUALIZATION

The human being is so conditioned by language that many philosophers and psychologists have assumed it is impossible to think without words. The outstanding turn-of-the-century linguist, translator, and scholar Max Muller, for example, was convinced that thinking without words was impossible. Renowned psychologist-philosopher William James gave some credence to this idea and pointed out that it was unlikely someone could think, say, the word "bubble," without involuntary and distinctive sensations arising in the larynx or voice box.

The relationship between thought and "internal speech" has been investigated by psychologists for decades, yet because we are dealing with the subjective world there is relatively little hard evidence one way or the other. What is clear is that speech, language, the dependency upon words become greater as our attention is directed outward, and become lesser as we concentrate our attention mentally inward. As one moves deeper into the inner world, images and symbols not necessarily so word dependent begin to predominate and absorb our attention. We begin to react in an instinctive way. It is this enhancement of nonverbal understanding that meditation techniques seek to develop. Once the meditator begins to relate to his internal imagery without first responding with words, without translating the inner symbols verbally, progress is being made.

In all meditative visualization the symbol is used primarily to hold consciousness, to still the "noise" of the mind, not to fill it with a picture or image. This may seem paradoxical, but learning to visualize and concentrate on an image is, in fact, a method for training the mind in a relatively painless, pleasant way. There are, of course, other ways to discipline the mind, but they are longer, harder, and demand much energy and dedication. This is not to say, however, that one can be casual with visualization exercises; they demand just as much commitment and labor as other meditative methods. It is just that visualization is easier in the sense that it is pleasant. It is a happy, creative lesson as opposed to a more strenuous, exhausting technique. As Ernest Wood has written on the topic of learning mind-control: "In all these matters we must do no violence. We are not hard and lofty masters, whipping a wild animal into sullen obedience. . . . To command the mind is one thing. To teach it as a willing and happy pupil continually finding new delights of experience in healthy functioning is quite another." The distinction between the hard and the happy discipline is especially important for the beginning meditator.

Usually an idea, an image, or a symbol is used to fill a void, whether it is caused by a dry, noncreative period or simply by confusion about what to do next. Normally, the idea that comes into consciousness occupies a space in one's mind that a moment before lacked what might be called an essential or central image. Frivolous imagery is quite constant during the early stages of meditation and should be recognized as a diversionary technique of the protective personality and a mind that has been conditioned to have its own way for years. Therefore, it might seem strange to

think of visualization as a means of stilling or eventually emptying the mind, but it is an important realization toward understanding how the meditator must use his mind. √

Unfortunately, the power of mental imagery has been consistently underestimated by modern science. Only in the last few
years has a fuller appreciation of the influence of imagery and inner
vision occurred. At Northern Illinois University, psychologist
Thomas Roberts has initiated visualization techniques to instruct
electric-shop teachers in how to involve the student in what he
calls "fantasy journeys." After asking the students to relax he tells
them: "Now imagine you are an electron in a wire . . . you are
hopping, swirling, leaping, brushing around with other electrons,
all pushing and bumping against each other—rapidly, heatedly.
Now you are outside the wire, feel the force, the pull and intensity of the electronic field. Now take a trip down an electric
coil itself, feel yourself sliding, bumping, intertwining with other
electrons in the rush of forces. . . ." Such evocative imagery and
directed daydreaming are being used in an ever-growing number of
classrooms, workshops, memory and hypnosis courses, and meditation classes. These same visualization techniques have been part of
most meditation systems throughout history, but have been particularly developed by Eastern religions like Tibetan Buddhism. √

One of the most intriguing scientific uses of visualization and
meditation is in medicine. Dr. O. Carl Simonton, a radiologist who
specializes in cancer therapy, initiated a meditation technique com-
bining relaxation and visualization. A firm believer in orthodox
medicine, he combines standard radiation and chemotherapy with
meditation. It is often hard, therefore, to assign the source of his
sometimes surprising results. In some cases, however, a patient
makes a remarkable recovery after standard therapies have been exhausted or have had little effect. While many of his patients seem
to lack the personality or mental attitude to complete successfully
the meditative discipline Dr. Simonton sets for them, enough do
recover so that his techniques may be considered very promising for otherwise terminal cancer patients. Simonton has found
that the "will to live" apparently has a great deal to do with his
success rate. It seems, he states, that "when the will to live goes
down, the will to die comes increasingly up." √

From his observations of cancer patients, and their recovery in
relation to personality factors like attitude and will to live, Simon-

ton is developing a theory that incorporates into therapy belief systems of the patient and doctor. As an expression of his holistic view of medicine, Simonton is fond of quoting the presidential address of Dr. E. G. Pendergrass delivered at the 1959 American Cancer Society meeting: "There is solid evidence that the course of disease in general is affected by emotional distress. . . . Thus, we as doctors may begin to emphasize *treatment of the patient as a whole.* . . . We may learn how to influence general body systems and through them modify the neoplasms [cancers] which reside within the body. . . . We can widen the quest to include the distinct possibility that within one's mind is a power capable of exerting forces which can either enhance or inhibit the progress of this disease."

Simonton has taken Dr. Pendergrass's words to heart and is attempting to use methods in which the patient's mind and body work together. He finds that three factors are extremely important for successful treatment. "One is the belief system of the patient. The second is the belief system of the family and those people who surround the patient and are meaningful to him. The third is the belief system of the physician." Thus all attitudes that may influence the patient's recovery are considered. Meditation and traditional visualization techniques are, therefore, essential elements in producing a functional relationship between the body and mind.

Dr. Simonton's first patient was one of his most dramatic cases, and helped convince him of the mind's role in healing the body. The first patient to use the meditation-visualization technique was a sixty-one-year-old man with advanced throat cancer. He had dropped from 135 pounds to 95. He couldn't eat solid food or even swallow his own saliva. He learned to relax and was able to visualize his cancer, his bodily functions, and immune reaction remarkably well. After seven weeks of meditation-visualization treatment, his cancer had left him. He has lived for several years now with no recurrence. With the advanced state of his cancer he had been given a 5 percent chance of surviving two years. In addition, this same patient suffered from arthritis and impotence, which had been plaguing him for twenty years. Using the same techniques he had learned from Simonton, he managed to relieve himself of his acute arthritis and his impotence. His impotence was "cured" after ten days of meditative work.

Simonton's techniques are similar to those of traditional visualization and meditation methods. Patients are asked to meditate
regularly for fifteen minutes in the morning, at noon, and before
retiring to bed. The first few minutes are used for the patient to
achieve complete relaxation while sitting comfortably. He then
visualizes a peaceful, pleasant scene. Whatever understanding of
his disease that is necessary is provided the patient before the
meditative sessions begin by using pictures, X rays, diagrams, or
verbal descriptions. The patient is also shown photographs of how
his own immunological system works, with pictures of white blood
cells destroying cancer cells. He may even be given positive suggestion about the therapy by being shown pictures of other patients
with visible cancers getting smaller and eventually disappearing.
All of this pre-meditation education theoretically creates a positive
state of mind that will aid the meditator's own body in responding
to his visualizations and suggestions.

During his meditation the patient is asked first to visualize his
particular lesion or tumor. Then he pictures the tumor cells in his
body as dead or dying, with the white blood cells swarming over
the tumor, destroying the cancer cells, and carrying them off. At
the end of the meditation the patient is asked to visualize himself as being free of his disease and in perfect health. He also pictures himself as active and enjoying life. (There are some healing
meditations and exercises for visualizing in the Appendix, and you
will see how similar they are to Simonton's methods.)

Through visualization, the aesthetic aspect of life has been
used in traditional meditation, particularly in Eastern religions
like Buddhism. Because the normal senses offer a ready and useful
medium by which effective meditation can begin, religions that
use meditation incorporate painting, music, objects of nature as
materials for actively involving the disciple's mind in the meditative discipline. While the meditator eventually moves beyond
images, symbols, or ideas, using such common and natural mental
material during the early stages helps him to learn concentration
and mind-control.

Christian religious art was primarily didactic. Its purpose was to
instruct, inspire, or solidify the Christian faith. In contrast, Oriental religious art was often used as a meditation device. Its structure,
theme, and color were all calculated to describe a religious scene
(and in this sense some of it could also be considered didactic), or

specific designs were used to induce special insight or even enlightenment. In fact, the primary function of Buddhist art seems
to have been to alter the consciousness of the viewer.

But different schools held varying beliefs. Indian Buddhist art
depicted many images, religious symbols, and mandalas. The
Chinese Ch'an Buddhist school, however, maintained that
"there is more religion in the study of a flower or an insect than in
all the images of Buddhist deities." Buddhist visualization techniques are extremely difficult, especially for beginning meditators.
Indeed, they are even difficult for practiced meditators. A basic
Buddhist visualization meditation is to close your eyes and recreate yourself in a spot several feet in front of where you are sitting. Not just a vague image, but a complete, detailed, vivid recrea-
tion of yourself. Buddhist art is therefore not created to please the
senses or to express any individual's vision of the world, but rather
is a map of consciousness and a symbolic tool for self-discovery.
This tendency eventually created an art form that has become
basic in meditative art—the *mandala*.

The word mandala means "circle" in Sanskrit and is used in
Hindu and Buddhist ritual, art, and meditation. A mandala is
usually circular in design, but can include squares, polygons, or a
variety of geometric patterns. In all cases, however, the design is
calculated to concentrate the attention about a fixed point. The
mandala is generally represented physically, as in paintings, wall
designs, sculpture, etc., but it does not in fact have to be an actual
drawing. It may be memorized, drawn in the mind or even in the
air in front of you. When it is used in meditation it is held before
the mind. In some religions the mandala is believed to contain centers of power or energy related to a specific god or demon. It is
also regarded as a cosmic intersection at which the physical and
spiritual worlds meet. To psychologists the mandala is considered
a kind of psychographic design that is projected upon the screen
of the mind, a picture of the universal macrocosm reflected in the
psychic microcosm of the human mind.

Meditating on a mandala is a difficult and advanced practice not
to be undertaken lightly. Two basic procedures are used. The first
is to create your own mandala composed of symbols you consider
positive and significant. For example, a Christian might create in
his mind's eye a simple mandala design of a cross within a circle,
with a nimbus or halo tracing an additional circle around the inner

design. Naturally, the more complicated the design the more difficult it becomes to hold the attention steady. Another method is to
use traditional mandalas found in books on Hindu and Buddhist
art. Here one must study them in detail and recreate them in the
mind's eye. If it is necessary to study the mandala and then close
your eyes in an effort to recreate it a hundred or even a thou-
sand times, then that is done until the pattern is clearly visualized
and held steady in the mind. But the mandala is a dangerous exercise because it encourages the imagination to run wild. Hallucinations, apparitions, and a wide variety of psychological responses
have been reported with mandala meditations. Buddhists emphasize that meditation itself is not so important as "right meditation," and very careful use of mandalas is exercised. They believe
that misdirected meditation is futile and dangerous. In fact, one of
the fundamental principles in the Buddhist religion is "right
meditation." √

The ability to form clear, vivid images in the mind is essential
for progress in meditation. The more thoroughly you develop the
ability to visualize, the easier it will be to perform actual meditation exercises. One of the simplest meditations, for example, is the
bubble meditation mentioned by Lawrence LeShan in his excellent book *How to Meditate*. The bubble meditation demands simply imagining yourself sitting comfortably on the bottom of a
clear lake and observing each thought, feeling, image or perception, etc., that occurs within you. As the perception occurs, visualize it rising slowly to the surface. Do not attach any emotional significance to the bubble containing your thought or feeling, simply
observe it dispassionately. As it rises beyond your vision, simply
wait for the next bubble. Do not try to be analytical about which
symbols or images occur: This is not an exercise in self-analysis.
The meditation accomplishes several things. It helps establish a
sense of inner timing. It allows you to observe each thought separate from any emotional framework. √

You can create other variations if sitting under water makes you
uncomfortable: for instance, sitting by a campfire in a peaceful
wood watching puffs of smoke rising, or lying on your back watching clouds in the sky slowly drifting past. Each cloud would, of
course, contain your inner images. But the point is that none of
these exercises, as simple as they are, can be accomplished without a basic ability to visualize. Because visualization is so essential,

and incorporates so many different elements of learning to meditate—such as learning to concentrate, enhancing the ability to hold images in the front of consciousness, etc.—a number of visualization exercises have been included in the Appendix. They are placed so they become progressively more difficult; thus, it is important to practice them in sequence.

RELAXATION

Once settled into a proper posture, the first action we take is to learn relaxation. A simple, basic technique for relaxing all the muscles can be used generally for most meditations. Because it is not desirable to spend too much meditation time relaxing the body, a fast and simple technique is preferable. From long habit we have conditioned ourselves to go through a wide range of tensions when we concentrate—clenching our teeth and our hands, tightening up in our necks and shoulders. So it is necessary to be alert for any tension creeping up on you and to keep the body relaxed. If, for example, you are fatigued after your meditation it is probably due to unconscious tensions developing in your body while meditating. So a short but effective relaxation exercise will help your meditation. After you learn this simple, basic method, you will be able to relax your body in less than a minute merely by focusing your attention over areas of your body. But in order for it to be effective, it is necessary to learn the technique thoroughly.

Begin by consciously slowing down the rhythm of your breathing, and with every exhalation either think or say out loud a calming word such as "peace" or "be tranquil." Any word that quiets your fast, tension-oriented rhythm will work. As you think "peace," exhale and continue to slow down your breathing. Do not slow down your breathing so that it becomes uncomfortable, for you will only build up further tensions. A reasonable time at first is to count six slowly for both inhale and exhale. Then lengthen to eight and ten counts. The more difficult breathing exercises should only be undertaken after you have some experience. If you know where your tensions tend to build up, focus your key calming word on that area of your body. Most people, for example, get tense between the shoulder blades where the neck and spinal vertebrae meet. Focus your attention on that spot and with every inhalation picture the air coming into your body to flow directly to that spot. Let your mind flood that area with the air you breathe in, thinking your calming word. When you exhale think of the tensions in that area as leaving your body with your exhalation, again repeating the calming word. Repeat this process with each area of tension in your body. Cover your whole body in this way.√

Other simple aids to relaxation include gently rocking while sitting in a meditation posture, humming quietly (which can act as a mantra or point of concentration), or—the easiest of all—going over each part of your body individually, first slightly tensing and then releasing that particular group of muscles. Starting from the feet and moving to the head, the body is generally completely relaxed by the time you reach your face, neck, and scalp. √

HOW TO SAVE ENERGY AND AVOID FATIGUE √

Russian philosopher G. I. Gurdjieff isolated three sources of fatigue that deplete our normal energy: loss of energy by unconscious muscular exertion; loss by mind-wandering, which involves unconscious exertion; and loss by anxiety, worry, or what one might call negative mind-wandering. These three areas of human energy loss can be imagined as a three-story house, with each floor devoted to a particular form of energy expenditure. The ground floor symbolizes where we carry on our physical work; the second floor where we carry on our emotional life; and the top floor where we carry on our intellectual life. To follow Gurdjieff's analogy, when we are working (expending energy) on any one of the floors, the others are frequently involved. But this is unnecessary and a waste of energy. When we are working on the ground floor of our physical life, for example, it is not necessary to have the lights turned on all over the house. It is clear that this would be a waste of energy; yet we indulge in this kind of waste in our own lives all the time. Another example: When we are thinking, we need not waste energy on the emotional or physical levels of our lives. We should learn to shut off or at least turn down the energy levels for the various functions not in use. √

The three sources of fatigue and energy loss just mentioned can be corrected by a few simple rules that are meditative in their discipline and in their use of awareness. All *unconscious* actions waste energy; therefore, *conscious* action can reverse this problem. The first principle of saving energy is always to be conscious of its loss, not to allow any activity that wastes our physical, emotional, or intellectual energy to escape our attention. During fatigue or energy loss in any one of the three ways just mentioned, try to become aware of the state of your muscles at that instant. You will undoubtedly find that you are sitting in a tense position. Your legs may be crossed like a fully strung, tense bow; your neck and shoulders are probably about two or three inches higher as the muscles are bunched up into a knot. If you consciously think "relax" to these shoulder and neck muscles, you may be surprised to see them literally drop several inches. This means that the lights are on in your ground-floor physical life when you are sitting and should be physically relaxed. The cure for this obvious waste of energy in the ground floor is turning off the lights there by relaxing the body and allowing the conscious mind to control the situation. By long habit your body does not relax when you no longer need its energy. And since it has not yet learned to shut itself off when, say, you have just finished running for a train and are now sitting down after a hard day's work, you must teach it to hang loose.

Likewise, letting your mind wander and thinking aimlessly (and often with an unrecognized emotional tinge) is wasting the energy in the top floor of your life's house. Everyone, of course, indulges in this sort of thing; but meditation relaxation techniques give you the control to turn off the lights on these various floors when they are exhausting you. Just as with your physical body, you must learn to catch your mind when it wanders without any direction. At first it may seem even more tiring to try and bring your mind back from a pleasant daydream, but remember that when you have learned to do it, you can also bring it back when it is involved in an emotional and exhausting recounting of the day's problems or irritations. Develop the awareness of what your body, mind, and emotions are doing at any given time. All this takes is learning to *remember* to do it. Once you have convinced yourself that you are contributing to your own exhaustion, use the testing and relaxing technique all over your body in order to "turn off" the lights on the ground floor. When your mind wanders have a key positive sentence (compose one yourself), an "affirmation" that you can concentrate on and repeat over and over to yourself until all the irritations of the day, all the energy-absorbing fantasies about tomorrow are quieted. The English poet Shelley wrote, "We look before and after and sigh for what is not." In fact, we do considerably more than simply look and sigh: We exhaust ourselves unnecessarily. By relaxing your body and repeating an affirmation, you can convert these energy wastes into energy savings. Those who practice these simple methods will find themselves with more energy than they need in a very short time.

POSTURE

The distinguished American psychologist Gardner Murphy noted that we deceive ourselves and prevent unpleasant information from reaching our conscious mind by body movements. In Murphy's words, "the striped musculature of the arms, hands, trunk, neck, and by implication, other parts of the body, may be conceived to be used all the time in the battle of thought, especially the battle *against* thought, specifically the battle against recognition of information, and most of all, against information unfavorable to the self." These body defenses that the mind uses to divert uncomfortable information from reaching awareness are similar to what Wilhelm Reich called "character armour" and include irregular breathing as well as those movements mentioned by Murphy. By slowing respiration (in combination with shallow breathing) the oxygen intake is lessened, and food for the brain is thereby denied. The drowsiness and comfortable haze that follows is ideal for escape. Psychiatrists have long recognized, for example, that when a patient deals with a repressed conflict, breathing suddenly becomes shallow and complaints of tiredness or exhaustion follow. Some therapists will simply say, "Breathe deeply!" and the repressed problem will often begin to manifest in consciousness.

In meditation the body defenses are quieted automatically by the initial stages of relaxation and by the sitting or prone posture. First the body is quieted; once the body defenses are down, it is easier for the mind to concentrate.

Choose a quiet place generally free from disturbance. A room should be comfortable for you in the sense that there are no unpleasant memories or associations, no tinge of discomfort while you are in it. Try to have plenty of fresh air circulating.

Once you have decided on the place, any comfortable position will do for basic concentration exercises. You can concentrate with varying degrees of success in most places, including crowded rooms. But for the more specific forms of concentration needed for training your mind and for serious meditation, certain specific requirements are demanded. Proper posture is the first consideration. It is important because it contributes to a general, overall tranquil attitude. With the wrong posture, tension and pain develop. The various postures used in meditation are usually difficult for beginners; if you cannot twist yourself conveniently into a lotus or half-lotus posture, do not be discouraged. Effective meditation can occur in most comfortable positions as long as a few basic criteria are followed: a straight back and neck; relief of pressure on the internal organs and breathing areas; and positions in which the blood can have an easy and clear flow through the main arteries and veins.

You should not turn finding a posture into a competition with Tibetan monks or desert Hesychasts of the Christian church. According to Buddha, extreme asceticism is unworthy and disruptive to meditation. Indeed, extremity of any sort is frowned upon in his teachings. One of his first principles is following "the middle way" that is free of excessive rigidity or self-indulgence. Asceticism is considered a violent and unhealthy extreme. "The true ascetic," Buddha teaches, "does not gratify his body; but he cares well for the body that he may advance in the spiritual life. Cared for, it is the better vessel for truth."

You can even lie down while meditating if it is absolutely necessary. But the single weakness of using this position is the tendency to fall asleep. And the aim of meditation is, of course, relaxed alertness, not sleep. Sitting upright sets the scene as one of alert dedication: It is not too easy and not too hard a posture. It enables the spine to keep erect and gives the breathing apparatus total freedom to function—without the unnecessary pressure bad posture induces. If you cannot use the traditional Yoga lotus posture, try the ancient Egyptian method of sitting in a straight-backed chair with your spine straight, feet flat on the ground, and hands placed on each leg.

In detail, then, the best basic posture should be a seated one— whether seated cross-legged on a cushion, or on a low seat, or upright in a chair—with the spine straight, head held high and slightly forward. The basic position should close the bodily circuit: that is,

the head-neck, spine, legs, and hands all in some form of contact. If you find the straight spine requirement too difficult at first,
rest your back against the chair back or a wall, with a small cushion placed in the hollow of your back. Your hands should be relaxed, generally on your thighs or knees, or they can be folded in
your lap palms up. If you use a chair you can either have your feet
flat on the floor or your legs crossed.

The most preferred posture is the full lotus in which you sit on
a soft mat or thin cushion. Place your right foot on your left thigh
and your left foot on your right thigh. Since this is a difficult
position for beginners to sit in, the half-lotus can be used. In the
half-lotus you do not place both feet on both thighs, but simply
place your left foot on your right thigh. Allow the right foot to remain on the floor under the left leg. Position your feet and legs until they are comfortable; it does not help your meditation if your
foot is squashed under your leg and pains you within a few
minutes. Loosen all your clothing—belts, shirt collars, etc. Place
your hands on your knees, with palms either up or down.

You will no doubt find yourself leaning forward, backward, or
to the right or left. You might find your head drooping forward or
your spine bowing out in the back. Be aware of these alterations
and correct them as they occur. Try to keep your body in a
straight line by picturing a plumb line falling from the top of your
head down your spine to your buttocks, which acts as the base
support. Your ears should be on a plane with your shoulders and
your nose in a line with your navel. Once you have achieved this
position close your eyes (unless you are using a specific meditation that demands leaving them open), and place your tongue
against the roof of your mouth so the tip is just touching the
back of your front teeth. Your lips and teeth should be shut;
breathe slowly and gently through your nose. Before you begin
your meditation rock your body gently from side to side, forward
and backward, to make sure you are settled into a steady, solid
position.

When you arise from sitting, do it slowly and gently. Try to feel
your body movements as fluid. Do not move abruptly. If your
muscles are stiff, ache, or are numb, gently massage them before
you get up. Do not be in a rush to rise. Give yourself time to re-
orient yourself—both physically and mentally.

SITTING MEDITATIONS

Sitting meditations are particularly recommended for those people who are too aged, ill, or injured to learn other postures. Indeed, it is a good position for anyone who is not inclined to learn more complicated postures—and it is just as effective if done properly.

All sitting meditations involve positioning the body for a straight back and neck, with the arms, legs, and abdomen relaxed, and with the body in what generally can be considered a state of balanced quiet. In order to keep the spine straight you must frequently remind yourself to do so. This also goes for your shoulders. During the initial stages of meditation you will find that even after relaxing your neck and shoulders thoroughly, they will tense up again; and if you consciously release the tensions you will be surprised to find that your shoulders will drop and your neck will become visibly relaxed again.

Another thing to watch for is leaning to the left or right, backward or forward. When you catch yourself doing any of these things do not be harsh or critical of yourself; just gently correct the fault in posture and go on with the meditation. The neck is just as prone to lean to one side or the other, or to the front or back. If you consciously remember to relax your neck and shoulders during the initial stages of meditation, it helps you to develop a proper posture for the more advanced, longer meditations. The straight back and neck are particularly important because they facilitate the flow of blood to the neck and back muscles, as well as to the inner organs, thus preventing back and muscle aches and tension from long sitting. Keeping the feet flat on the floor helps balance the whole body. Proper balance is important because it aids the muscles and joints in keeping the right position for a long time without developing pressure or irritation. If the body is correctly balanced, with a natural alignment of bones, tendons, and muscles, weight should be directed down the spine with the total weight spread evenly over the buttocks and thighs. If any part of the body is twisted from its natural alignment—even to the slightest degree— tension and pain will develop.

This is different from the pain felt in knees and ankles when using the lotus posture, because in the lotus you are initially deliberately creating pressure in the joints in order to loosen them, which will allow you to use that posture more comfortably as you become a more experienced meditator. In other words, the pain associated with learning a new difficult posture has a beneficial purpose, just as pain associated with exercise initially makes muscles sore. In contrast, if pain develops when you are using a posture designed to relax all the muscles and joints while in a natural position, you are doing something wrong with your body.

The same attention to proper balance and relaxed sitting can be applied to your everyday life. Even if not meditating, you can develop awareness about your body posture while driving or riding in cars, watching a movie or television, or sitting at your desk at work. Relaxed, proper sitting provides maximum circulation for your body and helps to prevent fatigue and muscle and nerve damage. This is particularly important for people who work sitting down. Office workers are the worst offenders, for while concentrating they usually acquire habits that twist or distort their bodies into a Gordian knot of tension. If you can learn to sit in a good posture and keep at it for a short time, it soon becomes natural.

For the sitting meditation, position your buttocks on the chair so that your lower back is an inch or so from the chair's back. As mentioned earlier, a simple device is to envision a plumb line that drops from the top of your head, down through your head, neck, and back to the base of the spine. It might help to move your body slightly from left to right until you feel the position that is exactly straight from the center of your skull down to the spinal tip or coccyx. Once you have found the right-left axis, you might push your belly forward and then your lower back into a curve toward the chair several times until you find the front-back axis. The proper axis is, of course, between the extremes.

Your feet should be firmly placed on the floor, your arms relaxed and your hands resting lightly on your thighs or folded one on top of the other in your lap. You can place your palms up or down, depending upon which is most comfortable for you. Close your eyes and breathe naturally, softly, and deeply. But do not push to breathe deeply; let it be a natural movement of the diaphragm. Breathe through the nose only, with your mouth loosely closed. In this position you can choose where to place your mind. The Chinese prefer to concentrate on the lower belly, a spot an inch or two below the navel. Christians often concentrate on their heart, on the spot where the two sides of the rib cage join at the breastbone. Many Indian sects prefer to concentrate on a point between the eyebrows, just above the bridge of the nose. Each of these areas of concentration is, of course, used by all the meditation schools at one time or another, and each has its own purpose and value.

Once you are in the proper posture, breathe gently and deeply, concentrate on a single spot, and you will find that your body relaxes and your mind becomes quieted.

BREATH CONTROL

Out of all the vital elements that converge to make life possible, nothing is more central, more pivotal, more basic to human survival than air and breathing. But for most of the meditative religions breathing is not simply a rhythmic taking in of oxygen and expelling of carbon dioxide. Breath is considered a life force, a central principle of energy that drives the cosmic engine as well as the human one. Breath is so important to Eastern religions that each has its own special term to describe its special qualities.

We think of breathing as being automatic, something we do unconsciously. And this is true as far as it goes. But the fact is that breathing is a volatile, changeable process that is profoundly related to our physical and psychic well-being. Short, uneven, shallow breathing often accompanies fright, neurosis, and physical illness. And since all meditations attempt to reduce the disruptive influence of minds and bodies, it is no surprise that a broad variety of methods have developed to control breathing. The breathing of the average person fluctuates according to stress, tension, and the bewildering number of situations each of us experiences every day. Learning to control your breath for a few minutes can help you turn away from these sources of difficulty and irritation.

Even Zen priests use basic and simple breath control techniques to return their minds to meditation when they wander. Dr. Tomio Hirai reported that the brain waves of Zen priests would vary strongly during meditation. As Dr. Hirai watched on his EEG machine, the brain-wave patterns of the priests altered from the calm, steady alpha that was common to their meditations into an outflow of beta waves, which indicated mental tension and emotional stress. Then, just as suddenly, the brain waves returned to their regular alpha pattern. Later Dr. Hirai asked what had happened and was told that the priest had had his meditation interrupted by "worldly thoughts," but once he had corrected his posture and regulated his breathing he again entered deep meditation. Whenever a meditator's mind wanders, this simple technique is invaluable, for all it takes is to make sure your posture is correct (straight back and neck) and that your breathing is regular and deep.

The delightful truth about breath control is that it can be practiced almost anywhere with strikingly good results. A good place to try out a little breath control is on the subway, train, or bus. If you find crowds and the tensions of the day difficult, you can do a breath-control exercise and the person sitting right next to you will not be aware of it. Simply close your eyes to block out the more obvious distractions and quickly inhale. Hold it for a second or two and exhale slowly. As you find yourself relaxing, inhale more slowly until your breathing is deep and regular. If you concentrate on the inhale-exhale rhythm of your breathing, you will be surprised at how quickly your tensions will be reduced and your energy level raised.

To practice a more controlled breathing and develop ability to move on to more complicated exercises, a good beginning exercise is simply to inhale for four seconds, retain your breath for four seconds, exhale for four seconds, hold the exhale for four seconds, and begin the cycle again. The idea is to breathe deeply and reduce the number of shallow breaths per minute. No one knows just how many breaths one ought to take, but eighteen breathes a minute are common for the average person in a relaxed state. For the practiced meditator taking only four or five breaths a minute is common.

There are more complicated counting methods that use first one nostril, then the other. The counting varies and can be used in a series of 2–8–4, or in a series of 3–12–6, etc. The numbers in sequence refer to inhale, hold, and exhale. In practice the meditator is allowed to count in any form he wishes. He can use beads, mentally count his heartbeat, snap his fingers, touch the thumb to each of his fingers, etc. But the one-to-ten count and a halving of the "holding breath" are the most common methods. In order to halve your "holding breath" you simply reduce by half the number of seconds you inhale and exhale. If, for example, you inhale for eight seconds, you should hold for four, then exhale for eight

5—20—10

seconds, and hold again for four. Then repeat the cycle. (For several easy exercises in breath control see the Appendix: Exercise 7, "Chinese Deep-Breathing"; Exercise 8, "Counting Breaths"; Exercise 10, "Rhythmic Breathing"; and Exercise 12, "Abdominal or Lower Belly Breathing.")

MANTRA: THE MAGIC SOUND

Another major yet easy method for concentrating one's mind is the use of sound. In its most fundamental form a mantra (sound) is hummed, sung, chanted (either out loud or mentally); it performs the same function as visualization or any other method of mind-control. The mantra also serves as a psychological trigger to prepare one for meditation. But many such "signals" exist in the preparation for deep meditation once they become a part of the established routine. In fact, all ritual can serve the meditator in the same way; even meditating the same time every day turns the clock and the approaching meditating time into a signal.

Perhaps because of its simplicity, the mantra system has been practiced in the West with wide success. Modern gurus like the Maharishi Mahesh Yogi use simple Sanskrit sounds to calm the anxious or stress-ridden individual. The Hare Krishna movement, led by A. C. Bhaktivedanata Swami Prabhupada, teaches that one can reach a "state of bliss" simply by worshipping the Hindu god Krishna and constantly chanting his holy name. Hare Krishna devotees believe that chanting is the most direct way to experience God. When pressed by Westerners about the simplicity and validity of their techniques, they reply that saying the rosary is really just another way of chanting. But the Hare Krishna chant, they say, is the most powerful of all, even though one can probably "get results using any of the bona fide names of God." And in this sense, chanting or using a mantra is indeed a universal method for invoking God's presence.

Some meditation schools that use mantras emphasize that the meditator should employ only meaningless sounds, which would tend to prevent him from getting "caught up" in the meaning or emotional content of the mantra. Traditional mantras brought down through the ages in Hinduism, however, are similar to the Holy Name mantras of Christianity. In fact, Hinduism has six categories of mantras, the first four of which are deity mantras.

But in this it is similar to most religions, in which the great majority of mantras invoke the name of God in one form or another.

A good example of this is in Sufism. (See the chapter "Meditation and Religion," and the Christian use of Jesus' name in Exercise 24, "Prayer of the Heart.") The meditator in Sufism repeats the phrase *la illaha* ("there is no god"), followed by the phrase *illa'llah* ("but God"). When everything but God is forgotten, the devotee repeats this mantra or *zikr* (mantra remembering God) until his movement, breath, and whole consciousness become united with God. There are some Sufis, however, that do not even bother to repeat the whole *la illaha illa'llah* ("there is no god but God") and reduce their mantra to the word "Allah," which they chant incessantly.

The purpose of such chanting of mantras is to remove all thoughts and desires from the mind, which, once empty, can be filled with God. Christian mystics agree that meditating on the name of God or a religious image keeps them from losing the mantra during the early stages of meditation as they sink into the unconscious, otherworldly state of mind they desire. For the religious meditator the image of his god becomes so powerful that it can take root in his unconscious, which in turn enables him to control more easily unconscious imagery during meditation. But the meditator can also be brought safely past the distractions of his unruly mind and body when chanting the sacred mantra.

One of the most elaborate and effective uses of the mantra occurs in Tibet. In the Tibetan chanting style *each* monk of a group produces a chord that sounds as if it consisted of a low bass note and another note more than two octaves higher. Acoustic experts have analyzed these peculiar "double" sounds and found that they involve complicated harmonics unusually sung. From time to time there are even other overtones clearly indicated—all produced by a single chanter at the same time. In the Gyütö Tantra sect, each monk is taught these special chanting techniques, which take at least three years to learn. The ability to chant a mantra in this remarkable way is significant: the tone, the ritualistic setting, the involvement of the meditator in producing the mantra all contribute to creating an effective *sadhana*. (A Tantric sadhana is basically a recitation of a meditation text during which the monk first visualizes and then unites mentally with his god.) During the sadhana there is the concentrated effort to connect the sound, breathing, and the attentive mind, and thereby to transform the meditator's awareness. The Tantric monk also sometimes uses a bell, which he rubs gently along the rib with a stick. This produces a continuous, gentle hum that helps him in his meditation.

It is a fascinating fact that while the actual sound of the Tibetan Gelug tradition is quite different from Christian liturgical music, there are intriguing similarities. The Gregorian chant, for example, was performed during ritual, during a procession involving prayer and a reading of the gospel. Much the same occurs in the Tibetan sadhana ritual. In the *ars antiqua* chant, the tenor generally sustains a long note that is juxtaposed by an upper voice that flows freely, almost as an accompanying song. Often, all the voices move in rhythm and tone at the same time, evoking a mantric quality that is amazingly similar to Tibetan chanting considering the distance in time and geography between the two cultures.

One of the most famous mantras in Buddhism is *Om Mani Padme Hum*. *Om* (which sounds like "aum" in Sanskrit) is the unitive sound of enlightenment. *Mani padme* means "jewel in the lotus," or stands for the joining of male and female organs, and symbolizes a state of completion, an infusing of energy that results in unity and ultimately wisdom.

For the more secular-minded Western attitudes, the nature of the mantra's effect upon the mind and body is more likely to be put in scientific terms. This is just what has happened as a result of research on TM. (To learn how to use a mantra the TM way, turn to the chapter "The Mysteries of Transcendental Meditation.") Dr. Herbert Benson is one of the best-known researchers who has experimented with mantras and, more specifically, the TM techniques. He has found that it is sound itself that produces what he calls the "relaxation response." He follows the basic prescription for most meditations: a quiet environment; a mental device for easy concentration; a passive, noncritical attitude; and a comfortable position. In his description of how to use a mantra, the only variation from the numerous other techniques described in this book is that he recommends *any* single-syllable sound or word as a mental device. The syllable is repeated in a low, gentle tone. As with other meditation concentration devices, this single-syllable sound is used to escape from the logical, externally oriented state of mind we are in for most of every day. Because of its simplicity and neutrality, Dr. Benson recommends using the "non-cultist" word (or syllable) "one." (See the Appendix, Exercise 6, for an exercise based on the use of single syllables like "one.")

THE HEALING EFFECT OF SOUND

No one yet knows the full effects music and sound have on our minds and bodies. But the basic principles of music therapy (which is based on the assumption that sound does have a profound effect) have been recognized throughout the world and in every ancient culture. The use of music and sound can be traced to the ancient writings of the Greeks, Egyptians, Persians, Hindus, Chinese, South American Indians, and other early societies. Perhaps the oldest "case history" in music therapy comes from Pythagoras of Samos, who is generally accredited with the discovery of musical interval and the diatonic scale. He also developed a philosophy that conceived of the universe as a vast musical instrument and that regarded all things as constructed upon harmonic patterns that could be influenced by purposefully created resonant or vibratory effects. In one example from ancient Greece the story is told of a young man who had been jilted by his sweetheart. In a rage he piled wood all around her house in order to burn it down. A follower of Pythagoras saw what was happening and realized that reasoning with the young man would have no effect. He took out a lute he was carrying and struck a few notes. The enraged young man stopped what he was doing, listened for a few moments, and then removed the wood and left. Another story relates how Pythagoras was dining with friends one evening when a demented young man whose father had recently been sentenced to death by one of the guests burst into the house swinging a sword in front of him. He approached the jurist, cursing him and threatening to kill him, when Pythagoras picked up a nearby lyre and struck a chord. At the sound of the music the youth suddenly stopped, as if in a trance. He was then led from the room.

An interesting fact in these stories is that the lyre, or lute, was the calming instrument. Compare that with the fact that music therapists are finding that the guitar is one of the preferred instruments of disturbed patients. Pythagoras actually preferred the stringed instruments for healing and therapy. He believed that the human body was a kind of sounding board that would immediately respond to the vibratory effects of sound. The idea of tonal sympathy, or course, is not new and can be easily demonstrated with the help of a tuning fork. If one vibrates a tuning fork and holds it about an inch or so away from a guitar string that has not been touched, the string will begin to vibrate up and down its length. Water glasses placed near church bells can be shattered by the bells's ringing. The story is told about how Enrico Caruso could tap the edge of a glass tumbler with his finger, listen to its tone, and then sing the corresponding note. The glass would shatter. It has even been found that candles can be extinguished by sound. Considering that every cell in our bodies possesses neuroelectrical properties, and that the very nature of atomic matter is resonance, it becomes less strange to theorize that the sound of a mantra can indeed have a profound effect upon our minds and bodies.

Peculiar facts are beginning to arise with the greater scientific attention music has received. Research at Kansas State University has demonstrated that loud noise played around cattle produces a change in their body physiology causing the animals to produce an undesirable type of beef called "dark cutters." With a control group of cattle not subjected to "stress sounds" like clanking of heavy equipment, the roar of jet engines, or the playback of normal traffic noise, cattle produced meat with no "dark cutters."

Research into the effect of sound upon the human body and mind is just now beginning, but even early tests show that sounds produced by instruments like guitars and bass drums dilate the capillaries in the body, increase the heart rate, and cause other physical effects. Dr. Gary Schwartz has stated that the pleasant, calming sounds of the mantra have a tranquilizing effect. "Psychophysical research indicates that sounds that rise slowly and are resonant can decrease heart rate, inducing relaxation."

The psychological effects seem just as interesting and promising. At a Long Beach, California, Veteran's Hospital music therapists are finding that even the most withdrawn and disturbed psychiatric patients are responding beyond expectations. Retarded and even brain-damaged children improve very rapidly. After beginning music therapy, one sixteen-year-old retarded girl with the physical coordination of a three-year-old child began to perform dance movements before mirrors. She is beginning to learn the basic skills of moving her body. Her limbs (after almost two decades) have understandably become atrophied to some degree, but therapists find that musical therapy helps improve muscle activity even in badly crippled arms or legs. At New York Hospital, psychiatrist Annamaria Nucci has used music therapy on retarded children with very beneficial effects, and has found that melancholy music improved the mood of depressed patients, but had the opposite effect on schizophrenic patients.

Research continues to show an ever-widening range of physiological responses to sound. In one study, for example, six minutes of listening to Dvorak's *New World* Symphony caused a significant drop in the listener's galvanic skin response, indicating an unconscious emotional arousal. Another experiment showed that the more one likes a piece of music, the deeper one breathes when listening to it. After decades of dependency on drugs, some doctors are beginning to suggest symphonies for their tense and anxious patients rather than tranquilizers.

Problems and Dangers
in Meditation

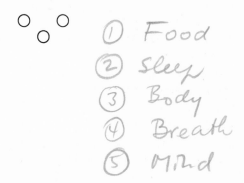

① Food
② sleep
③ Body
④ Breath
⑤ Mind

THE MASTER CHIH I DESCRIBED the meditator's tools with the usual Chinese practicality: "A potter who wants to make earthenware should first prepare proper clay that should be neither too hard nor too soft, so that it can be cast in a mold; and a lute player should first tune the strings, if he is to create melody. Likewise in the control of the mind, five things should be *regulated.*" These five are food, sleep, body, breath, and mind. Chih I is not denying either the body or physical pleasure, but rather, as in practically every other major religion with meditative techniques, he is emphasizing that the mind and body are intimately connected, and that the mind cannot be controlled without the body being equally controlled, and vice versa.

The attunement of body and mind is necessary for either to work efficiently. This is especially true in meditation. If the regulation of the mental and physical realms is not complete, then trying to learn meditation can lead to fearsome mental and physical disturbance. Depression, irritability, restlessness, and even neurosis and insanity are not unknown. Common sense and a modicum of self-discipline, however, can avoid these serious problems. But these are only some of the dangers to be aware of when learning to meditate.

Dangers exist even in those disciplines that move the novice along deliberately and slowly, such as Yoga. It is well known in India, for example, that some Hatha Yoga practices are dangerous and can lead to insanity. The Persian word *mastana* and the Sanskrit *avadhoot* are both used to describe an initiate or disciple who, while learning to meditate, succumbs to the unexpected powers he encounters. These are not commonplace, however, and are most often the result of moving ahead too rapidly without creating the necessary foundation of mental discipline and control. But it is good to keep in mind, and to move along the inner paths of the mind cautiously and gradually, like a child learning to walk before he can run.

Meditation is not an escape or an indulgence. It involves hard work, discipline, and understanding. For example, if someone believes in evil demons, or Satan, it is likely that this belief system will manifest itself during deeper states of meditation. If someone has a specific psychological problem with, say, sex, it is also likely that images and symbols that occur in the mind when meditating will be sexual. In other words, during the initial stages of meditation the content of one's individual emotional and psychological temperament will be reflected in one's experiences. It is this fact that makes meditation both a blessing and a difficult discipline, for when opening the depths of the mind to conscious manipulation, one is also opening the consciousness to the psyche's repressed energies. To begin thinking seriously about one's life can be a painful enterprise. It is even more painful when one begins to doubt previous assumptions and beliefs. Belief systems are like muscles, once exercised they begin to bulge and occupy space. If not exercised carefully they can crowd out other essential exercises of the mind such as objectivity, reflective self-evaluation, self-criticism, and applied will.

The human psyche is full of wounded symbols, images that tend to divert constructive action, destroy calm, and stir up psychic trouble. These wounded symbols are part of the neurotic baggage we all carry with us. The only effective measure of neurosis is determined by how much it incapacitates us, by how much our optimal functioning is cut short. It is the wounded symbol that will first disrupt meditation, that will come floating across the span of conscious attention. As we work our way through these experiences, however, the benefits are great; for problems that have been repressed for years are aired or dissipated when we redirect our attention to more positive goals. In this sense meditation is similar to psychotherapy both in purpose and result.

Another danger in meditation involves endowing objects with qualities, with becoming so absorbed in an object one is concentrating on that an imagined empathy and identification develops. If the purpose of meditation is to better define what is real, then allowing yourself to become so identified with objects can be as misleading as charging objects with an alien menace. In both cases the external world retains a distortive otherness, and prevents a clearer, more complete relationship between our internal feelings and the external world. Meditation on objects is basic when learning how to concentrate, and it is valuable when it gives added dimension and qualities to objects we once considered exclusively in simpler terms of form, color, or function. But if you go too far and allow a distortive empathy to develop, or begin to accept objects as real extensions of yourself, then you are defeating the whole purpose of meditation.

For example, while it is true that the world can be seen as a unitive whole (we are all atoms and molecules resonating forms of energy), there is clearly a difference between, say, a hand and a tennis ball. The difference is necessarily real. Relating to a tennis ball as if it were a hand may well lead to an inability of the hand to pick up the ball. A difficult paradox exists here, for there is truth in both visions: The world is indeed a unitive whole, yet on a functional, mundane level its separateness is valuable and necessary. The functional reality between the internal and external worlds must be maintained, even while this perception of separateness is being modified by meditative practice and newly developed ways of "seeing." It is vital, however, that the distinctions between these various levels of existence are kept clear.

Another danger, perhaps the greatest of all, comes once the meditator has made a satisfactory beginning, and then becomes either scared or let down once the meditative exercises begin to get serious. What at first seemed easy now becomes difficult. What was once rewarding seems to be utterly impossible. The mind just doesn't seem to work the way it did at first, and the peace and fulfillment initially felt have disappeared. Even the concentration that you felt some pride in may seem worse than when you began. Fantasies may return and imagination is harder than ever to control.

There are many traditional terms to describe this condition—lack of confidence, spiritual inertia—but the most poetic and ac-

curate explains it as a passing trial called the "night of the senses."
This type of experience was quite common with ascetic monks trying to lead a contemplative life in the desert. The Christian
church generally considered it a serious problem and felt it indicated that the meditator had somehow started his discipline
wrong. Generally it was the disciple's attitude that caused a chasm
to appear between his "inner life" and the rest of his existence.
The belief had set in that the "inner world" was in fact more real,
spiritual, or exalted in some way, and that the external world was
material, sensual, and somehow evil. This rejection of the natural part of one's world occurred quite often, for the inner life is
very seductive in this way. But this attitude is a key point—the
same point missed by those who identify too completely with
objects. Such people do not accept reality as it is and use that realization as a foundation on which exploring the subjective inner
world can be safely made.

St. Augustine observed wisely that in order to successfully explore
the unreal world, one had better have a strong foundation in the
"real." If you retain respect and affectionate contact with *both* aspects of the world, you can avoid the inertia and repulsion some
experience during the early phases of meditation. Avoiding a false
supernaturalism that sees the magical as a kind of ideal world can
often be achieved by simply respecting and enjoying fully the concrete realities of daily life—one's physical body, friends, environment, and nature generally. As Trappist monk Thomas Merton observed, "meditation has no point and no reality unless it is firmly
rooted in life."

The *wrong* attitude was expressed recently to a traveler to
Ceylon, where a monk he was talking to admitted: "I do not know
the things of your world, but I believe that I should have to leave
my order if I did get to know them, for I should succumb to that
world. I can imagine it. I cannot know it. In any case I am afraid of
it, but most of all, I fear my own weakness." This is not, then, an
ancient problem but one that exists today. This monk's attitude of
fear and apprehension cannot possibly lead him to the integrated
vision he desires. How can he find what he is seeking when he fears
so much? The fear acts as a barrier and a delusion. Much of his
world must be seen through its opaque filter, through the gorge of
his anxiety.

Put simply, if you alienate the external world by exalting the internal one, you may also succeed in imprisoning yourself. The same may be said for excessive attitudes toward anything, for each thing carries within itself its opposite. But ask this: Is it really any better to be a prisoner of one's fantasies and subjective anxieties than to be trapped into believing the external world is the only real one? Of course not. The basic idea of meditation is to create a harmonious relationship between the two, not to alienate either one in favor of the other.

Indian philosopher Krishnamurti has attacked the "specialness" of meditation techniques as practiced by some groups. He argues that meditation practices must be directed toward the whole of one's life, not only a special, isolated area. His criticism has a point, since modern psychotherapy has indicated that people who habitually engage in practices designed for personal growth tend to separate these special practices, and the resulting attitudes of "specialness," from the rest of their lives. True growth obviously has to take place in the context of an individual's whole life, the impact of change being consistently spread throughout the life-style generally. In a very real sense, life is the only arena in which growth can take place. But "life" here means not only our every-day life patterns, habits, feelings, ideas, and so forth, but the sum total of our internal and external experience.

A synthesis is obviously necessary. What we are confronted with is the constant challenge of adjustment, of balancing and accommodating opposing but complementary forces and alternate realities. To utilize meditation techniques—indeed, any method that helps us expand our awareness properly—is difficult but possible. If meditation is not incorporated into everyday life, a fundamental fact of the process has been missed. Meditation is meant to influence the whole person, to reintegrate the disintegrated elements of the deeper self. There is a Zen anecdote that illustrates this point perfectly. The great Zen master Dogen was studying in China while still a young man. One day while walking he struck up a conversation with a monk. After a while Dogen asked the monk, "Why don't you stay in your temple and practice *zazen* instead of working the kitchen or making such long journeys to out-of-the-way places just to do some shopping?" The monk smiled and replied to Dogen, "My Japanese friend, it seems that you don't know yet the meaning of religious practice in search of the Tao (Way)," and walked off with a laugh. Thereafter, Dogen realized that Zen was not for monasteries alone.

There is some basic advice on handling the inevitable emotional material that floods into one's awareness during meditation. As you begin to meditate try to avoid being afraid of not doing the right thing. Do not cling to the idea that everything should be perfect, clear, and easy as you start. In other words, do not be judgmental with yourself. Do not be afraid of making mistakes and having to do something over again. The simple, noncritical, nonjudgmental attitude is what you seek—especially in the beginning. Do not waste time or emotional energy on regret or disappointment over your progress. If you are persistent and patient, you automatically become more sensitive to the nuances of your concentration, the inner movement of your emotions, and your unconscious energies. You will find that distractions will occur with disturbing frequency at first, but as you progress you will be able to recognize them dispassionately and return to your meditation with ever greater ease. But complaints about your "performance" only create frustration and irritation. So whatever happens during your meditation, just observe it as it is. In this way you become more and more objective when dealing with your inner thought processes and emotional imagery. As you become more objective, your ability to move beyond the many mini-obsessions that occur during meditation improves.

Few problems in meditation are as difficult to conquer as irrelevant thoughts, unwanted images that arise spontaneously in the mind. The advice to empty the mind or to concentrate on one point or a specific thing is always made with the qualifying thought that (1) you have already developed some power of concentration to use, and (2) you know how to deal with the constant rising of disruptive impressions. The many exercises included in the Appendix were in fact created to help in learning mind-control. But it must be admitted that even with steady practice the troublesome interruptions continue to invite themselves into your private meditation party. There are, however, specific methods for dealing with these problems.

One Zen priest explained to his disciple that when distracting thoughts occurred to him during meditation he should make no effort to drive them away, but simply wait until they leave on their own. This is more difficult than the old priest makes it sound. It is one of those things that is only simple once you learn how. But then, any discipline once conquered seems simple. It is the initial grasping of the dimensions and reality of the problem and how to solve it that is difficult. In the Zen discipline mental control is learned as you allow the distracting thought to appear in your mind and then use trains of associations to lead to the dissolution of the original disruptive thought. According to this technique, you do not try to press the thought out of the mind—a method that the Christians, for example, do recommend—but let it follow its own course until it ceases. This involves a kind of co-consciousness in which the image arises in the mind and, yet, there is a part of the mind that is watching the idea or image and is aware that it is only a fleeting thought that will soon pass and allow you to return to meditation. You are supposed to simply watch the image or thought dispassionately so that you can simultaneously think about meditation and observe the troublesome thought. This is an especially valuable method if you are often interrupted by obsessive images. The more obsessive or stronger an idea or image, the more power you give it by struggling to push it away. With less potent images one can use the blackboard method of picturing the idea or thought on a blackboard and with the mind's eye simply run an erasure gently over it until it disappears.

Another similar method is to gently press the troubling image to the side of the mind, and, as if it were on a stage, let it disappear in the wings or beyond the frame of your "mind-stage." This simple, gentle removal often works with casual images that come into the mind, but if a strong image pops up time and time again the Zen association technique is best. With this Zen method the goal is a state of no-thought, or one in which the mind is calm and totally free of any distraction. In short, strong distractions cease to be distractions when you can incorporate them into the meditative process. In this way you learn to concentrate on one thing while allowing the mind to follow associative patterns dealing with something else.

To give an example, Zen priests advise us that as thoughts arise they usually begin to form a series. If you give these thoughts little more than the slight attention required to remain aware of them, you can see that each thought or idea tends to slip relatively quickly into another. One Zen priest, for example, related that he experienced the following series of thoughts during his meditation. While in meditation he suddenly heard the sound of someone walking quietly in the corridor outside. This reminded him that his Zen teacher had said that it was essential to walk quietly in buildings where others were meditating. (Notice that already the first interrupting thought has disappeared and been replaced with an association.) The thought then occurred to the meditating priest that young monks are no longer considerate enough and that he would discipline them at the appropriate time. This thought brought to mind a young monk who had been particularly skillful at ringing the bell to call the other priests to meditation. This brought to mind the idea "discipline" and the problem of how to discipline young monks. How one disciplines is important, and he thought to himself that in the modern world gentle scolding was preferred in contrast to the harsher methods of ancient days. And here the series of associations ended and the priest returned to his meditation until the next interruption. According to Zen, irrelevant thoughts paradoxically cannot be stopped by trying to stop them, but only through learning not to interfere with them. Thus the meditator learns to use various ruses and techniques to finesse the problem.

In one Soto Zen sect, for example, one master teaches disciples to concentrate on their hands during meditation. But because the mind will often wander and even tends to "sink," the disciple will transfer his attention to the top of the head or concentrate on the space between his eyebrows. The Soto Zen priest will correct wandering thoughts by having the young monk concentrate on the lower abdomen. When the mind seems to wander unattached to any specific image or thought, it is recommended that you concentrate on the feet or hands.

These, however, are very specific methods used by Zen priests for particular ends. For the purpose of the beginning and even the practiced meditator, it really doesn't matter much what you concentrate on. It is the discipline of learning to control the mind that is important. Choose a spot on your body, within your mind, a tree outside your window in the distance, a book against the wall, or a crack or stain in the ceiling.

An ancient Ch'an Buddhist master said that "one should be intimate with the unfamiliar and distant towards the familiar."

During meditation you may experience surprising visions, fascinating fantasies, shocking images or ideas. You may even experience what has been popularly called extrasensory perception, and have visions, or feel that you have left the body and are looking down upon the world from an alternative reality. It is not surprising, however, that these effects have been reported for ages by meditators, for during meditation you are exploring unfamiliar terrain in the unconscious, the source and home for all these powerful aspects of the mind. But even if one accepted the idea that such things as clairvoyance, out-of-the-body experiences, and so forth, are real, they are not important in the context of meditation except for the fact that they can be distracting.

Such inner fascinations present a continual problem for practiced meditators, but they can even be a hazard for beginners. Zen Buddhists call these impressions *makyo*, or sensory distortions. Makyo are not negative in themselves but are to be avoided because they disrupt the meditator from his goal. If too much attention is given to seeing "auras" or "colored lights" then one is diverted from the greater benefits of meditation by sensory game-playing. Therefore, it is better not to become too fascinated by these makyo. After you have established your meditative goals, gently return to the task you have set for yourself.

The cause of makyo seems to be a great deal of "crossover" between the various states of consciousness; one state of consciousness "bleeds" its effects over into another as you reduce the conscious mind's dependency on the external world. There seem to be no hard or rigid lines separating these various levels, and the constant mixing of impressions one gets in deep meditation may possibly induce confusion and emotional turmoil in the beginner. Because these makyo are so commonplace it is important to discipline the mind, to learn mind-control before plunging deeply into meditation and the farther reaches of the psyche.

It is harder to ignore makyo than might be imagined. Many of the effects are quite attractive. A real psychological danger is the overlapping of memory traces into the present, and reliving the memory as if it were occurring in the present. And because these are *your* personal memories they have an exceptionally strong appeal. In fact, you can become enraptured watching the unfolding of such memories—something like watching an old film once loved but long forgotten. Then again, the memory might be painful and reliving it during meditation can turn into an ordeal; yet this fact does not make it any less interesting.

The best way to avoid the whole problem of unconscious memories is to ignore them when they start, before the recognition turns into emotional attachment. A good defense is to maintain an attitude of detachment, of dispassion toward the whole process of meditation. This is, in fact, one of the basic principles of successful meditation. Disruptive thoughts and makyo impressions will certainly occur. As soon as you become aware that you have been diverted from your meditation, gently return your attention to it. If you can maintain an alert, noncritical, dispassionate attitude, you will have succeeded in creating the right state of mind to meditate.

Appendix:
Meditation Exercises

Friend, let this be enough. If thou wouldst go on reading,
Go and thyself become the writing and meaning.

—ANGELUS SILESIUS

INTRODUCTION

THE FORMS OF meditation in the appendix of this book are grouped
in a generally progressive manner; that is, they are placed with the simpler exercises first and move on to the more difficult. Some people
will prefer certain types of meditations over others and therefore may
wish to use an exercise that is in the middle rather than in the beginning. This is all right, for when a meditation is particularly difficult, that
fact has been noted in the exercise itself so that the beginner will be
warned.

Many of the exercises in the appendix involve pictures, visualization,
etc., and are not "pure" meditations in the strict sense of the word;
rather, they are concentration techniques to be used during the meditation period. Actual meditation is hard to describe, for it is an effortless
dwelling within the "process" of meditation. Both the "fact of" and the
"activity of" meditation become melded when that deep state of true
meditation is reached.

The following are some general guidelines, suggestions, and advice
on learning to meditate. I have also tried to answer questions that might
develop as you progress.

It is best for beginners to "tune up" their minds for meditation with
simple exercises. Those who have already done similar exercises need
not repeat them again here before turning to other more appealing
exercises. Try to do the easier exercises first and not jump ahead before
you are ready. If you choose a meditation exercise that is too hard for

you, the discouragement might put you off meditating for some time, if not permanently.

If you approach meditation with the idea that there is a meditator doing meditation, your basic assumption about it is wrong. This attitude immediately introduces the ego into the process.

Do not hesitate to try a variety of different forms of meditation. If you have learned the basic principles of meditation, you can grasp the essentials of practically all methods of meditation.

Practice. It is a word that we all have heard many times. But in meditation, practice is not only essential, it is imperative. Without regular practice you might not even begin. We all tend to revert back to ingrained habit patterns unless we continually integrate the newly learned lesson into our everyday life. This is why every meditation method emphasizes the necessity of regular practice. Without the daily routine we immediately revert back to old patterns. So if you meditate for a week or two, or even months, and then begin to miss one day, then several days a week, don't be surprised that the expected benefits fail to develop.

There can be no final rules for how long one should meditate. It can range anywhere from a few minutes to days. Most experienced meditators agree that in the beginning meditations should be kept short. If you try to do too much too quickly you will merely set yourself back. Meditation is a discipline unlike any other you have ever attempted. Fifteen to twenty minutes is a good length of time. Increase the time only as it is comfortable for you. You are after the quality of the time spent, not quantity. Also seek a place where you will not be disturbed. For it is not the amount of time spent in meditation that counts, but the amount of *uninterrupted* time. Meditation does not involve an escape from reality or a loss of consciousness or physical mutilation. In fact, the greatest problem is one of discipline—of constant, persevering attention to the task you have set for yourself.

The best time for meditation is in the morning, as the first act of the day. It is then that the mind is comparatively peaceful. The morning is also especially good for beginners because success in quieting the mind is more likely before rather than after the ordeal of a "normal" day at work. On the other hand, it is equally important to quiet yourself after a full day of activity and before sleep. If morning is not possible, the next best time is evening. Meditating both morning and evening is best of all. Once you have chosen your time and place, stick to them. It has been found that it is best to meditate at approximately the same time and place every day.

When choosing the right meditation, try many and select those that appeal to you the most and are the easiest to do. It is important that

you choose and stick with a meditation that is compatible to your present stage of growth and your own unique personality. Each meditation
is a good one—once you have perfected it.

How do you tell when you have had a good meditation? There is no
clear signal, no green light or buzzer that goes off in your head telling
you that your meditation is successful. A good indication is how you feel
after the meditation. Do you feel more rested, at peace, energetic than
when you started? Within a few weeks most people are able to begin to
distinguish between the various levels of awareness. Things begin to happen automatically and with a greater ease than when you began. In the
deeper stages of meditation there is an inner silence. During this deeper
stage one is simply aware of "what is," without comment or context.
Opinions, thoughts, emotions, desires are all forgotten. In Buddhism
this phase has been described as "gathering within the temple to observe the thing itself." The silence of the mind is so complete that unexpected external sounds wash over the body in waves but leave you
unmoved, unresponding to its character. This is true whether the sound
is a car horn outside, a child crying, voices arguing in the distance, a cat
meowing. None of the sounds carries emotional weight, and none seems
capable of disturbing this deeper inner silence of mind.

As for summing up how to concentrate or learn meditation in simple terms, it cannot be done adequately. But if one were forced to state
a principle on how to meditate, it should probably be "Begin and persevere."

THE EXERCISES

1. *Meditation on Developing the Will*

In order to meditate one first needs the "will to will it." More than
most modern psychologists, Roberto Assagioli has emphasized the need
for developing one's will. His exercises in training the will are valuable
for beginning meditators; they will familiarize you with meditative and
visualization techniques as well as help establish the necessary will to
persevere in the greater rigors of meditation. The first step is conviction. You must mobilize your energies and commit yourself to developing your willpower. The progression of Assagioli's exercise moves from
simple, basic emotion visualizations to autosuggestion. I would suggest,
however, reading Dr. Assagioli's complete chapter on training the will in
his excellent book *Psychosynthesis.*

First, put yourself in a comfortable position. Relax your muscles,
breathe slowly and evenly. Visualize as vividly as possible all the un-
fortunate consequences that have actually occurred to you and others as

the result of your inadequate will in the past. Then visualize those un-
fortunate events that might occur in the future through your lack of
will. Examine them carefully one by one, formulating them clearly; then
make a list of them in writing!

Allow the feelings these recollections and forecasts arouse in you to
affect you intensely: shame, dissatisfaction with yourself, fear of repetition, the desire to change, etc.

Second, visualize as vividly as possible all the advantages training your
will can bring to you. Examine carefully each benefit and satisfaction
that will come to you and others. Enumerate and then write down each
item. Allow the feelings aroused by this examination to consume your
attention and fill you with emotion: the joy of future possibilities, the
desire to realize each one, and the strong urge to begin to accomplish
them at once.

Third, visualize as vividly as possible being possessed of a strong, persistent will. Picture yourself walking with a firm, steady stride; acting in
various situations with decisiveness, persistence, strong concentration,
and focused intention. Picture someone trying to intimidate you but
failing. Use your ability to daydream and fantasize in order to create
situations in which you show strong will and determination. Specifically
choose situations in which you previously have either failed to exert
sufficient will in real life or in fantasy and alter the situation. See yourself acting in different and more desirable ways. Such visualization is
not a delusion if done with the clear idea that you are developing your
strength of will and not merely indulging in neurotic fantasies.

It is important to try to transfer these visualizations into everyday life.
Set yourself reasonable tasks like going to bed at a certain time regardless of what you are doing, of exercising or reading one book a week and
following through on it. Do not set impossible or even especially difficult tasks, but rather reasonable goals that you are sure you can meet.
If you fail in the beginning do not be overly critical with yourself.
These are exercises to develop will and you don't help by flagellating
yourself or by feeling guilty. Those are exactly the feelings of powerless-
ness that you are trying to overcome. Be patient, noncritical, and persistent.

2. A Chinese Squatting Meditation

The ancient Chinese developed a simple but effective posture for
meditation that is meant to strengthen the leg and back muscles, help
straighten the spine during meditation so the internal organs can function unimpeded, and facilitate digestion. The squatting position is, of
course, taken from the fetal position in the womb. The image is of an

unborn child in a state of inactivity, with eyes, ears, and mouth shut, the mind devoid of any disturbance. The Taoists were very fond of emphasizing the origins of things and believed if you could succeed in returning to an original condition of peace and harmony, life would take on a new dimension and greater clarity. As Lao Tzu, the founder of Taoism, said: "Things appear multifarious and plural, but eventually they all return to the common root; when they return to the common root there is quiescence."

You do this posture as a simple exercise or as a meditation—or both. Sit in a squatting position and cover your ears with the palms of your hands. At first it will probably be better to squat with your back against a wall or something solid to give you support. But try to get to the point where you can do the exercise without using any back support at all. Make sure your back is straight, however, and that your shoulders are at right angles from your neck and trunk, your elbows forward as your hands cup your ears.

Proper breathing is essential. Inhale and exhale slowly and deeply through your nose. Focus your mind on your lower abdomen, two inches below the navel. Breathe gently, for after a while you will begin to hear the inner workings of your body. What is inaudible during your normal waking hours will begin to rise in volume as you become more quiet in your breathing. The gentle, deep, quiet breathing during this exercise is called "heel breathing" by Taoists, and is meant to focus attention on your inner being. Try to perform this exercise-meditation at night, in a quiet, well-ventilated room before going to bed. It is very relaxing and puts your conscious awareness in comfortable communion with the inner workings of the body.

3. Zen Meditative Sleep

As far back as the fifth century the Chinese used what they called a meditative sleep to enhance their health and longevity. Meditative sleep was traditionally believed to cure nightmares, morning fatigue, sore neck, cramps, and catching cold while asleep. The ancient Chinese believed that healthful sleep is nature's way of restoring the mind, body, and spirit. But its benefits can only be had when one sleeps in the correct way: the sleeper must be fully relaxed in a specific position in order to allow the body the opportunity to restore itself. Since the Chinese were prone to use metaphor, it's not surprising that they describe the meditative sleep as "to sleep like a dog." To curve the body while reclining on either side is recommended. The underside arm should be bent and the hand placed between the head and pillow and used as an added cushion. The other arm rests along your side, the hand on your

hip. The under leg is in a short curve, while the upper leg is bent more sharply into a full right angle.

If you are completely relaxed you should feel the bed's contact along the full length of your body. The arms and shoulders should be especially limp. Your chest, pelvis, abdomen, and back should be free of all tension. Your mouth should be gently closed, while you breathe naturally, keeping your mind free from all distracting thoughts by concentrating on the lower abdomen. Do not press your concentration on the navel area, but when you become drowsy and begin to fall asleep, continue to concentrate your mind and let your breathing be natural and relaxed.

Your state of sleep often varies in relation to psychical and physical conditions prior to the sleep period. The important thing is to remain mentally and physically relaxed, without any anxious thoughts about the day just past or the day to come.

4. Meditating on a Dream

A simple yet rewarding meditation is to use an important, recent dream as the central theme of a meditation. First, try to recall the dream in as vivid detail as you can. If you don't recall all of it at first don't worry; much of it will return as you meditate on it. Second, take each detail of the dream, each major symbol that has clearly presented itself, and meditate on its overall symbolic meaning. Don't analyze or dissect it intellectually. Try to reexperience the symbol fully. Deal with it in an intuitive way. Place the symbol in a pleasant, uncomplicated environment, like the night sky. Or visualize the smooth surface on a tranquil lake and see the symbol or detail rise up from its depths to reflect fully and vividly in front of your eyes. As it gently floats before your eyes, hold an expectant attitude. Listen carefully, and watch the lake for any other impression that might rise to the surface. Do not press, but learn to wait patiently watching the symbol and waiting for further insight into its meaning.

As each symbol reveals its meaning go on to the next detail that you want clarified until the central theme and meaning of the dream is clear. Do not be concerned about finding the solution immediately or even during the dream-meditation. The desired insight may come later when you're busy doing something else during the day. Or it may appear in another dream. What you are doing with this meditation is setting in motion the deeper forces of the unconscious, and they may not answer you at once. Repeat the meditation several times if necessary, and if you are not pressing or viewing the symbol or dream in logical terms, deeper insights into its meaning will surely occur. Stay in the dream-meditation as long as you care to. It is a good basic meditation, for it helps develop concentration and visualization abilities as well as supplying interesting answers to dreams.

5. Meditating with a Mantra

The preparation for this meditation is similar to most of the others. Find a quiet place where you won't be disturbed or inhibited by being overheard, and sit in your favorite posture (using either a chair or a cushion on the floor). As with the breath meditations, it is especially important that your clothing be loose and nonbinding. Do some slow, rhythmic deep breathing (as described in other exercises) while you visualize a peaceful scene.

Once you are completely relaxed begin repeating the mantra (word, sound, or phrase) that you have chosen. The only restriction on your choice is that the sound or word should have a pleasant meaning or quality for you and should not be disturbing or disharmonic to your ear. Repeat the mantra at a speed that is comfortable for you. If it seems natural that the rhythm pick up or change in any way, follow your impulses. As you repeat the mantra consciously continue to relax your body. When thoughts interrupt gently press them aside. Do not be irritated or disturbed. Be kind to these disrupting images and thoughts because, after all, they are swelling up into your consciousness after years of absolutely free reign. You shouldn't get angry at a puppy or kitten for doing something that it hasn't been disciplined not to do, so don't be angry with your unruly mind. Simply keep pressing the thoughts gently out of the way and continue to repeat your mantra. You will find that your mind is capable of doing both the repetition and dealing with any disruptive thought.

As your concentration improves try to feel the vibrations in your chest, throat, and head. Visualize the vibrations as moving all over your body, making your body one large resonating chamber for the sound you are repeating. To help this feeling along, place both your hands lightly against your chest with your fingers resting gently on your collarbone where the bones meet at the base of your throat. Feel the vibration in your fingertips as you chant.

Feel the vibrations going into your fingertips, moving down your hands and into your arms. Once the feeling of the vibration is strong in your hands, lower them again into your lap or onto your thighs with the palms up. They will continue to tingle with the vibrations. Use these lingering vibrations to envision the vibrations moving from your hands into your legs, filling your stomach and hips. It is almost as if you are holding in your empty hands an invisible musical instrument that is still ringing with the feeling of music played on it. Fill your body with that feeling and picture the mantra as setting your whole body vibrating with its force. Do not be frightened if you actually do begin to feel strong vibrations throughout your body. If you find them disturbing at first, simply relax and slowly cease to chant. Sit in your posture relaxing your mind and body by concentrating on your regular breathing.

When you want to stop your meditation, picture each breath that you inhale as invisible energy filling your body. Where there were vibrations before, picture energy and a feeling of healthy well-being.

This meditation can be modified easily into a healing meditation. If you wish to use this meditation for self-healing, do everything as before but when you remove your hands from the base of your throat place them on your body and visualize the vibrations as traveling through your hands and fingers into the affected area. Picture the vibrations as destroying the diseased parts just as sound waves can shatter glass. Or use any alternative visualization that is effective for you. See the vibrations as destroying the bad cells. After you have done this, picture the vibrations leaving your fingers and hands as energizing your body's own immunological system. See the white blood cells as being awakened and becoming so active that they attack and overcome the disease. Make up any variation on this theme that pleases you. Conclude the self-healing mantra meditation with the same visualization of inhaling energizing, healthful air. Take five or ten minutes and carry the energizing breath to the diseased area of your body, making it healthy.

6. A Simple Mantra Exercise Using Single-Syllable Sounds

The key to Dr. Herbert Benson's relaxation-meditation program is the use of any single-syllable sound. He recommends neutral sounds like "one." Either use "one" in the following exercise or any other single syllable that appeals to you. The important thing to remember is not to rush or press yourself. Practice this meditation once or twice daily but not within two hours after eating. Benson has found that the digestive process seems to interfere with the desired physiological response.

As with other meditations, sit in a comfortable position in a quiet environment. Close your eyes and relax your muscles. Begin at your feet and work up to your face, relaxing each muscle group individually. Spend as much time as necessary on each muscle area until you feel it is relaxed. Breathe through your nose. Become aware of your breathing, and as you breathe out say the word "one" silently. Since your breath takes a second or so to exhale, the sound of the word will necessarily be elongated, which is, of course, the reason mantras always take on a chanting quality—even such simple, "non-cultic" sounds like "one." If you wish, think a relaxing word, perhaps "peace" or "calm," as you inhale; and as you breathe out repeat "one." If you find using two words disruptive, stop the practice and use only the single syllable.

Following the TM practice, Dr. Benson recommends doing the "one" sound for twenty minutes twice a day. He also suggests not using an alarm to tell you when twenty minutes are up (this might destroy the very relaxation response you are after) but, rather, opening your eyes when you think about twenty minutes have passed. After a while you will be surprised at how accurate your sense of timing becomes. When you finish, sit quietly for a few moments with your eyes closed and then a few minutes more with your eyes open. Try to transfer the feeling of relaxation and peace beyond the meditation time and carry it with you through the day.

BREATH MEDITATIONS

7. *Chinese Deep-Breathing Exercise for Meditation, Sleep, or Relaxation*

Lie on a bed or mat. Use a high pillow for your head. Softly close your eyes and rest your hands on your abdomen on each side of your navel. Your arms and legs should be relaxed. Make sure your chest is relaxed, and let your diaphragm and abdominal muscles do the work of breathing. Deep breathing must be done slowly, six to eight in-out cycles per minute, but don't force yourself to breathe this slowly immediately; let your body relax completely first and simply breathe deeply and comfortably. Once you are comfortable and your breath becomes naturally slower, begin a slow six and eight count: Exhale through the mouth (with a six count), inhale through the nose (with an eight count). As you exhale deflate the abdomen completely, using slight pressure from your hands. After you exhale, close your mouth and inhale gently through the nose again. Do not force by taking in too much air.

Once this rhythm is comfortably established, concentrate your mind on the point two inches below your navel, and let your diaphragm control your breathing naturally. When your inhalation is complete, begin the exhalation by using slight hand pressure again. Keep up this cycle bringing your attention back to your lower abdomen whenever your mind wanders.

Do not pressure yourself if all the rhythms fail to come easily or immediately. Keep at it until you can concentrate on the in-out rhythms of your lower belly comfortably for fifteen or twenty minutes. This meditation relaxes the body and mind and prepares you for sleep or for deep meditation. Once this deep-breathing exercise is comfortable for you, it can be practiced anytime in order to relax tensions and relieve stress.

8. Counting Breaths

This is a variation of another breathing exercise similar to the yogic technique of simply observing your breathing. In observing your breath, there is no other task but to observe the rhythm and process of your natural breathing action. All of these exercises have in common the desire to teach the student to learn the nuances of his body's rhythm and to learn concentration. The major difference with this exercise is that it involves counting from one to ten.

Any comfortable posture can be used with this exercise. But the same requirements exist: straight back and neck, relaxed body with hands, arms, and legs comfortably positioned. There are two basic ways of counting. Either you can simply count "one" as you inhale, hold, and exhale, and so on; or you can visualize luminous numbers in front of your closed eyes. Hold the number in front of you for the full duration of the breathing cycle. Sit either on a cushion on the floor or in a straight-backed chair. If you use a chair place your hands, palms down, on your thighs. The fingers should be slightly spread an equal distance from each other. Place your tongue lightly against the roof of your mouth. If you are sitting on a cushion on the floor, your legs are crossed in the traditional lotus or half-lotus posture and your hands are in your lap with palms up, the right hand resting on the left with the thumbs lightly touching. In both positions your eyes are kept slightly open. In fact, if you are seen from the side it should look as if they are actually closed. Direct your gaze about one yard in front of you and count each breath. This is the basic zazen meditation, except with zazen there is no counting—just sitting.

9. *A Simple Sensory Breathing Exercise*

Breathing involves your senses as well as your body, and it is valuable to recognize the subtle relationship that occurs among them all. Find a comfortable position and close your eyes. Try to become aware only of your breathing for three minutes. Try to experience the deepest movement of your breathing as it goes into your lungs, and the air as it exhales. After you feel you have experienced the relationship between your inner body and your breathing, try to feel the air moving in and out of your nostrils. Feel its temperature, its strength. Now return to the whole cycle of your breathing, as you inhale, pause, exhale, pause, and repeat the whole cycle again. Allow the breathing to function uninterrupted. Do not try to regulate it. Feel this breathing cycle for as long as it is comfortable, but concentrate and do not fall asleep, which is very possible with this exercise. In fact, this is an excellent breath exercise to cure insomnia.

10. *Rhythmic Breathing*

The first step in rhythmic breathing is to choose a song, phrase, piece of poetry, or anything that can be repeated over and over with the same rhythm. Zen priests use the opening line of the famous *sutra* "Prajna-paramita-hrdaya": *Makahannya hara mitta*. Hindu meditators often use lines from sutras. One of the most popular is *Om Mani Padme Hum*, which is repeated endlessly as the meditator begins the process of excluding the external world and the disruptions of his mind. While it doesn't matter what kind of rhythm is used, it is important to use pleasing words and phrases. Success in learning to breath rhythmically depends on repetition. You develop the idea more quickly if you concentrate on the rhythm more than the words or their meanings. As you swing into the rhythm of the sounds, your breathing rhythm will automatically follow. It isn't necessary to worry about the length of your inhalation or exhalation; they will also follow your chanting. You will naturally inhale as much air as you need. But as you inhale during the natural pauses take the air in deeply. Do not allow yourself to rush the phrase and fall into breathing shallowly.

Rhythmic breathing is not primarily concerned with reducing the number of breaths, but rather strives to concentrate the mind with the different rhythms of breathing. For anyone who finds the other breath control methods difficult, rhythmic breathing is highly recommended. It is one of the simplest yet most effective methods of learning to control breathing. The rhythmical breathing exercise is effective for the same reasons as the mantra meditations: the mind concentrates on the rhythmic sounds and the breathing regulates itself automatically. (For a specific Yoga rhythmic breathing exercise, see Exercise 13, "Rhythmic Breathing in Yoga.")

11. Zen Breath Control

A Zen method for learning to breathe fully, taught to a European student in Japan, is both safe and simple. Begin to breathe slowly and deeply, the lips closed, both inhalation and exhalation being taken through the nose. As you inhale you will distend and raise the chest, pull in the abdomen, and push down the diaphragm. This way of breathing is exactly the opposite of most methods, for when you are inhaling you will think of pulling up as far as possible the wall of the diaphragm, and when you are exhaling of pushing it down and out against the solar plexus. As you continue, and do not have to concentrate too much on the muscular control of the breathing, you will find that you can press the diaphragm still further down until the final pressure seems to come just below the navel. Note that it is to the exhaled breath that one puts one's attention. The exhaled breath should be considerably slower than the inhaled breath, the exhaled breath and the downward pressure continuing so long that the inhalation is a reflex action from the exhalation.

Once this method of breathing is clear in your mind, begin to count the breaths, concentrating entirely on the counting. This exercise has been used by Buddhist monks for centuries, is still used today, and is much more difficult than it sounds. There are many methods for breath counting, involving a variety of rhythms. One of the most frequently used is to cut in half the number of counts you take when holding your breath in, then to breathe out for the same number as you used breathing in. For example, if you breathe in six, you hold for three, and breathe out six. A Zen student relates the Zen method for counting: "Begin to count the breaths up to ten. Then begin again at one and continue the counting up to ten indefinitely. You will keep your mind on the breath count and on that alone. When other thoughts come in don't try to get rid of them, but just keep on counting and push them out of the way. A willful attempt to keep away other thoughts only seems to make for more disturbance. Just keep patiently coming back to the counting. I found this exercise very difficult at first. Three hundred counts—that is, ten counted thirty times—is considered the goal to aim for, but these three hundred must be made without another thought of any kind coming in during the entire course of the practice."

12. *Abdominal or Lower-Belly Breathing* ✓

The Chinese have a saying: "Abdominal breathing is proper breathing. A baby breathes from the abdomen, an adult from the chest, an elderly person from the throat, and a dying man from the mouth."

Taoists believe that there are two kinds of breathing: one is outer breathing, which is the common action of inhaling and exhaling. The other, inner breathing, is considered the highest form of respiration and leads the individual to physical and psychical harmony. The lower-belly breathing starts with outer breathing. Sit comfortably in the lotus or half-lotus posture, with back straight, hands on your lap, tongue against the palate, and eyes half-closed. Inhale air through your nostrils and exhale through your mouth. Center your mind at a point between and behind your eyes. As you breathe, watch the air from your nose travel down to the abdomen to a point one to two inches below the navel. With your mind's eye, watch the air when you exhale as it rises and rushes from your mouth and nose at the same time. Repeat this deep, regular breathing from some time. When your concentration is strong and your meditation deep, the breathing becomes "inner breathing" and you observe the cycle of breath move from nose to lower belly, and the exhale rise from below your genitals and move up your spine to the top of your head and down and out through the nose. Keep up this cycle throughout the whole meditation. ✓

Another variation of this basically Taoist meditation is to concentrate completely on the lower belly. As you inhale press your belly out, and as you exhale press it in until the movement is easy and natural. Picture the air filling your lower belly and emptying as you inhale and exhale. After a short time steady your mind at a point several inches in and two inches below your navel. Hold your mind on this point as your belly extends and deflates, as you breathe in and out. ✓

13. *Rhythmic Breathing in Yoga*

One of the easiest to understand (but difficult to do) of all the Yoga *asanas* (postures) is the Savasana. This exercise combines relaxing the body, concentrating the mind, and developing rhythmic breathing. Lie down on your back and mentally go over each group of muscles and relax them. The body should be completely relaxed, and, therefore, this posture is sometimes called the "death pose" by yogis. Choose each section of the body separately. Concentrate your mind on the part and imagine all the tissue of the muscle group as relaxed, even flabby. Repeat this as often as it is necessary to relax your body fully. ✓

add other figures until you are unable to hold together the series of numbers.

Again, don't be discouraged if you can't immediately hold a ten-digit number in front of your closed eyes. This exercise is more difficult than it seems. The numbers have a tendency to jump about, change color and form. Sometimes they seem to be literally jumping like water in a hot pan before your eyes. But while this may seem humiliating the first time it happens, learn the valuable lesson that it teaches: We really don't have as much control over our minds as we like to believe. And besides, if you do this exercise often enough you will be surprised at how steady you can begin to hold the numbers. This is, of course, what you are working for: the ability to control your own mind, to create images *you* consciously desire to occupy your attention, and to hold them in your mind as long as *you* like.

16. A Blossoming Flower

This third visualization exercise, "The Blossoming of the Rose," is the most difficult so far because it incorporates a variety of different elements: form, color, smell, movement, etc. It is similar to color meditations, but here your goal is to create the form more than the color or other subsidiary qualities of the flower. In the color meditations your task is to include all elements with equal intensity. These exercises are progressive and it is necessary to do these simpler ones before trying the color meditations.

Imagine a small, closed rosebud. Visualize the stem and leaves beneath the bud. It is green at the base, where the leaves enclose the flower, but at the top you can see a small rose-colored point. Visualize this as vividly as you can and hold the image in the forefront of your consciousness. After holding it confidently for a short while, begin a slow movement of leaves encasing the rosebud. They gradually start to separate, turning their points outward, peeling back to reveal the deep red petals of the rose itself. They continue to open until you can see the whole of the small red flower. The petals now begin to open up slowly until it is a perfect, fully opened rose. Study this perfect creation of yours for a moment or two and then see if you can catch the faint perfume. Try to smell it, inhale its unmistakable scent. Next, expand your vision to include the whole rosebush, with bright red flowers blossoming all over it. Examine the rosebush in detail, see its base and the stem going into the earth. Picture the earth in its full, rich color. Finally, try to identify with the rose itself, with its strong urge to blossom, to open itself to the sun and sky. Try to feel the vitality in the plant's roots, stem, branches, leaves, and flowers.

17. Color Meditations *

Using color as the focus for meditation has several advantages. One is that some people respond to the visualization meditations better than other types. For these people color has a strong impact on their lives and possesses an emotional and psychological attraction that transcends all other forms of sensory perception. And for those who are not particularly attracted to color, a color meditation offers a good opportunity to develop an area of their senses that has probably been badly neglected. Doing these exercises for a month can develop an acute appreciation of color where none existed before.

As with all other forms of meditation, using color helps develop one's powers of concentration. It is a vibrant, magnetic, and enjoyable way to involve oneself in the meditative process. As with other meditations, fifteen to twenty minutes in the morning and evening should be spent on the exercise. As usual, before meditating the body should be relaxed and slow, rhythmic breathing established while you are comfortably seated or lying down. In doing the color meditations keep in mind that the colors should be as full and radiant as you can make them. It is easier to do this by relating all colors to the pictures that build up in your mind. You will find that the colors become clearer, brighter, and easier to evoke as you persevere in the meditations.

As you do these color meditations think of color as different modes of light, and as you contact this light as "color," the light strikes your eye and mind and evokes a similar light-energy mode from within you. In this way the use of color-light becomes a means of expanding your conscious awareness in which you are passing from *effect* to *cause* rather than the other way around. If you wish, think of the "cause" as a Divine Principle, or a Cosmic Energy that permeates everything you look upon and everything within you that reponds to it. The color meditation thus helps diminish the boundaries betweeen you and the objects you perceive.

Traditionally, color possesses certain meanings to those who use these types of meditations, and you can create as many more as you like; simply be sure the colors in your meditation always contrast sharply and that you concentrate completely on each thing to which you attend. You need not follow the meanings of traditional color psychology, but they can act as a basis upon which you can attribute your own values to each color you use. To find how you respond to color generally, visualize your mind filled with a particular color by choosing something of a

* The color meditations are freely adapted from S. G. J. Ouseley, *Colour Meditations* (London: L. N. Fowler & Co., 1949).

single outstanding color—for example, a red rose, a blue sky, a white
china vase, pottery, or anything else that appeals to you and is easy to
visualize. As you look at this object move your mind's eye closer and
closer as if you were in a shop, for example, and actually moving
closer to examine a beautifully colored piece of pottery you want to buy.
As you move closer to the object it fills your whole field of vision.
Hold the color within your field of vision as long as you can. Concentrate on the color, and if it slips away go through the whole process of
approaching the object again until once more it fills your mind's eye
with color. Once you can hold the color in your mind, allow feelings to
rise up within you. See what thoughts, ideas, images, fantasies are
evoked by that particular color. Compare your own "feeling" about the
color with these traditional relationships: Red—courage and strength;
Green—hope and faith; Scarlet—victory, bravery; Emerald—joy, exulta-
tion; Bright Blue—happiness, peaceful enjoyment; Yellow—guidance
and wisdom; Amethyst—spiritual awareness; Golden White—cosmic
union, oneness, unity.

I

Picture in your mind a cluster of *white* flowers (acacia, almond blossoms, white gardenias, orchids, etc.) waving softly amid pale *green*
leaves and grass. The blossoms cover a hill and contrast to a clear *azure*
sky surrounding the whole scene. A few trees with deep green leaves
dot the landscape. Look closely at each color, at the details of the petals
and of the veins in the leaves. See how the green from the leaves gives
a slight pale green reflection on the white flowers, how the bright sky
lightens both the flowers and the leaves. Examine carefully all the details of each thing you look at in your landscape. The more details you
evoke and concentrate on the better. If you cannot hold a particular
image in your mind after a serious effort, move on to another image
that comes more easily into fullness in your mind. Hold and examine
it. Try to actually love what you are looking at. See the radiance within
the object. A flower is not simply a color, but a whole, complex fusing
of life forces, light reflections, organic juices flowing in its leaves and
petals. Look beneath the colors to what makes the color. The more
deeply you look *into* the color, realize that the colors possess a power or
vibration of their own that differs according to its own unique existence.

II

Visualize mentally a great tree (oak, beech, birch, maple, etc.) changing slowly to autumnal coloring. The leaves are altering from their nor-

mal *green* to a burnished and shining shade of *copper, red-brown, gold.* The straight, strong trunk remains its rich, dark, reflecting rough surface. (If you desire, envision a white mother-of-pearl and silver beech trunk or anything else that comes easily to you. You are not limited to my descriptions here. Create whatever scene evokes the deepest, strongest response from you.) The autumn sky behind the tree and filtering through the leaves and branches is deep *blue.* It is a clear, deep sky with an occasional cloud that puffs across the landscape. As the leaves turn to their reds, browns, and golds, they flutter to the ground and land softly on a carpet of dark green grass. Picture them rocking their way down, the bright colors shifting as they twist and fall. Study them carefully as they come to rest on the earth. See how they are glistening, but drying before your eyes. The moisture in their leafy texture dries up and turns them a deep rust, and then an antique gold. They curl slightly at the edges. Occasionally a breeze rocks them and sends them tumbling over each other only to settle again on their curved backs.

Create as many of these color meditations as you like and follow the simple outline above. Just make sure the colors are bright and the forms basically easy to visualize. If at first you find it difficult to visualize color, place a strongly colored object before you. Study it in detail, then close your eyes and recreate it in detail. If after seriously trying you fail to recreate some detail of the form or the color just doesn't come, open your eyes and study it some more until you can successfully recreate it. You can perform exercises like this as often as you like, and for as long as you like.

18. Receptive Meditation

This is a slightly advanced meditation that involves holding the mind still and alert on an object or idea until a new insight or inspiration about it occurs. It should not be practiced until after simpler exercises like "A Blossoming Flower" have been mastered. The best state of mind for this meditation is one of expectant but dispassionate attention. An analogy might be waiting quietly as you listen for something that will make a sound in the far distance. The state of receptive listening should be blended with a positive attitude, free of tension or anxiety. You may sit at this meditation for a long time even before achieving the proper attitude for the actual "receptive listening," and even then you may not be able to hold it for long at first. As the father of Taoism, Lao Tzu, put it: "One cannot remain forever on tiptoe." The acute awareness needed for this meditation involves a mind-control that comes only after long practice, so don't move on to this meditation until you have thoroughly mastered the earlier exercises.

Sri Krishna Prem in his book *The Yoga of the Bhagavad Gita* describes this meditation in detail: "Essentially the method consists of gaining such control over the mind-processes that they can be stilled at will, thus enabling the consciousness to perceive the Truth like a calm lake reflecting the eternal stars. . . . The state (of mind) is not one of mental vacuity, as represented by some critics, and still less is it one which is produced by some 'occult' mechanism or other. The centre of consciousness withdraws its attention from the world of outer phenomena, whether of sense or of thought, passes through the central point, which is itself, and emerges in the spiritual world of the *buddhi*."

An analogy used to describe this meditation is that of a searchlight scanning the depths of the sky, trying to uncover what lies beyond normal perception. Once you can successfully sit in this meditation you may receive a variety of reactions from within. A frequent phenomenon is seeing a brilliant illumination. The light may be seen in your head, before your eyes, or as a diffuse area of illumination. Other colors and images may appear from the deeper levels of consciousness and should be ignored. When that happens bring your attention back to receptive listening. If you begin to hear voices, ringing of bells, or music that seems celestial, these are all impressions from your own psyche and should be turned away from and receptive listening begun again. If you are a musician, however, this kind of phenomenon becomes fascinating. For the spiritual seeker such impressions are diverting from their primary goal of enlightenment, but for others these inner responses are helpful in their lives or professions. Mozart, for example, reportedly remarked that writing music was not difficult for him; it seemed to pour forth from his mind and he simply wrote it down. Thus these deeper states of awareness can be used for creative insights and for problem-solving that escapes your normal, everyday consciousness.

First, prepare yourself by relaxation techniques. Find the posture and quiet your mind. Do deep breathing until your body and mind are thoroughly at peace. This meditation begins where earlier, simpler meditations ended.

Visualize a quiet, peaceful lake set among some trees and high mountains in the background. After you have created a complete picture of the scene, attend to the lake. Be receptive to its numerous qualities, especially its reflective surface. Its surface is like a blue mirror that can recreate on its face the trees, mountains, and clouds surrounding it. Realize that this symbolizes the ability of the tranquil mind to perceive the world surrounding it. See the clouds on its surface and realize that the lake's gleaming surface penetrates into the deepest recesses of the sky.

Be receptive to this relation between the lake's surface and the depths of the sky reflected upon it. Keep control of your mind and hold consciousness open to receive any impression that may press itself upon this clear, tranquil mirror. Your state of mind should be one of expectancy, that some truth *can* be revealed to you. Hold as the center of this expectancy the theme or subject on which you seek insight and understanding. If you have a problem you desire solving or lines of a poem you wish to complete, hold these ideas quietly behind the receptive listening. Keep positive, alert listening. But above all remain receptive to anything that may occur.

Anchoring any impressions that may come to you during this alert silence is important. As something appears in the sky or on the lake's surface, bring it forward into consciousness and reflect on it for a minute or two so that it becomes anchored in your conscious mind and will be recalled later. If you wish, and have made the proper arrangements, write down your impressions concisely and in general terms. That way you may be sure it won't be forgotten.

Some recommend closing this meditation with an affirmation, such as sending out a thought of gratitude into the still sky.

19. Meditation and Self-Healing

Self-healing through meditation is an ancient practice, regardless of its recent publicity through Dr. Carl Simonton's research. Over seventy years ago Yogi Ramacharaka described a simple technique involving both autosuggestion and meditative breathing. Notice that all of the ingredients of Simonton's techniques are in this yogic healing method: strong images, intense concentration on the body (including the diseased organ), and positive visualization. In his advice Ramacharaka refers to *prana*, which is the Hindu word for the life energy that Hindus believe permeates the universe and enters the human being through the breath. As with all the major Eastern religions, this pranic energy can be directed by the mind. As Ramacharaka points out, the main principle to remember is that by rhythmic breathing and controlled thought, one is able to absorb a considerable amount of prana to use as one wishes.

I

Lie down in a relaxed condition, breathe rhythmically, and command that a good supply of prana be inhaled. With the exhalation, send the prana to the affected part for the purpose of stimulating it. Vary this occasionally by exhaling, with the mental command that the diseased condition be forced out and disappear. Use the hands in this exercise, passing them down the body from the head to the affected part. In using the hands in healing yourself or others, always hold the mental image that the prana is flowing down the arm and through the fingertips into the body, thus reaching the affected part and healing it.

A little practice of the above exercise, varying it slightly to fit the conditions of the case, will produce wonderful results. Some yogis follow the plan of placing both hands on the affected part and then breathing rhythmically, holding the mental image that they are pumping prana into the diseased organ and part, stimulating it, and driving out diseased conditions, as pumping into a pail of dirty water will drive out the latter and fill the bucket with fresh water. This last plan is very effective if the mental image of the pump is clearly held, the inhalation representing the lifting of the pump handle and the exhalation the actual pumping.

Specific autosuggestions by Ramacharaka are also part of his self-healing program. His autosuggestion consists of suggesting to oneself the physical condition one wishes to bring about. The autosuggestions should be spoken (audibly or silently) just as one would speak to another, earnestly and seriously, letting the mind form a mental picture of the conditions referred to in the words. For instance: "My stomach is strong, strong, strong—able to digest the food given it—able to assimilate the nourishment from the food—able to give me the nourishment which means health and strength to me. My digestion is good, good, good, and I am enjoying and digesting and assimilating my food, converting it into rich red blood, which is carrying health and strength to all parts of my body, building it up, and making me a strong man (or woman)." Similar autosuggestions, or affirmations, applied to other parts of the body, will work equally good results; the attention and mind being directed to the parts mentioned will cause an increased supply of prana to be sent there and the pictured condition to be brought about. Enter into the spirit of the autosuggestions, and be thoroughly in earnest over them; and, so far as possible, form mental images of the healthy condition desired. See yourself as you wish yourself to be.

II

Dr. Carl Happich, an M.D. and psychotherapist who developed specific meditative-healing techniques, emphasizes using what he calls the meditator's "symbolic consciousness," which he theorizes lies between consciousness and unconsciousness. Dr. Happich is an internist who has involved himself in Oriental meditation techniques, physiology, and the psychology of meditation. To Happich, symbolic consciousness is the level of awareness in which all creative production begins, and through which the use of symbols in the healing process can also reach deeper levels of the unconscious. In contrast to standard psychotherapeutic methods in which the patient is encouraged to maintain a passive attitude, in the meditative healing techniques one takes an active, goal-directed role. In this sense the healing meditation is different from traditional meditations in which goals are not sought. But a healing meditation takes on an autosuggestive quality, which is not normal meditative procedure, even while employing basic meditative techniques. The healing meditation attempts actively, consciously to evoke unconscious powers in order to influence bodily conditions.

Happich used a visualization technique to prepare the meditator for working with deeper, healing symbols. After some initial breathing exercises Happich has his meditator visualize walking out of his room, through his village or city, and into the country. There he finds a meadow covered with fresh grass and flowers. This is Happich's "Meadow Meditation," and after the meditator repeats this exercise and can visualize each step clearly, he goes on to the "Mountain Meditation."

The meditator retraces his steps through the country, walks through the meadow until he comes to a mountain. He slowly climbs the mountain and passes through a forest until he reaches its peak, where he can view the whole countryside. This exercise is also repeated until it is clear. Then the meditator moves on to the "Chapel Meditation," in which he visualizes walking through the previous meadow and mountain and on through a grove until he reaches a chapel in the woods. He enters and remains there for a long time. Finally, Happich has the meditator visualize sitting on a bench by an old fountain and listening to the sound of the water.

All of these symbols—the meadow, the mountain, the chapel, and the fountain—have more significance in the deeper levels of consciousness than in ordinary, everyday consciousness. Psychotherapists such as Happich believe that each symbol stimulates responses on a primordial level when experienced during deeper states of meditation. The archetypal significance of the meadow, for example, would be nature in its serene, fertile, and beneficent aspect and is therefore a valuable beginning symbol. It initiates the meditator into a fertile, creative world. It also symbolizes the world of the child, the newly born, the seed blossoming into its destined form. As Dr. Wolfgang Kretschmer says of this image, when one meditates on the symbol of the meadow, "he regresses to his psychic origin, his childhood." Once there he returns to the creative, positive, beginning of his life.

When climbing the mountain the meditator will frequently envision some obstacle in his way. In overcoming the obstacle he must prove himself. The climbing symbolizes movement, growth, a strengthening and maturing through demonstrating his ability on a deep symbolic level. The passage through the forest allows the meditator to familiarize and harmonize himself with the fearful, dangerous aspect of nature. The shadows and lurking dangers of the forest are exorcised through familiarity, and even this mysterious element of nature becomes compatible to the human adventure.

The chapel symbolizes the inner chambers of his own psychic being, where the meditator should spend enough time to face the central problems of his life. Once the meditator recognizes the significance of the chapel, he can use it as a stage to confront and resolve his basic confusion and conflicts. Happich's use of these symbols is not haphazard, for there have been numerous dreams recorded in which a mountain occurs in a landscape, and a church stands on top of it. In normal meditation such symbols might occur during the long process of moving deeper into the various levels of the unconscious. But with a healing meditation these symbols must be evoked and used by either the therapist or the meditator to affect the ill body or mind.

SERENITY MEDITATION

20. *A Meditation on Being Serene*

Relax all your muscles and nervous tensions. Breathe slowly and rhythmically. Visualize your face and body in a serene condition. See your face with a serene smile. *Believe* yourself to be serene.

Think about serenity, its quality, its value and use, especially when you are faced with a normally tense situation. Praise serenity in your mind, concentrate on feeling it in your body and mind. Evoke it directly by feeling it in specific places in your body. Feel it in your heart, and feel it slowly expand in peaceful waves like the gentle ripples moving across the surface of a placid pond. Feel its waves expand throughout your chest, into your neck and shoulders and head; down into your stomach, hips, legs, and feet. Feel the tension and tautness leave your muscles, tendons, and nerves as it radiates throughout your body.

Repeat the word "serene" over and over again in your mind or use some other word that appeals to you more, such as "peace," "calm," "tranquil," etc. If you wish, you can repeat a phrase or sentence from a book that appeals to you. Any positive, suggestive phrase will do.

A variation on this technique is to insert a visualization in which you picture a hostile person confronting you in anger; or place yourself in danger; or see yourself surrounded by rapidly moving events to which you must respond—and then picture yourself calm and serene in the midst of it all. Visualize yourself facing and dealing with the hostile person calmly and with patience.

Before you conclude this meditation you might suggest to yourself strongly and repeatedly that you will remain serene throughout the day regardless of what happens. Determine within yourself that you will radiate serenity and be a living example of peace and calm.

CHRISTIAN MEDITATION

21. *Prayers of the Heart*

An example of the spiritual and meditation advice given to the monks by the church fathers emphasizes the same criteria of concentration of the mind and the withdrawal of the senses typical of meditation the world over. From "Theoleptus of Philadelphia":

Thus, sitting in your cell, remember God; and, moreover, withdrawing your mind from everything, prostrate it speechlessly before God. Pouring out your heart to Him, cleave to Him with love. Remembrance of God is contemplation of God, who attracts to Himself the vision and striving of the mind and illumines it with His light. Having cut off all images of existing things and turning to God, the mind sees Him without form or image, and thus has its vision cleared despite its imperfect comprehension of the Object of its contemplation, Whose glory is utterly inaccessible.

In another section of the *Philokalia*, St. Barsanuphius advises: "The approach to perfect prayer is when a man is freed from dispersion of thoughts and sees his mind, enlightened in the Lord, filled with joy. A man has attained perfection in prayer if he makes himself dead to the world with its ease. But when a man does his work diligently for the sake of God, it is not a distraction but a thoroughness, which pleases God."

In direct contrast to Eastern teachings that advise *never* resisting intruding thoughts while meditating, the Christian invocation of the Lord's name frequently was used as a bludgeon against unwanted ideas and images. Philotheus of Sinai says: "Guard your mind with extreme intensity of attention. As soon as you notice a hostile thought, immediately resist it and at the same time hasten to call on Christ our Lord to wreak vengeance. . . . Here come waves of thoughts, more numerous than ever, again rushing against you, one after another, so that the soul is almost engulfed in them and is about to perish. But Jesus, being God, when the disciple appeals, again forbids the evil thoughts and they become subdued."

The prayer of the heart is ideally a silent prayer. The disciple attempts to "come to a steadfast resolve always to remain in silence of the heart. And when moved by our love for Divine things, we begin zealously to work at attention and prayer in the mental workshop of our heart."

Hesychius of Jerusalem sets down a basic meditation:

We should always be turning the Name of Jesus Christ round the spaces of our heart, as lightning circles round the skies before rain. This is well known by those who have spiritual experience in inner warfare. Let us conduct this mental war in the following order. The first thing is attention; then, when we notice a wicked thought draw near, let us wrathfully hurl a heartfelt curse at it. The third thing is to turn the heart to the invocation of Jesus Christ and pray Him to disperse forthwith this phantom thought, lest the mind runs after this fantasy like a child attracted by a skillful juggler. . . . It is impossible for a man to look at the sun, and the pupils of his eyes not glitter with the light. So too a man, who constantly penetrates into the air of the heart, cannot but shine with light.

The Christian commitment to passion is complete. Even when there is recognition that passionlessness is a desired state leading to God, the admonition is for intense prayer: "Passionlessness of mind is one thing and true prayer is another—the latter being higher than the former."

The Hesychasts (young monks who practiced silence) were taught a method of meditaton by attention to breathing, together with saying the prayer: "Lord Jesus Christ, Son of God, have mercy upon me." The prayer becomes a mantra as it is repeated throughout the hour that the young monk is praying. As the monks say, this method "contributes greatly to the concentration of thoughts."

You know brother how we breathe: we breathe the air in and out. On this is based the life of the body and on this depends its warmth. So, sitting down in your cell, collect your mind, lead it into the path of the breath along which the air enters in, constrain it to enter the heart together with the inhaled air, and keep it there. Keep it there, but do not leave it silent and idle; instead give it the following prayer: "Lord, Jesus Christ Son of God, have mercy upon me." Let this be its constant occupation, never to be abandoned. For this work, by keeping the mind free from dreaming, renders it unassailable by suggestions of the enemy (evil thoughts) and leads it to Divine desire and love. Moreover, brother, strive to accustom your mind not to come out too soon; for at first it feels very lonely in that inner seclusion and imprisonment. But when it gets accustomed to it, it begins on the contrary to dislike darting about among external things. For the kingdom of God is within us, and for a man who has seen it within, and having found it through pure prayer, has experienced it, everything outside loses its attraction and value. It is no longer unpleasant and wearisome for him to be within. Just as a man who has been away from home, when he returns is beside himself with joy at seeing again his children and wife, so the mind, after being dispersed, when it reunites with the soul is filled with unspeakable sweetness and joy.

MOVEMENT MEDITATIONS

22. *Taoist Jogging, or "High-Striding" Meditation*

The typical American jogger simply runs, his primary attention only on the physical involvement of his exercise. To the Chinese such exercise is a wasted opportunity. To understand the Taoist viewpoint compare the beginning swimmer with the practiced one; the beginner thrashes his arms and legs, flailing the water and wasting enormous amounts of energy and receiving very little in return. If he floats he feels he has accomplished a great deal. The expert swimmer uses the water to help move him along; he uses the buoyancy of his body, the full length of his arms, and the even rhythm of his feet and legs to propel him through the water far faster and with less expense of energy than the beginner. Similarly, the Taoist uses a high-striding walk as a method for concentrated activity and as a means for uniting his mind, body, and environment. He is the expert swimmer using the water and his body in unison, so each is a partner with the other.

Taoist jogging is different from ordinary walking and jogging, for it concentrates on total involvement. The Taoist believes that this meditation exercise dispels negative emotions such as anger, hate, sadness; it calms the mind as well as increases the body's blood circulation and oxygen consumption and utilization. But most important, this exercise helps the meditator extend his awareness beyond the physical body. If done properly the body, mind, and nature converge to create a feeling of unity between the jogger and the external world. The wandering Taoist, who would supposedly sometimes cover hundreds of miles without any destination, used this exercise as an aid in his meditation.

The exercise should be done every day, either morning or evening. In the beginning it should be practiced for a short time, and gradually increased to three hours. Initially, you may be tired, but as you learn to relax and allow the body to move fluidly, you will gain both momentum and energy. Once you reach this point you will feel like you are coasting rather than briskly moving. If you are meditating on the lower belly properly, you will feel a warmth there that will extend throughout your body. Following this, the body will feel lighter than air and you will even forget that you are actually doing a physical exercise.

Your eyes should always be straight ahead for this exercise, the tongue held against the roof of the mouth on the hard palate. This helps promote saliva and prevents thirst.

Your body should be erect, the back and head in a straight line, your shoulders relaxed with the arms hanging down along your sides. As you walk, your arms and hands should be allowed to move freely.

Most important, you should place your attention just below your navel (technically, just more than one inch). According to the Taoist this is the body's center of gravity, and it is the key center for all forms of Zen and Taoist martial arts and exercises. Envision your breath entering your body and traveling to this spot. As this becomes easier visualize your breath as coming in and going out to and from the lower belly.

You should not actually run, or even jog as in the American exercise. The foot starting to step forward should be a little higher than when walking normally. This is why the exercise is called *shien chio*, or "walking with high strides."

The body should be completely relaxed during the *shien chio*. And if you are meditating on breathing in the lower belly, relaxation will follow.

Although walking is a basic experience, many people do not walk in a relaxed way that is regenerative for both the mind and body. For meditative walking the important element is parallel placement of each foot as it contacts the ground. While the mind is concentrated at the body's center of gravity in the lower belly, the walking should be synchronized with your breathing. It should be one, two, or three walking cycles per breathing cycle. It is important to concentrate on the stability of your striding and on remaining relaxed.

23. T'ai Chi Exercise-Meditation

When doing t'ai chi several fundamental ideas must be learned: (1) Breathe naturally. Avoid forcing your breathing and after a few minutes of movement it will become deep and easy without conscious effort. (2) Keep a low center of gravity and think of the lower abdomen as the body's center. When you move use your hips and waist as a pivot point. (3) Remove all tension. When moving, avoid tensing any muscle. When you move, imagine that that part of your body is moving as if by itself. For example, when raising your arms let them float up as if they were being slowly raised by invisible strings. Make sure your shoulders and neck stay relaxed. (4) Move as if your body were a part of the surroundings. When you move your hands, for instance, see if you can feel the air as a tangible, real substance such as water. (5) Concentrate. Each movement demands full attention. Direct your mind completely to each task. Avoid letting extraneous thoughts or ideas clut-

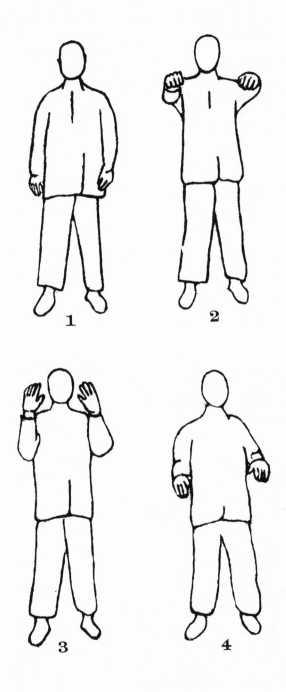

ter up your movements. Remember that your mind is an equal partner in each small activity, in each minute movement. Such concentration develops after practice so do not become discouraged.

The beginning form of t'ai chi is basically a simple arm movement, but it involves concentration and understanding:

Stand with your hands relaxed at your sides, palms facing backward. Face forward with the weight evenly distributed over both feet. Your head is up; chest, shoulders, neck, and abdomen are all relaxed. Breathe naturally, easily through your nose. Your tongue should be lightly held against the roof of the mouth, the tip behind your front teeth. Check your body alignment, and follow a plumb line from the top of your head down through your spine to your heels. Feel the center of gravity just below the navel. Concentrate on this point throughout the exercise. If your mind wavers, gently bring it back without feeling guilt, remorse, or irritation with yourself. (See figure 1.)

Allow your arms to rise slowly in front of you. It is an effortless move, as if your wrists were being raised by invisible strings. Let them rise until they are shoulder height. Listen to your body and feel its inner workings as the arms rise. (See figure 2.)

Straighten your fingers and palms slightly until they are parallel with the ground. Slowly draw your wrists toward your shoulders; the palms and fingers should hang loosely. (See figure 3.)

Move your elbows slightly back as they pass your sides. Press your hands gently forward as they sink downward to where they began. Let the heels and palms of your hands fall back into position along your sides. (See figure 4.) Think of the rising and falling of your hands as a circular movement.

Repeat the exercise as often as you like. It is a good all-around movement meditation and releases tension, anxiety, headaches, etc.

INNER MIND MEDITATIONS

24. *Flow Meditation: A Meditation for Learning to Feel Body Rhythms*

Lie or sit in a comfortable position. Make sure your arms, legs, body trunk, neck, and head are in an extended relaxed position. Move through your body with the standard tensing of each muscle group for a few seconds, and then relax them. Pay particular attention to the chest, neck, and shoulder muscles. Take a deep breath and hold it for five or six seconds. Release the air and let your breathing become deep, easy, and normal. Picture the breath as a fluid energy connecting your body and consciousness with the world outside your skin. Concentrate on the ease with which these two worlds communicate on the pathway of your breath.

Next, think about your blood circulating throughout your chest; feel your heart beating, pumping blood through your veins up to your head, out to your shoulders, arms, and down through your stomach, hips, pelvis, legs, and into your feet. Feel it flow in each of these places; feel it flow through your face and into your toes. After you have traced the blood pulsing throughout your body, relax even more and feel it softly moving in your chest. Join the rhythm of your heartbeat; tune into its resonance and regularity.

Now relax and feel the multiple rhythms of your body. Visualize your body as a whole. Your mind and consciousness are a part of this rhythm. See your body as an alive, vibrant electrical being. Each cell, each small blood vessel, each fiber is alive with pulsing blood, with electrical energy that extends from your body in all directions. Watch the patterns as the energy flows out of your body into the space around you. Visualize an enlarging electrical field that extends beyond the room, beyond the house, beyond the earth and into the sky, in all directions.

As you watch these lines of energy rhythmically extend from your body into infinity, feel your conscious awareness expanding along with the energy, moving out on the electrical lines beyond your body and the room or building you are in. Imagine yourself floating higher and higher until you can see the earth below you for miles. Rise still higher until you can see the slight curve of the earth's horizon, until you can see the towns and cities beneath you. Envision the earth turning slowly as you float higher into the sky. Be aware that the sky and earth are touching, and that your body is still in contact with the earth through the vibrating lines of energy. There is no anxiety in this floating, for you are a part of both the earth and sky, with the gentle rhythms connecting all that your awareness can encompass. See the stars glittering in the sky around you, the moon in the distance slowly changing its shape as it floats around the earth. As the moon changes its shape, see its gravitational pull on the great bodies of blue water on earth. Feel the warm energy of the sun as its rays join the many other particles rhythmically passing around and through you. Feel yourself move still higher, passing beyond the orbits of the solar system's planets. Your own body continues to radiate lines of particles that mingle with the constant energy of the universe around you. You are an integral, perfect part of all that is happening. Not only do you still feel comfortably connected with the earth, but now you are intimate with the moon, the sun, and the planets. As you float outside of the solar system, join in their graceful cycle. And as you move further into space, watch the solar system become smaller and more distant until it slowly dissolves into just another bright, blinking star.

Now you are a bright light of consciousness, of radiating light, just as all the other stars are. As you extend your particles of energy to all the stars around you, receive waves of light from them and let yourself be bathed in their streaming lines of undulating particles. Visualize yourself as being on the edge of the immense Milky Way, looking toward its distant center, which is an intense point of light many times brighter than the sun. Watch as the Milky Way turns slowly and majestically in its circle and you float out beyond its rim, beyond all the bright stars, toward other galaxies, beyond other slowly turning galaxies of milky light that shifts its colors all across the spectrum.

As you move farther and farther into the universe, realize that all the planets and stars within the galaxies are alive and breathing, a pulsing part of the whole galaxy. Be aware that each galaxy is circling slowly on its own axis, yet is spinning in relationship to all the other galaxies. Realize that all of this movement throughout the whole universe is identical to your own body back in that small room on that distant planet; it is identical to your heartbeat, your soft regular breathing, and the electrical rhythms of your mind and brain. Feel the unity within this vast, unending being you call the universe. It is alive, yet calmly, rhythmically, unendingly functioning just as you are. Feel the immense calm throughout the universe, within all the dark spaces between the galaxies. Feel this peace within your own mind and body. There is a calm that underlies all the pulsation around you: identify with it and let it embrace you. Become aware of this calm inside of you. It is beyond alteration and sustains all the activity around you. Feel yourself a part of this universally sustaining peace and allow yourself to float in its immense, unending comfort.

When you are ready to return to the earth and your body, begin to visualize the particles of energy intensifying, moving faster. Feel the quickened pace of the vibrations in your mind and body. If you feel like remaining in that immense universal peace, remind yourself that it will always be there for you to return to. You have a body to enliven and utilize. Visualize the vibrations becoming so intense that they form cloudlike groups and interact with your physical brain and body. These particles are highly energized and they form the basis for organic life. Visualize these cloudlike particles entering the cells of your body. Feel the billions of cells in your body interacting with each other to form the organs of your body. See the particles and cells pulsing in your heart as it pumps blood to your lungs, stomach, neck veins, brain, legs, arms, feet, and hands. Feel each of these cells filling your body with energy.

Feel your bones and muscles being filled with these energetic cells; feel them spill over in their rush to energize your body and skin.

Now relax and feel the many rhythms of body and mind together. Feel your body working in unison with the billions of cells sending energy and vitality throughout your body until your skin seems to glow with its strength. Listen to your heartbeat, your regular breathing. If you are sitting, trace all the surfaces of your body that are being touched by something. If you are lying down, do the same thing. Allow yourself to breath regularly and feel your whole body in relation to its surroundings. Feel your body and mind rhythmically working, and feel your relation to the room, the house, the neighborhood, the city or town in which you live. You are a part of a community of beings, a community of living things. Relax and simply feel your body-mind and its contact with the world around you. When you are ready, move your body very easily, slowly. Gently stretch your muscles and tendons as you get up. Retain that feeling of unity with the world as much as you can throughout your day.

Note: Since this is a complicated meditation, you may not want to read it through the several times necessary to get the sequence and images clear in your mind before using it. It might be easier for you to read the meditation slowly into a tape recorder and play it back during your meditation, which will allow you to follow it exactly and effortlessly.

25. Ten Yoga Concentration Exercises

Swami Sivananda, one of the most respected and renowned of the modern gurus to travel to the West, recommended that one should practice concentration on a wide range of various subjects, both "gross and subtle," of this world and the abstract. The basic technique for practicing the following concentration exercises of Sivananda's should be to fix the mind on some object either in or out of the body. The trick is to keep your attention there steadily for some time. It will, as with all other meditative disciplines, have to be a daily practice.

1. Ask your friend to show you some playing cards. Immediately after he shows you a card, describe it in detail. Give the number, name, color, etc.

2. Read two or three pages of a book and then close it. Now think about what you have read and abandon all distracting thoughts. Focus your attention carefully and allow the mind to associate, classify, group, combine, and compare what you have read. If you concentrate carefully,

you will receive a clear, strong impression. In addition to practicing concentration, this exercise helps you develop your memory as well as reading abilities.

3. In a quiet room, sit in your favorite meditative posture about one foot from a watch. Concentrate on the tick-tick sound. Whenever the mind runs away, try again and again to hear the sound. See how long your mind can stay fixed continuously only on the sound. Practice this exercise until you have improved your original length of concentration by tenfold.

4. Sit in your favorite posture and close your eyes. Close your ears with your thumbs or plug them with cotton or wax (make sure the wad is large enough to pull out easily). You will hear various sounds of the body like your heartbeat, etc. These are the "gross" sounds. Listen to them for a while and then try to hear only a single sound among all the others, a sound that underlies the others. Try to isolate this "special" sound from the others and concentrate on it. If the mind runs away, you can shift back and forth between the gross sounds of your body and the subtle single sound. You will often hear sounds mainly in your right ear. Occasionally you will hear it in your left ear also. Let this experience happen and try to retain the sound in one ear or the other. Shift the sound from one ear to the other. In this way you will also develop one-pointedness of mind. Sivananda says that this is an easy way to capture the mind, "because it is enchanted by the sweet sounds, just as a snake is hypnotized by the notes of a snake charmer."

5. Keep a candle flame in front of you and try to concentrate on the flame. When you are tired of this, close your eyes and visualize the flame. Do this for half a minute (approximately) at first and increase the time to five, ten, fifteen minutes, or longer, depending on your preference. This exercise moves the meditator into deep concentration.

6. In a prone posture, concentrate on the moon (or a star, or even a spot on your ceiling). Whenever the mind runs away, bring it back time and time again to the image. This is a very beneficial exercise for calming the emotions.

7. Sit by the side of a river where you can hear its subtle sounds. Listen to the overall sound the rushing water creates. Sometimes it even sounds like "Om." Concentrate on that sound as long as you like. If you don't live near a river choose a special piece of music you enjoy and listen to it over and over again, following every rise and fall of tone, volume, and quality. Listen to the music as many times as you can. You shouldn't become sick of it if you are listening to it properly. You

should literally try to identify with the sound so thoroughly that when it moves you "feel" the action—the music seems to become a part of you and you of it. You should not become tired of that piece of music any more than you would become tired of a single mantra sound —if you are concentrating properly.

8. Lie in the open air and concentrate on the blue, expansive sky above. If you live in a city, or it is inconvenient to lie outside for other reasons, try to position yourself near a window so you can lie down and look out of it. As you concentrate on the blank, blue depths, your mind will expand. Think of the sky as an expression of the infinite nature of the universe and the inner self.

9. Sit in a comfortable posture and concentrate on any one of numerous abstract virtues such as mercy, kindness, understanding, gentleness, love, forgiveness, etc. Concentrate on this idea for as long as you can.

10. Take any piece of furniture and use it as the object of concentration. This means getting full, detailed knowledge about the object. If you are concentrating on, say, a chair, notice the type of wood, its construction, workmanship; imagine yourself sitting in it and establish its degree of comfort, and whether the parts need polish or not.

26. Basic Simplified Meditation Instructions of Patanjali
(Adapted from Patanjali's Yoga Aphorisms*)

Zero	Study preliminary Yoga. Read a simple introductory book on Yoga. Do not try too hard at the following. Do not move on to the next number without thoroughly completing each stage.
1. *Posture*	Sit or lie in a simple meditation posture. For example, lie on a mat or rug and relax each part of your body in sequence from the feet up to your neck, face, and scalp. Or, alternatively, sit in a high-backed chair with your feet flat on the floor. Your hands relaxed, palms up in your lap, your eyes closed. Relax your body as described above. Adjust your position until your body becomes accustomed to the posture.

* Following the traditional "Yoga Aphorisms of Patanjali" and his instructions in concentration and meditation, Dr. John Clark of Manchester University created a simplified graph of the yogic meditation procedures. It is a clear and helpful—but not complete—description of the meditative process. These instructions have been freely adapted from Dr. Clark's construction in *New Society* magazine, July 23, 1970.

2. *Hearing*

Pay attention to all you hear. List mentally everything you hear: voices, cars, footsteps, distant radio or TV, and so on. Next, listen to the sounds without labeling them. Don't try to identify any of the sounds, but listen as you would to music until your verbal thinking drops away.

3. *Breathing*

Be aware of your breathing—breathe normally. Concentrate on breathing more deeply and slowly for a minute or so. Do not force or create stress. Keep chest, stomach, diaphragm, neck, and shoulders relaxed. Keep back straight while breathing deeply. Return to normal breathing for a moment or two, then return to deep breathing until it is comfortable, easy, and regular.

4. *Sensations*

Become aware of all your sensations. Mentally list them as they occur. Locate where your body touches the external world. Let each sensation linger for a moment in your mind, examine it, and consider its qualities and its source. Trace the outline of your body with your mind's eye. Keep your mind calm and your body relaxed.

5. *Emotions*

Attend only to your emotions. List them as you isolate them. Let each emotion appear gently, without pressure. No matter how pleasant or unpleasant the emotion, remain calm. Impart that calmness to the emotion. Once you feel you have control over each emotion that arises, go on to the next stage.

6. *Thoughts*

Let each thought enter your mind. Do not resist its entrance into awareness. Calmly list each thought that occurs. Do not intellectualize or analyze—simply observe it until it dissolves or another enters your awareness. Continue until you feel comfortable with the technique. Reestablish your body's relaxation, your mind's calmness, and your regular breathing, if necessary, before going on to the next stage.

7. *Concentration*

Visualize a funnel into which your mind is slowly moving. As your mind descends into the funnel think of it narrowing its attention span.

Narrow your thoughts to one thing alone that is within the smallest end of the funnel. That object, image, symbol (choose whatever positive, strong idea you wish) is the single thing you keep in mind. Every time you lose it, return down the funnel again and reestablish contact with the image. Once you have succeeded in thinking of one thing only for even a short time, relax the effort. Allow a comfortable time to pass before returning to ordinary consciousness.

8. *Contemplation* Slowly, gently, even lovingly let your mind become empty. It may help initially to use the object of your previous stage of one-pointed concentration. Visualize the object or idea slowly dissolving until nothing remains. Repeat this exercise until your mind remains unoccupied at least for several seconds. Then relax for a short period and allow the object of your concentration to remain intact. Repeat the dissolving exercise until you succeed in having your mind unoccupied for a slightly longer time. Relax the effort and allow a little time to pass before returning to ordinary consciousness.

9. *Awaking* When returning from meditation breathe deeply. Picture your stomach, chest, head, and whole body being filled with energizing air. Continue to fill all extensions of your body with air until you feel totally energized. Move your hands, back, neck very slowly at first. Then you may get up.

10. *Summation* Keep in mind Patanjali's basic three stages of consciousness that encompass the above exercise: (1) *Concentration* is the binding of the mind to one place. (2) *Meditation* is continued effort there. (3) *Contemplation* is the same when there is the shining of the object alone, as if devoid of one's own form.

Index

Read:

Merton, Thomas: "The 7 Story Mountain"

Furlong, Monica: "Merton: A Biography"

Merton: "Seeds of Contemplation"

Calan, Pierre de: "Cosmas, or The Love of God

Huxley: Doors of Perception

Philokalia

Candle of Vision

Cage, John: "Silence"

Luria, A. R: the Mind of a Mnemonist

Keyserling, Hermann: The Travel Diary of a Philosopher

Sri Paramananda: Concentration & Meditation

Bailey A.A. Light of the Soul

Assagioli's: Psychosynthesis